CALL BACK YESTERDAY

O call back yesterday, bid time return.

Shakespeare, *Richard II*, iii. 2. 69.

I have seen so many sunsets, so many radiant dawns. This man has failed and that man has succeeded, and both have grown tired of it all. But what right have I to grieve, as Thoreau said, who have not ceased to wonder?

C. F. G. Masterman, *In Peril of Change*.

There is the two-edged sword that will never fail you, with enthusiasm for one of its edges and irony for the other. There will be always joy and loyalty enough left to keep you unwavering in the faith that politics is not, as it seems in clouded moments, a mere gabble and squabble of selfish interests, but that it is the State in action. And the State is the name by which we call the great human conspiracy against hunger and cold, against loneliness and ignorance; the State is the foster-mother and warden of the arts, of love, of comradeship, of all that redeems from despair that strange adventure which we call human life.

T. M. Kettle, *The Day's Burden*.

AT THE FOREIGN OFFICE, 1930

HUGH DALTON

CALL BACK YESTERDAY

Memoirs 1887–1931

FREDERICK MULLER LTD
LONDON

FIRST PUBLISHED BY FREDERICK MULLER LTD
IN 1953
PRINTED AND BOUND IN GREAT BRITAIN BY
HAZELL WATSON AND VINEY LTD
AYLESBURY AND LONDON

CONTENTS

V—WAR

VI—L.S.E.

VII—FIVE QUICK ELECTIONS

VIII—M.P. FOR PECKHAM

IX—ABOUT PEOPLE

X—M.P. FOR BISHOP AUCKLAND

XI—FOREIGN OFFICE

XII—END OF THE SECOND LABOUR GOVERNMENT

NOTE—MY UNCLE HUGH AT JUTLAND

Fifth Battle Squadron stationed five miles from Beatty's flagship—When Beatty turned in pursuit of the enemy, Fifth Battle Squadron did not turn at once—For this delay Mr. Churchill and the so-called *Admiralty Narrative* blame my uncle—But Jellicoe disagrees, and is supported by the official Naval historian, and by Admirals Bacon and Harper—They blame Beatty and the signalling staff of his flagship—The signal to turn was made by flags, could not be seen by my uncle owing to heavy smoke, and was not repeated—Later stages of the action—Fine gunnery of Fifth Battle Squadron—My uncle replies to Mr. Churchill

LIST OF ILLUSTRATIONS

ACKNOWLEDGMENTS

The author wishes to acknowledge with thanks the permission of the following publishers to quote from books listed below:

GEORGE ALLEN & UNWIN, LTD., *Keeling Letters* by Ben Keeling; JONATHAN CAPE, LTD., *Remembering Good Friends* by M. A. Hamilton; CASSELL & CO. LTD., *A King's Story* by H.R.H. The Duke of Windsor; CONSTABLE & CO. LTD., *King George V* by Harold Nicolson; RUPERT HART-DAVIS, LTD., *Two Memoirs* by J. M. Keynes; WILLIAM HEINEMANN, LTD., *Arthur Henderson* by M. A. Hamilton; *Collected Poetical Works* by Algernon Charles Swinburne; HODDER & STOUGHTON, LTD., *The Life and Letters of David Beatty* by Rear-Admiral W. S. Chalmers; LONGMANS GREEN & CO. LTD., *Life of George Lansbury* by Raymond Postgate; *Our Partnership* by Beatrice Webb; MACMILLAN & CO. LTD., *Henry Ponsonby: His Life from His Letters* by Arthur Ponsonby; METHUEN & CO. LTD., *With British Guns in Italy* by Hugh Dalton; ODHAMS PRESS LTD., *The World Crisis* by Winston S. Churchill; ROUTLEDGE & KEGAN PAUL, LTD., *Practical Socialism for Britain* by Hugh Dalton; *Towards the Peace of Nations* by Hugh Dalton; SIDGWICK & JACKSON, LTD., *Complete Poems* by Rupert Brooke; H.M. STATIONERY OFFICE, *History of the Great War, Naval Operations* by Sir Julian Corbett; and the executors of Viscount Snowden's estate for permission to print excerpts from Viscount Snowden's *Autobiography*.

PREFACE

THIS book covers the first forty-four years of my life, which has been active, varied and controversial. I hope to carry on the story in a second volume up to the end of the Second World War, and in a third volume from 1945, when the Labour Party won power in Britain for the first time, to whatever shall seem the most appropriate stopping-point.

I began to keep a diary in the First World War and have gone on doing so intermittently—sometimes with long breaks—ever since. In this book I have quoted a good deal from my diaries, and much that is not direct quotation is based on what I wrote down at the time. This gives a surer foothold in the past than dim memories and wise hindsight.

I have written frankly and without much reserve, not hiding either my sympathies or my antipathies, or my reasons for both. Otherwise one is only half on the record, and it may be the more important, or even sometimes the more amusing, half that is suppressed.

I hope that I may have thrown some new light on policies, personalities and personal relationships within the Labour Party during a period of rapid growth and some mental uncertainty; new light, in particular, on the political events of 1931. Many versions have now been published, both by participants in these events and by others. But a true picture has not yet emerged. I have tried, drawing on notes made at the time, to fill some gaps, to correct some misconceptions and to distribute praise and blame more justly than some writers have done.

I must thank Her Majesty the Queen for gracious permission to quote from a letter written by King George V to my mother, when my father died.

I regret very much that, though it is now thirty-eight years since his death, none of Rupert Brooke's letters, except those quoted in Sir Edward Marsh's Memoir of 1917, have been published. But I must thank Mr. Geoffrey Keynes for agreeing, on behalf of Rupert Brooke's literary trustees, to my publishing "anything he wrote to you".

xi

I am also grateful to the First Lord of the Admiralty, Mr. J. P. L. Thomas, and the staff of the Admiralty Library, for enabling me to study the various accounts of the Battle of Jutland; to Lord Vansittart for allowing me to reproduce a Minute on Style, which he circulated in the Foreign Office; and to Mr. Raymond Postgate for letting me make use of the admirable character studies of certain Labour leaders contained in his *Life of George Lansbury*. Finally, I must thank my secretary, Peggy Hughes, for her indispensable help in preparing this book.

HUGH DALTON

House of Commons
January 1953.

CHAPTER I

CHILDHOOD

IN 1882, my father, still a bachelor at the age of forty-three, was ship's chaplain to H.M.S. *Bacchante*. He was also tutor to "the young Princes", Prince Eddy, the Duke of Clarence, who died in 1892, aged twenty-eight, and Prince George, the Duke of York, who later became King George V. The *Bacchante* was taking the Princes, still in their 'teens, round the world and, in particular, round the Empire. My father was strongly in favour of this trip, though not of this ship—doubt having been cast on her stability in a storm. There had been much discussion beforehand, and some difference of views, about the voyage. Queen Victoria, the Prince of Wales, the Admiralty, my father and the Cabinet of Lord Beaconsfield all took part in this.[1]

---

[1] Sir Henry Ponsonby, the Queen's Private Secretary, thus recorded "the confusion of opinions":

"I am much perplexed about this *Bacchante*.

1. Plan proposed to the Queen, who did not at all like it.
2. Dalton sent by the Prince of Wales to urge it. Queen's objections not pressed.
3. Unanimous condemnation by the Cabinet of the plan.
4. Indignation of the Queen and Prince at their interference.
5. Cabinet said they didn't. Plan adopted.
6. Controversies on the selection of the officers. The Queen supporting what she believed to be the Prince of Wales's choice. Sometimes it appears he wished for others. Final agreement on the officers.
7. The *Bacchante* announced to be the ship. Who chose her, when and where I don't know.
8. Chorus of approbation.
9. Strong whispers against her. No stability. The Queen doubtful. The Prince of Wales doubtful. Dalton very doubtful—prefers *Newcastle*.
10. Smith (First Lord) furious, outwardly calm. Offers to turn over crew to *Newcastle*—an old ship full of bilge water. Sends reports in favour of *Bacchante*.
11. Scott ordered to cruise in search of a storm, so as to see if she will capsize.
12. Scott returns, says she won't. Dalton not satisfied. Wants to separate Princes.
13. Queen says this is what she first thought of, but Dalton said it was impossible. Let him consult Prince and Princess of Wales.
14. Queen mentions doubts to Lord Beaconsfield.
15. B. observes he has been already snubbed—but, if his advice is wanted, he will give it.
16. Knollys says Dalton is wrong."

Henry Ponsonby, His Life from His Letters by Arthur Ponsonby, pp. 105–6. (Macmillan.)

It was finally decided that both Princes should go together on the *Bacchante*. This summary of events is also quoted by Harold Nicolson, *King George V*, p. 19.

In the *Bacchante*'s ship's company was a midshipman named
Hugh Evan-Thomas, who more than thirty years later was to
command the Fifth Battle Squadron at Jutland and become
the centre of a sharp naval controversy. He and my father
became great friends, and he showed my father a number of
letters which he received on the voyage from his sister Kitty.
My father said he would very much like to meet this girl. The
midshipman said this could easily be arranged. When the
cruise was over, my father was invited down to the Gnoll
House, Neath, the home of the midshipman's parents, and
there he met, and within three days proposed marriage to, the
midshipman's favourite sister. She was only half my father's
age. Her parents and the midshipman's five brothers were all
a bit taken aback, and her younger sister Molly, who had had
many flirtations and fancied herself a good deal, was the most
astonished of all. But the proposal was pressed and accepted.

The marriage did not take place at once, for my father, at
the end of the cruise of the *Bacchante*, spent six months with the
Princes at Lausanne, where they learned French, and then
went back to Cambridge, as Tutor to Prince Eddy, while
Prince George continued in the Navy.

In 1884 my father was appointed Canon of St. George's
Chapel, Windsor. He and my mother were married in 1886.

I was born at Neath, on August 26th, 1887, in my grandparents' house, "on a Welsh hillside, just above the Neath
football ground", as I used to put it in later years. As a boy I
often climbed through the wire fence separating this ground
from a wooded slope belonging to my grandparents, so as to
watch the match without paying. My grandmother told me
this was very wrong. But I saw some wonderful games. And I
heard crowds singing, as only Welsh crowds can, when the
game warmed up.

I spent most of my early years at Windsor, next door to St.
George's Chapel and under the shadow of the Castle. My
father occupied a Canon's house in the Cloisters, a large house
with a north view, looking out across Eton and the Home Park
and the river. I suppose that these surroundings stimulated in
me a certain irreverence towards authority. I have shown this
characteristic at many different stages of my life and, when in

due course I became authoritative myself, I have enjoyed and even encouraged it in others, particularly in younger people of whom I approved.

When I was four years old I went to a children's Christmas party at the Castle. Hundreds of us were there. My behaviour on that occasion was reported in the local press, and several different versions have been in intermittent circulation ever since. The true version, to the best of my belief, is as follows. When we were all seated at long tables, enjoying a very good meal, the door opened and Queen Victoria entered, accompanied by a Lady-in-Waiting. We were all called to attention and told to stand up and stop eating. The Queen passed slowly along each table, saying a few words to each child. She was told by the Lady-in-Waiting, I suppose, who we all were. Perhaps they had a Table Plan. I had just greedily grabbed a lot of grapes and piled them on my plate. When the Queen reached me, she said: "What a lot of grapes you've got." And I replied, shrilly but audibly, "Yes, Queen." Then she said: "I expect you'd like me to go away, so that you can eat all those grapes." And I replied again, "Yes, Queen." Whereat she turned to her Lady-in-Waiting and said: "What a loud voice that child has, just like his father!" For he, of course, had often preached to her, and no one could ever fall asleep during one of his sermons. This I believe to be the true version. Others, less agreeable on both sides, have been put about, some, I suspect, by my political opponents in my maturity. But I must here testify that I did *not* say: "Go away, Queen, I'm eating cake," nor did she say: "What a horrid little boy!"[1]

My first and, I think, my only meeting with the Prince of Wales, afterwards King Edward VII, was in my parents' house at Windsor. This, I am afraid, is another greedy story. He had come to tea, and I had been produced for inspection. I remember only that he was standing up, holding a plate on which lay a muffin fairly running with butter. Violently attracted by this luscious object, I snatched it off the plate, tried to put it in my mouth and covered my face and hands and clothes with butter. The inspection was soon over.

[1] Indeed, Harold Nicolson relates that Prince George, visiting my parents at Windsor in December 1888, wrote in his Diary: "They have such a nice little boy, fifteen months old." (*King George V*, p. 41.)

One more story I must tell here, because it is the best answer I can give to the question I am sometimes asked: "When did you first become a Socialist?" I was being wheeled in a pram by my nurse down the Long Walk, between the splendid lines of great elms, later all cut down. I saw a poor old thing, in rags, picking up odds and ends of firewood under the trees. "Look," I cried, "there's a lady picking up sticks!" But my nurse, well trained in the stiff class structure of our society, replied reprovingly: "That's not a lady. That's only an old woman." I said no more, but, on our return home, was taken in to tea in the drawing-room to be presented to some most important, titled and authoritative visitor. "Come", said my mother, "and say 'how-do-you-do' to this lady." So I went, and looking her straight in the face said sternly: "You're not a lady. You're only an old woman." From that incident I date my sense of social equality.

When I was eight I began to go as a day boy to St. George's Choir School, at the bottom of the hill on which our house stood, reached through the great Chapter Garden used by the Dean and Canons of St. George's and their families in common. I did not sing in the choir. They tried my voice and said, "A good clear voice, but absolutely no ear". But I did some Latin and some mathematics and played some cricket and football, and ran up and down the hill two or three times a day.

In 1898, when I was eleven, I went to Summerfields at Oxford. Quite a good school, then as now, though with a tendency to cram. At this stage in my life I was thought to be rather a delicate child. I was constantly going down with asthma and bronchitis, having to stay in bed or indoors, missing both work and games. And I was growing very fast and was, therefore, clumsy and ungainly. I appear, at this time, to have been a mild and well-behaved person, somewhat lacking in energy and vitality.

From Summerfields in 1901 I went to Eton. Henceforth I had no more bronchial or asthmatic troubles. That nonsense was finished! And I soon became, and steadily remained, physically very fit. Otherwise, for the next fifty years, I could not have lived the life I have.

My father and mother and my sister and I spent many holidays at the Gnoll, Neath. My sister, four years younger than I, was christened after two Queens—Alexandra Mary—but was always called after a King, Georgie. A younger brother died in childbirth. Had he lived he would have been christened George.

The Gnoll was a large Victorian house, with big rambling gardens, soft and hard tennis courts, a fives court, kitchen gardens, shrubberies, some good trees, including two well-grown Californian Redwoods, a temple, three large ponds, and woods, in which pheasants were reared and rabbits bred, and stables whose smell I still remember better than any other smell in the world. My grandfather, Charles Evan-Thomas, had many interests and was active in the public life of South Wales. I only remember him dimly as a rather formidable figure. He died while I was still too young to know him well. He had a large practice at the Parliamentary Bar, but gave this up in order to have more time for public work and for his private interests in Glamorgan and Breconshire. He owned land in both counties, and served on both county councils, and as a magistrate and Deputy Lieutenant. He was a strong advocate of better educational opportunities, at all levels up to the University, and represented the Neath Borough Council on the Board of Governors of the South Wales University College. After he died, my grandmother lived on at the Gnoll until her death, when I was at Cambridge. She used to spoil me and all the rest of her large army of grandchildren, my cousins.

I have very happy memories of days spent at the Gnoll. I learned to ride, on a little Welsh pony called Nobby, and to shoot rabbits and an occasional pheasant or partridge. But I did not keep up my shooting.

I often asked my Granny to let Mr. Phillips, the postman, come up and play his harp in the evening. He used to play in the big billiard hall and whistle the accompaniment—Welsh tunes, like "Llwyn-on" (The Ash Grove) and "The Bells of Aberdovey".

I regret very much that I never learned Welsh when I was at the Gnoll. It would have been quite easy to arrange this. Mr. Phillips himself could have taught me.

There were wonderful walks on the hills all round, in those borderlands between nature, still almost undisturbed, and the new mining and industrial developments. Once, I think in my first year at Eton, I went off by train to Brecon and climbed the Beacons all by myself, and coming down lost my way in the dusk and was taken care of by a farmer who could speak only Welsh. He put me up for the night, and next day I returned to find the whole household at the Gnoll in a state of great commotion, wondering what had become of me.

I used to tell my Granny, when I went up to Cambridge and was already harbouring Socialist thoughts, that this big house of hers and all these grounds and gardens ought really to belong to the people of Neath. This shocked her sense of private property, but after her death it came to pass. The house was too big for any of my uncles, the grounds too expensive to maintain and poaching impossible to control, so that the sporting value of the estate was much diminished. My uncles, therefore, presented it as a gift to the Neath Borough Council. The gardens and the woods are a fine public property now, and are enjoyed by many thousands. The lower lake is a public bathing-pool, beautifully sited between the hillside and the woods. But the house is now a ruin, since the Council could not make up their minds what to do with it and, while they debated, it decayed. In the Second World War it was used for battle training. It might have been turned into a school, or a sanatorium, or a nurses' home, or simply a place for refreshments, concerts and other entertainments, as part of the new public estate. I hope something may yet be done with the site on which this unsightly ruin still stands.

My mother's brothers made this gift to Neath, and Neath made me a gift which I was proud to receive. In 1946 they gave me the Freedom of my home town. They gave it me, first, because I had been born among them and spent part of my childhood there and, second, because they thought I had done something, through politics, to banish unemployment from their midst, and to bring new industries and new hope to the distressed areas, of which Neath was one. But all that comes later in this story.

My mother had six brothers and one sister. I liked them all, but her favourite and my father's favourite was my Uncle Hugh, after whom I am named. He had a distinguished career in the Navy. Apart from sea commands, he was private secretary to three First Lords of the Admiralty between 1905 and 1908, Cawdor, Tweedmouth and McKenna. I remember his telling my father once, when we were together at the Gnoll, how Tweedmouth had come back to the Admiralty after a Cabinet in which he had fought an unsuccessful action with "Lloyd George and other clever talkers", who had reduced his Naval Estimates, and how he had burst into tears in front of my uncle. That was one of my first insights into High Politics. It sounded fascinating!

At Jutland my uncle commanded the Fifth Battle Squadron. It was said by some that if he had turned his four great ships a few minutes sooner, in response to a signal from Beatty, we might have destroyed the German Fleet and scored a victory instead of a draw. It was retorted by him, and by others, that he never got the signal. In tribute to his memory, I have made a note on this controversy at the end of this book.

In the Navy in those days there was a Jellicoe school and a Beatty school—caution against daring. My uncle trusted Jellicoe's judgment more than Beatty's. Mr. Churchill, as he explains in *The World Crisis*, took the opposite view, though he says of Jellicoe "it might fall to him, as to no other man— Sovereign, Statesman, Admiral or General—to issue orders which in the space of *two or three hours* might nakedly decide who won the war. The destruction of the British Battle Fleet was final. Jellicoe was the only man on either side who could lose the war in an afternoon".

My uncle, in the course of a varied career, was Commandant of the Royal Naval College, Dartmouth, from 1910 to 1912. I remember spending a weekend with him there, and that he and I went for a run with the College Beagles. His last Command, as Full Admiral, was at the Nore from 1921 to 1924, when he retired. He died in 1928.

He thought some of my ideas decidedly odd. I was once reading a lot of John Morley and talked to my Uncle Hugh about him. I said I didn't think Morley believed in God. My uncle replied, very seriously and with the air of having settled the matter, "If John Morley ever found himself falling over a cliff, I bet he'd say 'My God!'"

My mother, as a girl, was devoted to my Uncle Hugh above all men; then, through all their long married life, to my

father; then, after his death, to me. She would never believe
that any one of the three of us was wrong, nor listen to any
criticism of us. She always stood up for my political views, even
if she did not wholly understand them. When I first stood for
Parliament as a Labour Candidate, some old pussy-cat from
the Castle condoled with her. "Oh, Mrs. Dalton," she said,
"I'm so sorry to hear this sad news about your son. I hear he's
gone the same way as poor Arthur Ponsonby." (The latter had
been Queen Victoria's page, and the son of her Private Secretary. He himself was Private Secretary to Campbell-Bannerman and, after a period as a Liberal M.P., joined the Labour
Party.) But my mother would have none of it. "I don't know
what you mean," she replied. "I think he's doing quite right."
She voted Labour from 1924 onwards.

So did my father in his last two general elections of 1924 and
1929. He died in July 1931, just before the break-up of the
Second Labour Government. What he would have thought of
that, I don't know.

He was very pleased that I was serving in that Government
as Under-Secretary at the Foreign Office, and hoped to see me
go higher. He thought well of Ramsay MacDonald, largely
because King George V thought well of him, and had lent my
father Mr. MacDonald's book about his late wife, which the
Prime Minister had presented to His Majesty. My father never
focused Arthur Henderson, my political chief, of whom I shall
have much more to say later. Though he was tolerant of
Scottish Presbyterians, he was allergic to Wesleyans. In 1924
he announced publicly at Windsor that he was voting Labour.
"I don't know the Labour Candidate," he said, "but I *do*
know the Conservative." The former was Mr. Birch Crisp,
well known in the City of London, the latter Mr. A. A. Somerville, an old Eton Housemaster who had unsuccessfully tried
to prevent me from being appointed to the Cambridge
University Statutory Commission in 1923, on the ground that
I would be politically biased. My father was very much
offended by this.

My father was the son of a country clergyman. He was born
in 1839, went to school at Blackheath and thence to Clare
College, Cambridge, as a scholar. He took a Third in Classics
and a First in Theology, and rowed in the Clare Second Boat.

He entered the Church and, while a curate at Whippingham in the Isle of Wight, at the age of thirty-one, he caught the eye of Queen Victoria, who in 1871 appointed him tutor to the two "young Princes". He was with them during their time as naval cadets on the *Britannia* at Dartmouth and their cruise on the *Bacchante*. Having been appointed Canon of Windsor in 1884, he there remained to the end of his life, for forty-seven years. He was domestic chaplain to Queen Victoria, King Edward VII and King George V.

He was a Broad Churchman with little sympathy for High Church practices and not much regard for Nonconformists, whom he always called "Dissenters". He did not take his Bible literally; told me that "Heaven is not a place, but a state of mind", and followed keenly and accepted fully all new developments in natural science. He was particularly interested in the discoveries of radio-activity and the transmutation of elements in the early years of this century, and was a personal friend and great admirer of J. J. Thomson.

He had the good Cambridge man's healthy contempt for Oxford, a place, he thought, of softness, affectation and too much money. In the Church he took some part in the work of Convocation. He published some suggestions of his own for the revision of the Prayer-book and made his own translation of the Psalms. He was a good Hebrew scholar.

He had a number of other interests. He never lost his love of the Navy, and he was a great believer in the future of the Empire. In 1901 he went in the *Ophir*, with the Duke and Duchess of Cornwall—later King George V and Queen Mary —to the opening of the first Parliament of the Australian Commonwealth. He formed a strong liking for several politicians whom he met on this trip—Alfred Deakin and John Forrest in Australia, and Sir Wilfred Laurier, with whom he talked much on a journey across Canada.

My father was much attracted by the idea of Imperial Federation, as propounded by Sir George Parkin, and by Seeley's and William Cunningham's writings. He made friends with Austen Chamberlain, when the latter was an undergraduate and my father was at Trinity with Prince Eddy.

He strongly supported Joseph Chamberlain's Imperial Preference Campaign, and transmitted some of his enthusiasm to me. When I went up to Cambridge from Eton, in my first term I stuck several pictures of Joe on my walls!

My father did not like Liberals. He was a Tory Democrat. No one I have ever known was less of a snob and less like the traditional picture of a courtier. He made friends, on equal terms, with all sorts and conditions of men. He had no use for lords, or for rich men, as such. When some wealthy nobleman was trying to bargain the Garter against a contribution to the fund for the restoration of St. George's Chapel, my father said to the King: "I'd give the old fool two Garters, one for each leg, if he'd give me a good big cheque."

Among his friends, with whom he maintained contact and correspondence over many years, were Edward Carpenter, a friend of his undergraduate days at Cambridge, known to British Socialists as the author of *England, Arise!* and *Towards Democracy*; Patrick Macgill, "the Navvy Poet" from County Donegal; and Arthur Benson, Eton Master, Public School Reformer, Poet and Master of Magdalene College, Cambridge. Benson was my father's best man at his wedding.

My father used to visit regularly, as part of his official duties, all the lodge keepers at Windsor Castle and in the Park. Once, finding the wife of one of the keepers ill in bed, he insisted on going down on his knees and scrubbing the kitchen floor himself. Some years ago I got a letter from the daughter of an old lodge keeper who had been in the Navy, in these terms:

"We lived in a lodge at Windsor Castle for thirty years, and the Canon thought a lot of my dear old Dad and used to visit him quite frequently.

"I well remember Christmas-time, the Canon striding down from the Castle, walking straight into the lodge, banging a bottle of whisky on the table and in his deep booming voice saying 'There you are, my old shipmate' to my Dad.

"He always called Mother his old sweetheart. They loved spinning sea yarns together."

A sense of social equality came naturally to my father.

Among his other interests were Church architecture—he wrote a book on *The Collegiate Church of Ottery St. Mary*—and the Drapers' Company. He was a very loyal son of the Drapers, was Master of the Company in 1919–20 and took a specially keen interest in its educational work.

He liked taking visitors, and particularly younger people, to dine at Drapers' Hall. He seldom drank wine at home, but he was a good judge of claret and hock.

My Uncle Corrie, my father's favourite brother and my favourite uncle on my father's side, was also a leading figure at Drapers' and in due course Master of the Company. He often came with his wife and daughters to spend Christmas with us at Windsor, and we sometimes spent summer holidays together by the sea. He was a heavily built man, with a beard, a sense of humour and, occasionally, a violent temper. He advised me not to go into the Church, because it would be so awkward if, afterwards, I ceased to believe in it. He did not much "believe in it" himself, and sometimes gently chaffed my father about miracles, and bishops, and Church organisation. He was a civil servant, in the Board of Trade. He too gave me some early insight into politics. He had been private secretary to Shaw Lefevre, and told me what a mess his chief had made of a speech in the House on bimetallism, though carefully coached and furnished with an excellent official brief. In 1906, when Lloyd George was President of the Board, my uncle put up to him a Patents Bill which became law in 1908. L. G., who knew nothing about the subject, asked whether this was Free Trade or Protection. "Whichever you like," said my uncle. "It protects the British manufacturer against foreigners taking out a patent and not using it, but, when the unused patent is revoked, it frees the trade." L. G. was delighted with this answer, became very keen on the Bill and got it through. Several previous Presidents had refused to be interested. My uncle ended his public service as Comptroller of Patents, a semi-judicial office of great dignity. He had an amused capacity for seeming pompous, which went well with his title of Sir Cornelius Dalton.

My father's friendship with King George V, from the time when he first became his tutor until my father's death, was one of his most precious possessions. This relationship was always one of complete frankness. Harold Nicolson in his *King George V* gives a good and well-documented account of my father's work and influence through the tutorial years. In later years my father was invited every summer by the King to visit Balmoral or Sandringham. Even when he went away nowhere else, he still kept up this annual visit—right to the end.

When my father died, the King wrote to my mother: "I shall miss him greatly. It is now just sixty years since I first knew him. I always had the greatest respect and affection for him and during those long years I greatly valued his kind advice. He was my oldest and most intimate friend."

The author of his obituary in *The Times* wrote that at Windsor "his antiquarian knowledge and his strong and forceful personality quickly gained him a unique position. He studied the history of St. George's, its buildings and its traditions with intense interest. He loved them wholeheartedly, and his appointment by the Chapter to the office of Steward gave him a post of responsibility in regard to the management of finance and the care of the fabric which he filled with a dominating vigour and a degree of independence that at times were not without embarrassment for his colleagues of the Chapter. Yet, even when differences on points of administration were acute and indeed, on Dalton's part, explosively violent, they could not obliterate his personal charm or destroy the real affection he inspired even in those who had most cause to mistrust his policy and his methods of achieving it.

"His sermons were more often interesting for their vigorous delivery than for their contents. Every hearer was impressed by the wonderful voice, ranging from a high falsetto to a thunderous bass, with which the sermon was spoken. And as a reader he had no living equal. He loved his Bible, and to hear Dalton read one of the more dramatic passages in St. George's Chapel was an experience indescribable and never to be forgotten. This power seemed scarcely affected by the passage of the years."

I inherited and learned much from my father that has helped me to make my own way through life—good physical health, after an uncertain start, and great stamina, a strong voice, a strong temper, strong views, some obstinacy and, I hope, a capacity for friendship on equal terms with a wide range, in age and class and type, of men and women and, I trust, beyond all else, an abiding loyalty to firm friends.

So, amid much that is different in his life and mine, some things, I hope, are the same. Certainly very different on the surface, for "it is an interesting commentary", says the Duke of Windsor, "upon the flexibility of British society that this man who played so influential a part in moulding the conservative character of my father should himself have produced under the shadow of Windsor Castle a son, Hugh Dalton, who became Chancellor of the Exchequer in a Socialist Government".[1] Perhaps less different deep down.

[1] *A King's Story*, p. 35.

CHAPTER II

ETON

I WENT to Eton at Michaelmas 1901. I was only seventeenth on the list for College. It was thought that, if I had been physically stronger while at Summerfields, with fewer interruptions through sickness, I should have been several places higher and made sure of getting into College.[1] So I became an Oppidan. I went first to Luxmoore's for two halves. Then, when he gave up his House, to Kindersley's. Then, with three other boys, to Luxmoore again for part of the summer half, after the fire which burnt out Kindersley's on June 1st, 1903, when two boys were trapped and burnt to death. My hair was singed and I smelt fire very easily for some time after that affair! Then back to Kindersley's.

On balance, I am sorry I did not get into College. There I would not have reached the lonely eminence of my last year as Captain of Kindersley's, but I would have found more mental stimulus and been a member of a more closely knit society. Most important of all, I believe I should have been quite good at the Wall Game, which, as an Oppidan, I never played. It would just have suited my build and temperament. Weight rather than pace; endurance; low cunning. I was clumsy and slow and heavy on my feet, but with steadily increasing strength and stamina. I was not good at the Field Game, nor at cricket, though my style as a bat, based on a study of the textbooks, was much better than my run-getting. Therefore I never took much interest in games at Eton and was lethargic and physically lazy. And I was still growing rather fast.

But I was not unhappy at Eton. That was a Tory story to explain why, when I was Chancellor of the Exchequer forty years later, I put up the surtax and the death duties on some of my old school fellows. Another Tory story, once repeated in a speech in the House of Commons, was that I was only a day boy at Eton. But this was mistaken identity, fortified by

---

[1] In 1901 only twelve got in; in 1903 sixteen; in 1904 fourteen.

mistrust! There *was* one day boy at Eton in my time—they
were very rare—a year or two my senior, H. F. Dalton, son
of an Eton Master known as "Piggy" Dalton.

I was not unhappy, nor bullied, nor much beaten in my
House, nor ever birched by the Headmaster—rather an easy,
lazy life, in short. Until my last year I was rather bored and
indifferent. But I loved that last year, when I was Captain of
my House and in Sixth Form. I liked marching up Chapel in
the Sixth Form Ram. And I created a great sensation, and
great animosity in some quarters, by going round as Headmaster's Praepostor, whose duty it was to summon boys to the
Presence, in pumps! This was a privilege of dress strictly
reserved by convention for members of Pop, that society of the
élite by co-option which dominates the social life at Eton.

My pumps were an anti-Pop gesture, a symbol of rebellion
and irreverence. Gladwyn Jebb, who will appear later in this
story, himself well described by someone as "every inch a
Pop", Captain of his House as well, and equally good at all
games, sports and studies, said, when I related this incident to
him, that it was like the beginning of the Class War in Ancient
Rome. I was leading the Plebs against the Patricians, a foretaste of Socialist politics. But there was no follow-up!

I greatly enjoyed, and was much developed by, the exercise
of authority and responsibility as Captain of my House. The
Liberal Government of 1905 had just come in and Grey was
Foreign Secretary. I told a party of grown-ups at my father's
dinner-table that "I have greater power in my House than Sir
Edward Grey has in the Foreign Office". What a sententious
little prig! But there was some truth in it, and the masters
encouraged us to rate our responsibilities very high.

I was against the Liberals. I was a Joe Chamberlainite, a
Tory Democrat, a self-confessed Imperialist. I gave a big book
about the Empire to Kindersley when I left. He was a Liberal
Free Trader and I wanted to educate him. And I knew that
Chamberlain had also asked "What ransom will property
pay?" and had declared that "the Monarchy can't long
endure". That strain of Radicalism appealed to me. Most sermons in Chapel bored me, but a Socialist sermon by Scott
Holland on conditions of life in the slums moved me a lot.

I sometimes hear talk, nearly all by people who haven't been to public schools, of the tyranny of fagging and the brutality of beating by House Captains, Games Captains and Fagmasters—or, as they are called at many schools, though not at Eton, by Prefects. I have always thought all this talk much exaggerated, both in fact and psychopathic fancy, and that there is much to be said, provided they are not allowed to get out of hand, for these traditional arrangements for personal service and for these simple sanctions. Anyhow, there wasn't much beating either at Luxmoore's or at Kindersley's in my time. Both, judged by this standard, were quite gentle Houses.

Indeed, it might have been good for me to have been beaten a bit more and a bit harder, since this would have made me run about a bit quicker and made me more alert and less lethargic, which at this stage of my life would have been an improvement. In later life, particularly when I got well started in politics, I did not lack energy, or keenness, or quickness of response to my surroundings. But at Eton I did. In 1940, when I was Minister of Economic Warfare, I was, I believe, known by my staff as Dr. Dynamo, and though that name may have fitted me then, it certainly would not have fitted me at Eton.

But I was reminded, more than forty years later, by Lord Winterton, when he was Father of the House of Commons and I was a Cabinet Minister, of an occasion when, as Captain of my House, I beat the whole House, below the top four, because no one would own up to having scribbled some objectionable remarks on the wall of the lavatory. One of my victims on that occasion was, at this later date, a most blameless-looking Tory M.P. who had related this incident to Winterton.

My closest friends at Eton were Bob Bourne and Geoffrey Morris, who were both at Booker's, and Algy Bligh, a good footballer and a stout supporter of mine in all rows and faction fights in my own House. I stayed with Algy at Minehead, where his father was a Master of Harriers, and we rode on Exmoor together. But he did not go to a University and we lost touch after leaving Eton. R. C. Bourne went to Oxford. He was a famous oar, by far the best of all his contemporaries. He stroked Eton to victory at Henley, and Oxford three times to victory against Cambridge, and one year created a new record. He won the School Sculls at Eton and the Diamond Sculls at Henley. He was not popular at Eton. When he won the School

Sculls, I was one of the very few who ran along the bank and shouted for him against a more popular opponent. He was an agreeably arrogant athlete-intellectual. A favourite saying of his was : "God gives us our relations. Thank God we choose our friends." He had read and heard something of Voltaire and of Nietzsche and of the modern rationalists and scientists, which made, at that age, a formidable combination. He influenced me a good deal. Many of my early beliefs, as we walked and talked together, were lost on the playing-fields of Eton.

I must relate, to give a faithful picture of the mood in which many of us found ourselves, that with others in my first year at Eton I had been duly confirmed according to the practice of the Church of England. Luxmoore prepared me, and no one could have done it more impressively. But the Bishop was not impressive. We had all been expecting something tremendous to happen to us. But it didn't. And, in the anti-climax, this one went the rounds among us:

BISHOP: My dear boy, if you were in a dormitory with twenty other boys, and they all got into bed without saying their prayers, would you have the moral courage to kneel down, all by yourself, and say yours?

BOY: My dear Bishop, if you were in a dormitory with twenty other bishops, and they all knelt down to say their prayers, would you have the moral courage to get into bed, all by yourself, without saying yours?

Bob Bourne became Tory M.P. for Oxford City, and would, I think, have been Speaker of the House of Commons had he lived. He had an amazing knowledge of Parliamentary procedure and remarkable quickness of decision. His early death in 1938 caused the famous Munich by-election.

Geoffrey Morris was a classical scholar. He was a wit, a cynic, a *bon viveur* and very ugly. He went to Cambridge as a Scholar of Trinity, and was later a Fellow, first of Jesus and then of Corpus, where he became Bursar. During the sittings of the University Statutory Commission in the nineteen-twenties I often used to dine in Corpus with Will Spens and meet him there. In University politics he was an ultra-Conservative. He spent much time at Newmarket, where he was often very successful in his bets. He died between the wars.

I gave up classics in my last year at Eton and specialised in mathematics. It was a near choice and perhaps a mistake, but it was thought that my mathematics were better than my classics. I was taught mathematics so well at Eton by J. M. Dyer, A. E. Conybeare and others, that after three years at Cambridge, mostly devoted to other interests, I got through my Mathematical Tripos Part I, with a Third, largely on the mathematics I had learned at Eton.

Mathematics at Eton, and afterwards, always had for me a certain elfin quality, as of a symbolic fairyland, wherein are found the Square Root of Minus One, the Fourth Dimension, and Infinity. I often went on the journey to Infinity and back. But why did I always come back on the other side of the Asymptote? I used to chew over all this when I felt meditative and solitary.

As for the Classics, I got most from Hugh Macnaghten, who made me and many other Etonians love Catullus.

> *Soles occidere et redire possunt.*
> *Nobis, cum semel occidit brevis lux,*
> *Nox est perpetua una dormienda.*

Not till 1951 did I read Sir Walter Raleigh's perfect translation:

> *The sun may set and rise;*
> *But we contrariwise*
> *Sleep after our short light*
> *One everlasting night.*

It is all there!

Another of Macnaghten's favourite quotations, which has stayed with me, is Aristotle's μεγαλῶν ἀξιούμεννι ἀξιοῖ—"Those who think themselves worthy of great things, they *are* worthy." By this message, with a wistful smile, he encouraged us, and I have often used it since to encourage others.

One day, a landmark in my life, I discovered Swinburne's *Atalanta in Calydon* in the school library. No one had told me about it, nor about Swinburne. It swept me off my feet, and gave me new songs to sing, or at least to declaim, for ever. I pressed on to the *Poems and Ballads* and there I found *The Triumph of Time*, inspired, as I learned afterwards, by the mocking rejection of the poet's advances by a young lady whose father was a friend of Ruskin and Burne-Jones, just as *Dolores*, which he

wrote a few years later, was inspired by a lady who rode horses
at a circus. I proposed to those in authority that I should declaim some twenty stanzas of *The Triumph of Time*, as my contribution to the Speeches to be made on the Fourth of June,
1906, in Upper School by members of Sixth Form. Much to my
surprise and, as I think, to their credit, those in authority
agreed. Swinburne, I am pretty sure, had never been declaimed before in Speeches at Eton. But the previous October I
had declaimed a large part of Tennyson's *Ode on the Death of
the Duke of Wellington*, a most orthodox choice. I enjoyed those
speeches, delivered before a large audience after much private
rehearsal. They were a foretaste of political oratory, and of
the Winchester Reading Prize which I won at Cambridge.
J. F. Crace, with whom I rehearsed, said that my style was
"rather parsonical", and I was certainly rather nervous before
the thing started. But I said to myself, to restore my confidence: "Don't be nervous. Think how much more nervous
most of your audience would be, if they had to do it. And
you know you can do it better than they could."

Those lines of Catullus, *The Triumph of Time* and Tennyson's
Ode are all about Death. I luxuriated in that theme at Eton,
and still more at Cambridge. It was not long to wait till 1914.
What grand stuff that Swinburne was to declaim!

> *Yea, I know this well: were you once sealed mine,*
> *Mine in the blood's beat, mine in the breath,*
> *Mixed into me as honey in wine,*
> *Not time that sayeth and gainsayeth,*
> *Nor all strong things had severed us then;*
> *Not wrath of gods, nor wisdom of men,*
> *Nor all things earthly, nor all divine,*
> *Nor joy nor sorrow, nor life nor death.*
>
> *You have chosen and clung to the chance they sent you,*
> *Life sweet as perfume and pure as prayer.*
> *But will it not one day in heaven repent you?*
> *Will they solace you wholly, the days that were?*
> *Will you lift up your eyes between sadness and bliss,*
> *Meet mine, and see where the great love is,*
> *And tremble and turn and be changed? Content you;*
> *The gate is strait; I shall not be there.*

And, later, the superb run of stanzas, beginning:

> *I will go back to the great sweet mother,*
> *Mother and lover of men, the sea,*

where the poet imagines himself drowning in ecstasy and, being dead,

> *I shall sleep, and move with the moving ships,*
> *Change as the winds change, veer in the tide.*

And Tennyson, too, in very different mood and style, had fine declamatory rolling lines, full of quotations, as the old lady said of Shakespeare.

> *Not once or twice in our rough island story*
> *The path of duty was the way to glory. . . .*

> *Peace, his triumph will be sung*
> *By some yet unmoulded tongue*
> *Far on in summers that we shall not see,*
> *Peace, it is a day of pain. . . .*

> *We revere and while we hear*
> *The tides of music's golden sea*
> *Setting towards eternity,*
> *Uplifted high in heart and hope are we. . . .*

> *Gone; but nothing can bereave him*
> *Of the force he made his own*
> *Being here, and we believe him*
> *Something far advanced in state,*
> *And that he wears a truer crown*
> *Than any wreath that man can weave him.*
> *Speak no more of his renown,*
> *Lay your earthly fancies down,*
> *And in the vast cathedral leave him.*
> *God accept him, Christ receive him.*[1]

---

[1] Mr. Churchill (*The Second World War*, Vol. V, p. 146) relates that, after Admiral Fraser in the *Duke of York* had sunk the *Scharnhörst*, "I reminded him of these famous lines . . .

> *Not once or twice in our rough island story*
> *The path of duty was the way to glory.*

The Admiral seemed all the more pleased, because, as I judged, he had never heard the quotation before. I hoped he thought I had made it up myself on purpose."

AT ETON, 1906

I hated leaving Eton—I was near the top of the tree and I
didn't want to come down—but I now look back on myself, at
the end of my time there, with disapproval. I had done much
better in my last year, and I had enjoyed, and benefited from,
being Captain of my House. I had gained self-confidence and
some sense of leadership. But I was still soft and self-centred,
sluggish, sententious, sentimental and sheltered from raw
reality.

Maybe it would have done me good physically, strengthened
my character and usefully widened my experience if, like many
Etonians during and since the last war, I had gone straight
from school to a period of military service before going up to
the University. Especially if I had started, without any
favouritism, in the ranks and had to earn all advancement
entirely by my own performance, with no social pull. As it was,
I went on living in a sheltered corner. I knew nothing of my
working-class contemporaries and only met some of them when
we were all a good deal older and, to that extent, much less
interesting to one another. But during the Long Vacation my
father sent me to France, to live with a family and learn French.
And that proved very useful later on.

At midsummer 1906 I was Fifth Oppidan in Sixth Form
at Eton. By Michaelmas 1906 I was gone. Thereafter I did
not see some of the faces I had known at Eton until in
1924, eighteen years later, I saw them again in the House of
Commons. Rows of Old Boys! Nearly all of them, I regret to
say, were sitting opposite me on the Tory Benches, supporting
Stanley Baldwin, an Harrovian Prime Minister, and Winston
Churchill, an Harrovian Chancellor of the Exchequer—with
Austen Chamberlain, a Rugbeian Foreign Secretary, thrown in.

There were only three Old Etonians on the Labour Benches
in that Parliament—Arthur Ponsonby, Pethick Lawrence and
I. And the attendant, on my first appearance as a new M.P.,
had thought from my demeanour that *I* was a Tory and
directed me towards the Government Benches. But look at
those Tory old schoolfellows of mine! *This* was political
apostasy!

The Eton Boating Song, both the tune and the words, always
haunts my memory, undistinguished dry-bob though I was.

Rugby may be more clever,
Harrow may make more row,

we used to sing, with accents of contempt.

But we'll swing together,
Steady from stroke to bow,
And nothing on earth can sever
The chain that is round us now.

Those Tory Old Etonians ought to be with *us*, in opposition to such a Government as *that*, fighting our traditional enemies, to chase them out of Downing Street!

I have already said that I was anti-Pop when I was at Eton. This, no doubt, was partly green-eye and partly my habitual irreverence towards authority. I did not, indeed, stand quite aloof from the affairs of Pop. With the help of Bob Bourne and Geoffrey Morris—who were both in Pop *ex officio* in my last year, the one as Captain of the Boats, the other as Captain of the Oppidans—I organised enough black balls to keep out, for that year anyhow, one aspirant whom I disliked, and whose election, since he was in my House, would have caused me local inconvenience and rivalry. But a kindlier feeling towards Pop as an institution, and towards many members of it, younger than myself, whom I met as years went on, soon grew within me and remains today. These grave constitutional and personal issues are best seen, not from the worm's-eye view of an adolescent contemporary, but from the high ground reached in the autumn of youth's ending, or even from the snow-peaks climbed in the hard winter of early middle age.

It is best if at school no too sharp line can be drawn between those who excel at work, those who excel at games and those who excel socially and in other ways. Excellence on a wide front, even when the whole front widens immeasurably, as it does at the University and after, is still the finest achievement. I have often so advised young men in later years.

Since I left Eton I have always steadily favoured Boarding Schools, as against Day Schools, for the great majority. In my Utopia most boys—and, I think, girls too—would, for several years, go to Boarding Schools well away from their homes, so that their parents could not always be looking over the gate.

They would live with one another, and with their teachers, well out of range of day-to-day parental interference.

Living in a community of your own contemporaries—say a five-year age-group—can be, if the conditions are right, the best of all educational experiences. At a Day School there is a daily strain of a split personality, of two worlds in conflict. And the influence of parents may be very bad and cramping. "Our object here", said Woodrow Wilson at Princeton, "is to make young men as unlike their fathers as possible." Too absolute an aspiration, no doubt, but not in all cases a mistaken aim!

The qualities, and defects, of the British Public Schooligan have often been debated. Training in leadership, power of decision, responsibility in running the affairs of a small but vital community, indirect rule by senior boys rather than direct rule by the masters, the virtues of the perfect prefect. We know all that. And, on the other hand, intolerance, conventionality, conservatism in a wide social sense, narrowness of outlook and experience. We know all that too. And some of this mud sticks. But in a more equal society, and with more Boarding Schools, many of these objections would disappear. And much, of course, depends on the masters, even if they only rule indirectly. And some, we know, are mediocre. But that is true of Day Schools too.

Really equal opportunity in education is one of the biggest steps forward now to be taken. But it should include an equal opportunity for all of education in a Boarding School. It is silly that this opportunity should be limited now to small sections of the nation—Eton and Borstal! Attacks on Public Schools as such always leave me pretty cold. What we need is a great increase in their number, and a real classless mingling within them. An improved and much extended Public School system, through which should pass the main body of the young life of the nation, could become one of the firmest foundations of that Classless Society which Socialists like me are busy building.

We must "democratise" the existing Public Schools, as we are "democratising" the Universities. And we must build new ones, classless from the beginning, far from the crowded towns where most of the parents live, deep in the country, in healthy and beautiful places.

CHAPTER III

CAMBRIDGE

ONE of my most distinguished contemporaries at Eton, a Colleger who went on to Oxford and then into the Roman Catholic Church, told one of my younger friends many years later that Eton had very little, but Cambridge very great, formative influence on me. Certainly, when I went up to King's in the autumn of 1906, it was as though the heavens had opened. A whole new world of persons, interests and emotions now spread out before me, and I advanced most eagerly into the very midst of it.

I did not win a scholarship at King's, but I held a Soley Exhibition, a family affair with limited competition. I stayed up four years, reading—nominally at least—mathematics for the first three and economics for the fourth. I was in lodgings in Peas Hill in my first year; in College, in Bodley's Buildings, in my second and third; in lodgings near Newnham in my fourth.

I gathered a very wide circle of friends, both in and outside King's, including athletes and æsthetes, intellectuals and innocents, politicians and playboys—these classes, of course, overlap—and I lived, for my first three years, a most intense and varied life among them all. In my fourth year I went out to a suburb and worked. I played no organised games, only tennis and, in my first year, Eton Fives. I liked these games because one picked one's company. I also walked considerable distances at a brisk pace with chosen companions—to Ely and back, along the river, was one of our favourites in summer.

My three primary interests at Cambridge were Personal Relationships, Politics and Poetry. I came to Economics through Politics, and to Ethics through Personal Relationships.

As Belloc wrote of his undergraduate days at Oxford, so I of mine at Cambridge.

> *Sure no one in our long decline,*
> *So dusty, spiteful and divided,*
> *Had half such pleasant friends as mine,*
> *Or loved them half as much as I did.*

The Germans, as I relate later, killed most of them.

King's in my time was a very male society. Among the Dons, at all ages, there was a high proportion of bachelors. There was also, and this was a very good feature of the College, a high proportion of young Dons, living in College and knowing the undergraduates.

As for women, most of us, while undergraduates, did not take much serious or sustained interest in them, though there were some outstanding exceptions to this rule among my friends. Lowes Dickinson used to say of the women who came to his lectures that he never could distinguish them; they all looked like cows. His lack of interest on this side of life was so well known that it caused great excitement among the undergraduates when it was once rumoured that he had been seen alone with a Creole woman in some remote rural solitude.

When I turned twenty-one I went, as I was then entitled to do, to the Dean—"Brookie", our greatest authority on the Septuagint, Rupert Brooke's uncle, and later Provost of the College—and said that I was not quite sure about my religious beliefs and did not, therefore, wish to attend Chapel compulsorily any more. But I should sometimes come voluntarily, I said, if only to hear the music.

He asked whether I did not think that I was still too young to have strong ideas of my own on these subjects. I replied that that was just what I had been trying to say.

Some of my friends then bet me that I would not stand on the Fellows' Grass in the Front Court—which was forbidden to undergraduates anyhow—wearing pyjamas and a dressing-gown, as the congregation streamed out of King's Chapel on a Sunday morning.

I won my bet. Brookie wrote me a note as follows:

"Dear Mr. Dalton,

"If I was not mistaken, I saw you standing on the Fellows' Grass improperly dressed after Service this morning. This must not happen again."

I cherished this note, and stuck it on my wall, with other trophies, till I went down. Then I destroyed it, with a lot of other letters and papers and fixture lists which I wish now I

had kept. But I was then in revolt against sentimentality towards inanimate objects, and against amassing records. I kept
all letters and postcards from Rupert Brooke—I felt *they* were
important—but almost nothing else.

The beauty of King's Chapel grew upon me with the years.
Close up against that tremendous background, physical,
æsthetic and spiritual, most men, especially most middle-aged
and elderly men, looked small and out of place.

Rupert Brooke and I were both born in August 1887. He
was twenty-three days older than I was. We went up to King's
together and we first spoke to one another on the first Sunday
in our first term, on the steps of the Provost's Lodge, whither
we had both been bidden.

No Cambridge friendship of mine meant more to me than
his, and the radiance of his memory still lights my path. Early
in our first term, with a few others, we founded in King's a
Society which we called the Carbonari, the Charcoal Burners,
after the name of an early nineteenth-century Revolutionary
Society in Italy. We met once a week to read papers and poetry
and to discuss. We dined officially once a year, and unofficially
more often. We added a few freshmen in our second year, and
a few more in our third. At the end of that year we let the
Carbonari die. It had had a good life. We did not want to risk
spoiling it by making it live too long.

At one of the first meetings Rupert read some of his poems
aloud; none had then been published. They belong to the
1906–8 section of his first thin volume of 1911. Both the poems
themselves, and his reading of them, moved me very deeply. The
best of those juvenilia, as I reread them now, amaze me still by
their imagery and by their music; *The Vision of the Archangels*
("Slowly up silent peaks, the white edge of the world"), *The
Song of the Pilgrims* ("What light of unremembered skies?"), *The
Song of the Beasts* ("Come away! Come away! Ye are sober and
dull through the common day, but now it is night!"), *Day that
I have Loved* ("Tenderly, day that I have loved, I close your
eyes") and *The Beginning* ("Some day I shall rise and leave my
friends"). Some he read to us just after he had written them.

He read verse better in a small company than anyone I have
ever known. His flowing rhythm and his emphasis and his
sense of drama were perfect. Speaking verse in a large company

he was less good, so that, to my great pride and surprise, Hugh Russell Smith, who had been at Rugby with him, and I defeated him and won the Winchester Reading Prizes, which were competed for each year in the Senate House, in 1909.

Rupert and I read and discussed much modern poetry together. I came to Cambridge rather drunk with Swinburne, and found that he was too. We read Housman's *Shropshire Lad* to one another, and he put me on to Belloc, quoting, very early in our acquaintance, those now familiar lines

> *From quiet homes and first beginning*
> *Out to the undiscovered ends,*
> *There's nothing worth the wear of winning*
> *But laughter and the love of friends.*

I was delighted to find that he liked some of Henley's poems as much as I did. And we went together into the Celtic Twilight with the early Yeats and stayed to see Synge's plays acted, as the daylight grew.

I find that I stay faithful to the poets of my youth. All these thrill me still. But it would be against nature if all the thrills were as sharp as forty years ago.

Most of Rupert's best poems were written after 1908, as his personal experiences widened and deepened, and his command of technique grew firmer. They are very varied in mood and theme. There is much in them that I still find very moving; much beauty and music, and laughter and irony and some deliberate, successful, ugliness. If I had to pick five from this second period I would choose *Jealousy* ("When I see you who were so wise and cool"), *Ambarvalia* ("Swings the way still by hollow and hill"), *The Fish* ("In a cool curving world he lies"), *Heaven* ("Fish fly-replete in depth of June") and *Retrospect* ("In your arms was still delight").

The five War Sonnets, written in the winter of 1914, stand by themselves. They are quite unlike anything else he ever wrote. They issued from him at a unique moment, in his life and that of us all. But having fitted so perfectly the mood of that moment, they have seemed to some to jar on later moods. Yet a strange felicity shines through them, and a very strong emotion.

The Carbonari also included Gerald Shove, Arthur Schloss (now Waley), Nigel Crompton, Kenneth Elmslie, F. A. Holt,

A. V. Jones, J. C. Jolly, J. Steuart Wilson, Philip Baker (now Philip Noel-Baker), Philip Morton Shand and Francis Birrell.

Waley became a distinguished Chinese scholar; Shand wrote an admirable book on wine; Steuart Wilson became a famous singer; Jolly—who was a butt for much good-humoured jesting at our meetings—became Recorder of Preston; Birrell a well-known figure in the Bloomsbury circle; Phil Noel-Baker and I went into politics; Gerald Shove became an academic economist. The others died in the war. Rupert, Gerald and Phil became Fellows of the College.

Of Gerald, who died in 1947, the author of *The Times* obituary wrote, having mentioned that he was a year junior to Rupert and me, in the same year as Arthur Waley, and a year senior to Phil, that "he soon became a notable, indeed a formidable, figure in the gay outspoken circle who discussed high Fabian policy and poetry and much else and were pleased to call themselves 'the Carbonari'". I was very fond of him, both in our undergraduate days and when, after the war, he was back in residence at King's. He married Maitland's daughter, but he wrote no book.

In fact, politics were barred in the Carbonari, though I was once allowed to read a paper on "Man and Masterman", in praise and exposition of Charles Masterman's writings, which, though mainly political, went wider. *In Peril of Change*, his collected essays published in 1905 just before the election in which he came to Parliament as one of the great Liberal majority, was a favourite book of Rupert's and mine. We both hero-worshipped him, and it was planned that I should meet him at Rugby.[1] We thought of him as the young leader

[1] Rupert wrote to me on October 7th, 1908

NATIONAL LIBERAL CLUB,
WHITEHALL PLACE, S.W.
Tra! La!

Dear Hugh,
    I stay here now.
    I meant to say—
        But you slid away—
    at that thing on Sunday
        This:
    That on *Monday* next, *Masterman* is going to speak at Rugby and dine and sleep at our house. I'll be there, and return to Cambridge on Tuesday. If you think it worth while to come across, and stay Monday night, and meet The Man, and hear him, do! I can't promise that you'll be able to talk a lot with him because there may be a lot of filthy Liberal provincial politicians hanging about. But at least we'll have him more lonely at breakfast next morning. He leaves early——
So come if you'd like. Rugby is hideous but you needn't notice it.

of the Radical-Socialist wing of the Liberal Party, which, we hoped, would soon split off and join the Labour Party to make a real Socialist Party in Britain. Nor did we hold it against Masterman that he was a confessed High Churchman.

Nor were we in the Carbonari, as our Italian founders were, republican. Not, at least, until one evening, February 5th, 1909, when we were holding our Third Annual Dinner in Rupert's rooms in College. There were seven toasts. The menu card, including the toast list, is the only such memento I have. It is Nigel Crompton's card, with our signatures scrawled on the back, and was given me by his sister Hazel many years after his death. The toasts were to the King; the Carbonari; the World, the Flesh and the Devil; our Better Selves; Life; Death; and the Great For-Ever. I proposed the fourth of these toasts and Philip Baker, our record-breaking half-miler, responded. Gerald Shove proposed the last, and Rupert responded. But Gerald, who was in the Chair that night, had earlier proposed the first—with a formula not according to the programme. This got out! Rupert's gyp, who also looked after Pigou, told him, and no doubt others. "They drank the King's health, sir, but not with much loyalty." Next day it was rumoured that there would be the hell of a row. But it all blew over.

At the ordinary weekly meetings of the Carbonari we all read papers in turn, mostly on literary subjects. After the paper everyone had to speak, the order of speaking being settled by drawing lots. Then the reader of the paper replied, and then the discussion ceased to be regulated. Sometimes, instead of a paper, we had readings, as when Rupert read his own poems, and other people's.

Of papers which he read I remember one on Modern Poetry, another on Hilaire Belloc, with a lot of quotations, and, most vividly of all, a paper on "The Life and Death of John Rump, an English Gentleman." There was a prologue in Heaven, when the soul of John Rump was launched for earth, amid great rejoicings and expectations. Then came the ironic story of his uneventful and unprofitable life. He became a master in a Public School and helped to make another generation as unprofitable as himself. In due time he died—there was a scornful death scene—and the epilogue, like the prologue, was staged in Heaven. It ended with a superb and angry dialogue between John Rump and the Almighty, John Rump winning and Heaven vanishing in a high wind. This paper, I fear, is lost, though I have kept a typed copy of the Death Scene and the Epilogue. Of the rest I only remember stray phrases, such as John's view of his duties as a housemaster, "to turn a blind eye to sodomy and prepare the boys for confirmation".

I wish that he had written more prose at Cambridge, even at the cost of his writing less verse. But poetry, and the idea of poetry, went very deep in him. "There are only three good things in the world", he said once, vehemently answering some Carbonaro Philistine, "one is to read poetry, another is to write poetry and the best of all is to live poetry!" And I remember his saying that at rare moments he had glimpses of what poetry really meant, how it solved all problems of conduct and settled all questions of values. Moreover, it kept men young, he thought. Late one night we were sitting at a high window overlooking King's Parade. We had been discussing some philosophical point about the nature of Beauty, when we saw and heard some drunken members of another College going home. "Those fellows", he said, "would have thought us very old if they had been in this room tonight, but, when they go down and sit on office stools, they will grow old quite suddenly and, many years hence, we shall still be talking and thinking about this sort of thing, and we shall still be young." I remember, too, that he once took me into Rugby School Chapel and pointed to the vacant space between the memorial tablets to Matthew Arnold and Clough, and said, half solemnly and half in jest: "They are keeping that place for me."[1]

After he became a Socialist, he was at one time seriously planning an epic poem on wealth and poverty, culminating in a triumphant Social Revolution. "Forward, the Dawn is Breaking!" But he found the theme intractable.

There is no socialism in his published poems, though in one of them, which I quote later, a vision that

> *. . . behind the night,*
> *Waits for the great unborn, somewhere afar,*
> *Some white tremendous daybreak.*

[1] Some of the preceding paragraphs are taken from some notes about Rupert which I sent to Sir Edward Marsh when he was preparing his Memoir. From these he made some quotations on pp. xxx–xxxii of the Memoir.

And in an unpublished poem, now probably lost, he hopes for a better world, where all shall have a larger life,

> *lest man at the last go down into the dark*
> *with his best songs unsung.*

But his paper on "Democracy and the Arts", read to the Cambridge Fabians in 1910 when he was President—I heard it— and published in 1946 by Hart-Davis, contains, if you care to use such language, some suggestions, still well worth considering, for a Socialist policy for the encouragement of artists.

In the Long Vacation Rupert and I and others slept out beside Byron's Pool, and in the field in the Backs at King's, just over the river.

One summer night he and I and two others from our College slept there and were spied by the Porter, who, not having approached us very closely, reported to the Dean that three men and a woman were sleeping in the Backs. Rupert wore his hair rather long.

I made a cult of sleeping out in those years, believing that one hour's sleep under the stars was worth two under a roof.

Another society which Rupert and I joined, with a membership in many Colleges, was the Fish and Chimney. We met to read plays. I have kept the Minute Book for the term before we joined. The President that term was Ben Keeling of Trinity, the Secretary Archie Campbell of John's. The former was also President of the Cambridge University Fabians. The latter went from Cambridge to be Professor of Latin, I think at Liverpool University. He had both Scots charm and Scots wit. He published in 1912 through Heffer at Cambridge a thin volume of poems, including this, one of four *Poems for Children*:

> *Put on your coat and come to my boat,*
> *And I'll row you away with me*
> *Till the land and the day are both far away*
> *And the night looks over the sea . . .*
> *And I shall row where the moonbeams throw*
> *A streak across the sea,*
> *And we'll follow the streak on the waters bleak*
> *To see what the end may be;*

For it may be the home where the dreams come from,
   Or it may be a dead city,
   Or a great rock wall, or nothing at all
   But a streak across the sea.

When we read *Man and Superman* in Keeling's rooms, I remember that I asked for my part, and was given, the Stage Directions—the best part in the play.

And this is how the Secretary kept the Minutes:

"The members of this brotherhood coincided in Mr. Keeling's rooms on the evening of Wednesday, October 24th. That gentleman opened proceedings by a modest announcement. Referring the Society to Suggestion 3b 'that Committees shall not be appointed but spontaneously generated', he begged to inform them that having constituted himself a committee by a process of parthenogenesis, he had unanimously created himself dictator. He further observed that this genesis of a dictator would be followed by an exodus of all mutinous members. The Society received this amiable pleasantry with a polite smile. Sheridan's *Duenna* was then read.

"On the evening of Wednesday, November 14th, the Fish met in a Shoal off the coast of Newnham. The play read was Beaumont and Fletcher's *Maid's Tragedy*, where the tragic element lies in the fact that she was not a maid. The Society made a noble effort to free itself from the oppression of the dictator. It was proposed to eject him from the Society under Suggestion No. 2, Section 2, the charge brought against him being that of celibacy; but the prosecution broke down."

In January 1907, at the end of my first term, I joined the Fabians and declared myself a Socialist. I exchanged Joseph Chamberlain for James Keir Hardie—and Sidney Webb. This change in my political beliefs was smaller than it may have seemed to others—and even to me—at the time. My dislike of unfair privilege and unjust inequality of every kind dated back a long way. Democracy was already one of the most emotive words in my vocabulary. Nor was the Fabian leadership against the Empire, and that reassured me.

Ben Keeling, the Dictator of the Fish and Chimney, netted me. He ran the Fabians as well. He was at that time the acknowledged leader of Cambridge undergraduate socialism, spoke often at the Union and eagerly sought converts everywhere. He was a History Scholar of Trinity, a Wykehamist— not the familiar smooth type, but the not-at-all-rare, rough type with a tendency to violence of thought and expression. He was a dominating person with immense vitality, and great fun as a friend. But his conscience tortured him.

When he left Cambridge he went to live in typical London working-class surroundings in the Walworth Road, trying to establish relationships of real equality with active workers in the S.D.F. and the I.L.P. He joined the first staff of the Labour Exchanges, which Winston Churchill, impelled by the Webbs, created when he was President of the Board of Trade, with Beveridge as the civil servant in charge. This took Keeling to Leeds and to a close personal friendship with Arthur Greenwood. Had he lived, more certainly than any of my contemporaries at Cambridge he would have played a big part in Labour politics. But he was killed by the Germans in 1916, a sergeant-major on the Somme. He had refused to take a commission. A number of his letters, and parts of a journal he kept, were published in 1918 with an introduction by H. G. Wells.

A memorable event for me and many others was Keir Hardie's visit to Cambridge early in 1907. He had just upset conventional people by some blunt criticisms of British rule in India. He was a red rag to all Tory bulls. So when it was announced that he was to speak in the Cambridge Guildhall, under Fabian auspices, the bulls got busy. There were moves and counter-moves. We let it be known that he was arriving by a certain afternoon train, which some of us went to meet. This party met one of our number, alighting from the train wearing a false beard and carrying a bag conspicuously stamped J. K. H. They greeted him respectfully and drove off in a hansom cab—there were no taxis then—triumphantly pursued by observant Tories in a second cab. The first cab drove as far as Trinity Great Gate, where the bogus Keir Hardie got out, then turned and ran, simulating panic as the Tories, with loud and threatening cries, descended from the second cab. He ran past John's, turned sharp left, hotly pursued, as far as Magdalene. Then turned again, pulled off the false beard and faced them with a loud laugh. They might, we thought, have guessed that an elderly Labour leader could not run so fast!

They then, leaving their deceiver unharmed, hastened back to Trinity. Here another hansom had drawn up, containing this time Keeling with V. H. Mottram, a Socialist scientist, even more persuasively made up as Keir Hardie, with appropriate hat, grey beard and hair, and red tie. After the ostentatious presentation to the great man of a number of Fabians, this party made its way across the Great Court to Keeling's rooms at the top of one of the towers. There, we had caused it to be rumoured, Keir Hardie would be dining before the meeting, and a meal had been loudly ordered from the College kitchens in his name. The enemy, according to a prepared plan, which had become known to us, screwed up the door. During this operation they heard voices within addressing "Mr. Keir Hardie", and a slow Scots voice replying. But he was not there either. That party later descended, outside the College, by a rope from the window, and went along to the Guildhall.

Meanwhile, another party, of which I was one, met the real Keir Hardie on a later train, and took him to King's for a meal and then to the meeting. This was soon broken up, before he had been able to say much, by stink-bombs and catcalls. An attempt was made to rush the platform and there were cries that he should be thrown into the river.

So we formed a bodyguard around him and fought our way across the Market Square and King's Parade into the shelter of my own College, where he held court awhile and then slept peacefully.

In a crowded room I sat at his feet, literally and spiritually. I admired his total lack of fear or anger, his dignified bearing, his simplicity of speech and thought and faith. That night I became a quite convinced Socialist.

That year, and for some years after, the Cambridge University Fabian Society had a terrific boom. The young poured into it. They were allowed to be Associates, if not yet prepared to "sign the basis", as the rather comical phrase was, and become Full Members. Politically there was nothing in the University to the Left of us. (There was an I.L.P. branch in the town, which some of us joined. It met in a pub, more for social intercourse than for serious discussion.) Classics and mathematicians and scientists joined the Fabians, and athletes too. We were very proud, in particular, of our Rowing Blue, Godwin Baynes, a medical student and a friend of Ben Keeling. He did splendidly in the street fighting on Keir Hardie Night. Some of the more attractive girls from Girton and Newnham joined too, including Amber Reeves, later Amber Blanco-White.

Rupert Brooke, Gerald Shove and about half the Carbonari joined. Rupert said he was "a William Morris sort of Socialist, not your sort of Socialist, but I want to join your society as an associate".

That was in April 1907. A year later he decided to go all the way. He sent me two postcards from Torquay. H. G. Wells had helped.

April 8th, 1908   3 BEACON TERRACE
   (and for 10 days)   TORQUAY (!)
Under the influence of
   (*a*) Talks with the wee, fantastic, *Wells*.
   (*b*) His books.
   (*c*) Fabian tracts.
   (*d*) Private meditation and prayer.
   (*e*) Arguments on the other side.
   (*f–z*) Anything . . .—etc.— . . .
I have decided to sign even the present Fabian Basis, and to become a member (if possible) of the Central Fabian Society.

The former part, I suppose, may wait till next term; as I have no Basis with me. Spiritually, the thing is done (not without blood and tears). But the latter—is it possible? What steps can I take, even now? Where write? What say? . . . Tell me . . . I am eager as a neophyte always is, for action.

I must have replied that there was no hurry. He answered— our hero Masterman had just entered the Government—

The Good Friday,   TORQUAY
   April 17th, 1908.   even yet.
Many thanks. The first strange fever flickered and died, and I am content to sit quietly till next term. So I have left Pease[1] in peace. 'Pease, perfect Pease', as the hymn says.

     [1] E. R. Pease was the Secretary of the Fabian Society.

My high young heart is withered and scarred by Aristotle and this popular resort; but I am convalescing. By next term I shall be able to sit up and take a little Webb-and-milk. I am quite brave and cheery. But ah! my Uncles weep.

So Masterman has . . . what has he? Spread his wings for a great flight? Or taken the second step down to the mire? Anyhow it is all very exciting.

Winston is a rather magnificent fraud.

Your remarks about the Licensing Bill are strangely like a passage of Ibsen. They haunt me.

We had a fine series of lectures after Keir Hardie—Sidney Webb and Beatrice Webb, Bernard Shaw, Granville Barker, H. G. Wells, Graham Wallas, J. A. Hobson, Will Crooks, George Barnes, Pete Curran and Ramsay MacDonald. I took the Chair, I remember, for Ramsay Macdonald, who drew curves on a blackboard, not very convincingly, to show how badly wealth was distributed. He was very nervous lest there should be a demonstration against him—he remembered Keir Hardie's experience—and asked me whether I thought it was really safe to hold the meeting. I was rather unsympathetic with his fears, and all went peacefully. He talked better afterwards with a small party. I never took to him, either then or later. His good-looks and his beautiful voice and his easy rhetoric never covered up his jealous vanity and his inferiority complex.

And I gave him an early bad mark for never even answering a joint letter from Rupert and myself and some others, inviting him to come and spend a few days with us at Clevedon in the summer of 1910, where Rupert's mother had taken a house, and there meet and talk to a number of keen young University Socialists. It was a very polite, humble, eager letter. But he ignored it.

In 1908, and again in 1909, a strong Cambridge contingent went to the Fabian Summer School at Llanbedr, between Harlech and Barmouth. Mrs. Webb has described us in her diary. The first year she rather liked some of us; the second she screamed with disapproval.

She wrote: "Sept. 15th, 1908. The Cambridge men are a remarkable set—quite the most remarkable the Fabian Society

AT CAMBRIDGE, 1909

has hitherto attracted—fervent and brilliant. I had seven of them to stay with me on their way to Wales." She praised two of us. "Keeling and Dalton—the one a fervent rebel (who reminds me of X in his generous vitality and incontinent intelligence) and the other an accomplished ecclesiastical sort of person—a subtle wily man with a certain peculiar charm for those who are not put off by his mannerism. The other five were, I think, commonplace—Schloss, Strachey, Brooke (a poetic beauty) and Shove—perhaps Dudley Ward was a little over the line of medium capacity and character. P.S.—This was the afterwards famous Rupert Brooke who put me off the track of his distinction by delivering a super-conceited lecture on the relation of the University man to the common herd of democracy. Also I am poetry blind, like some persons are colour blind." (*Our Partnership*, p. 415.) But a year later: "A little group of half-a-dozen Cambridge men—Hugh Dalton, Rupert Brooke, James Strachey, Clifford Allen, Foss—came for a week. . . . We have had interesting and useful talks with these young men; but the weather, being detestable, must have made the trip appear rather a bad investment for them, and they are inclined to go away rather more critical and supercilious than they came. . . . They don't want to learn; they don't think they have anything to learn. . . . The egotism of the young University man is colossal. Are they worth bothering about?" (*Ibid.*, pp. 456–7.)

And there was, I remember, some unedifying horseplay, too visible, one of our number pushed out, chamber-pot in hand, and locked out, on a balcony; and jokes late at night, too audible, about the Webbs themselves. We were, I am afraid, cliquish, rude, ribald and irreverent.

In 1908 a number of us reached Llanbedr via Rugby and Llanfairfechan, whence we walked for some days in the mountains of North Wales.

Rupert wrote to me from Rugby on August 18th; he was just twenty-one and I was within a week of the same river-crossing.

"Your letter is admirably precise and leaves me utterly undecided. I should love to sleep out with nothing but a few extra socks on. And yet . . . you in your low-lying Cambridge

may not realise how cold it is o' nights. . . . I don't know what
to do. I shall do what the majority do. Tell me what the
majority will do.

"If you and Ben are passing through this City on Wednesday,
you'd better drop in and take lunch here, play tennis if you
like, and take me on. The invitation holds good to *all* Fabians
who pass through, Walesward, that day.

"I don't know Mr. Service or his works.[1] I don't think I
should like them. I mistrust Sourdoughs. What *is* a Sourdough? Pronounced Sour-dô or Sour-duff?

"Human conversations are ever inconclusive. I told my
mother that the chief end of Life was Pleasure, and she burst
into tears. I await your Epiphany, your bright and glorious
coming with many attendant daemons, to snatch me from my
drab household. My Uncle the Dean will be here. No matter.
It will add to the Comedy. But Ben must be not-blasphemous.
I told the family a lot of people would be lunching here that
day. 'Who and what kind of?' they said. 'Oh! all right,' I
vaguely smiled at them, 'practically Liberals. There's Dalton,
son of a Canon, rather a Sourdô, you know—a Sourduff, I
mean.' 'What's a Sourduff?' said my mother menacingly. 'A
Colonial Sentimentalist,' I said, and drifted through Explanation for four meals. . . .

"The rumour about my age was quite true. I did it a fortnight ago. Leaving my unprofitable Youth and its fancies, I
stepped across the Threshold of Manhood, jauntily, manfully;
leaving a company of dancing children behind. I stumbled a
little on the step which I did not perceive.

"I strode forward, saying in a thin flat voice 'Ha! Ha!
talkin' of the Joy of Life, the Board of Trade Returns for Exp——'
and then I found a black square room, and sitting all round,
their faces to the walls, staring at me with the backs of their
bald heads,

rows of—
Adults—

P.S. Beatrice Webb's eye. . . .

"Can such things be? No, No, I am too old.

Hush."

---

[1] I had praised, in a letter, *Songs of a Sourdough*, by R. W. Service, the Canadian
poet.

Ben Keeling was one of the founders of the Cambridge University Fabian Society in 1905. He thus ends a short account, written some years later, of its early days and adventures.[1]

"Hugh Dalton abandoned Tariff Reform for Fabianism in the second year of the Society's existence, became its Secretary, and succeeded me as President when I went down in 1908.

"Writing this has made me feel for the first time in my life a wish that I could live again through all the crudities of those Cambridge undergraduate days. I will blush for nothing. It was a past worth living in—not merely to be lived through. If a Fabian friend or enemy of those days—man or woman—sees this, let him know that in my soul I have this moment drained yet another quart to him from the big blue mug. Prosit! The Cause!"

I spoke a great deal at the Union, making my maiden speech as a Tory Democrat in my first term. I spoke against a motion "welcoming the development of a Nationalist rather than an Imperialist spirit". Thereafter I spoke as a Socialist.

I got a lot of fun out of the Union, and made many friends there belonging to all political parties. I became, as time went on, almost too fluent. But this was good basic training for political speaking outside; though the styles required are different.

I was elected to the Committee in my second year. But I was never President. I stood twice for Secretary. The first time I was beaten by Alexander Ramsay, a Scots Liberal friend of mine, in a three-cornered fight; the second time by Geoffrey Butler, later Tory M.P. for the University, in a straight fight. In those days the succession from Secretary, through Vice-President, to President, was uncontested. No Socialist was elected President of the Cambridge Union till my friend David Hardman in 1925.[2] But some, before this date, had been what

[1] *Keeling Letters*, p. 12 (Allen & Unwin).
[2] I spoke at David Hardman's Retiring Presidential debate on December 8th, 1925, in support of a motion moved by him "that this House not only approves of the principles of Socialism, but believes that the practical application of these principles will promote the happiness of the English People". The motion was only defeated by 203 to 164.
I am reported to have said, "alluding to a remark of the previous speaker, that

would now be called fellow-travellers with socialism, while several eminent ex-Presidents became avowed Socialists later; Pethick Lawrence and Phil Noel-Baker among others. And a number of Socialists, of course, have been elected President since 1925.

I spoke several times, while an undergraduate, at the Majliss—the society of Indian students. Some of these debates were very animated, and once a Sikh drew a knife on a Moslem, and we had to separate them. Nehru was up with me, having come to Cambridge from Harrow. I knew him slightly, but did not foresee that "forty years on", in the words of his old school song, I should greet him as the first Prime Minister of Free India, and that, as a member of the British Cabinet, I should share responsibility for the policy which led up to this historic event.

We took ethics very seriously in the more intellectual of my Cambridge circles.

The impact of G. E. Moore's *Principia Ethica* upon some of us was immense. Everything suddenly became clear and, as it seemed to us, incontestable. The best account I know of how this hit us, and of how much there was in it, is in Keynes' Memoir on *My Early Beliefs*, written in 1938 and published after his death in *Two Memoirs* in 1949.

Principia Ethica came out in 1903. But many whom its teaching conquered did not read the book carefully—or at all. They got its essence from conversation with their friends. I read it first in October 1908—I inscribed this date in my copy. But I had already been taken by storm.

Moore's "influence", says Keynes, "was not only overwhelming; it was exciting, exhilarating, the beginning of a renaissance, the opening of a new heaven on a new earth. We were the forerunners of a new dispensation, we were not afraid of anything. . . . Nothing mattered except states of mind, our own and other people's, of course, but chiefly our own. These states

they were not there to discuss when capitalism began, but when it was going to finish (laughter and applause) . . . The Socialist indictments against the capitalist system were that it failed to deliver the goods, that its standards of production were miserably low, as compared with the possibilities of this modern age, and that of the goods which it did deliver, most of them were delivered at the wrong address (laughter and applause)." I still remember that I enjoyed myself that night.

of mind were not associated with action or achievement or with
consequences. They consisted in timeless, passionate states of
contemplation and communion. . . . Their value depended, in
accordance with the principle of organic unity, on the state of
affairs as a whole which could not be usefully analysed into
parts." Keynes adds: "I myself was always an advocate of a
principle of organic unity through time, which still seems to
me only sensible." Surely he was right, for how otherwise can
one value anyone's personality or character? But Moore, I
think, did not accept this extension of the principle. Keynes
continues: "The appropriate subjects of passionate contemplation and communion were a beloved person, beauty and truth,
and one's prime objects in life were love, the creation and
enjoyment of aesthetic experience and the pursuit of knowledge. Of these love came a long way first. . . . Our religion
closely followed the English puritan tradition of being chiefly
concerned with the salvation of our own souls. There was not
a very intimate connection between 'being good' and 'doing
good'; and we had a feeling that there might be some risk that
in practice the latter might interfere with the former. . . . It
seems to me, looking back, that this religion of ours was a very
good one to grow up under. It remains nearer the truth than
any other that I know, with less irrelevant extraneous matter
and nothing to be ashamed of. . . . It is still my religion under
the surface. . . . I see no reason to shift from the fundamental
intuitions of *Principia Ethica*; though they are much too few
and too narrow to fit actual experience, which provides a richer
and more various content." This last qualification is certainly
true, but it *is* a qualification only, and not a denial.

In Chapter V of *Principia Ethica*—and there are only six
chapters—"doing good" finds its place. Moore regarded this
part of his discussion as very important, though much more
difficult than other moral teachers, or writers on ethics, had
supposed. Few general rules of conduct, or of duty, could be
established, except as propositions in probabilities. Each case
must be judged on its merits, and every action in the light of its
probable consequences. "It was an important object of Moore's
book", as Keynes observes, "to distinguish between goodness
as an attribute of states of mind and rightness as an attribute
of actions." And it is much easier—and I am wholly in

agreement here—to be sure what it is good to be, than what it is right to do.

Fully accepting Moore's distinction, I was always inclined, and still am, to widen his category of things good in themselves. And this may lead to some greater degree of coincidence than his early followers recognised, between "being good" and "doing good" at the same time.

To accept Moore never meant to disinterest oneself from doing good. Otherwise such men as Pigou and Lowes Dickinson would never have accepted him. But the younger of us were at first inclined to separate rather sharply those people who were means to good (i.e. *did* good) from those who were good as ends (i.e. *were* good). We thought, for instance, of the Webbs as mainly means to good. We had no intense admiration for their states of mind.

General rules of conduct, consistent with Moore's teaching, are not, I think, so difficult to frame. Thus, in broad terms, no one should prefer his own good to the greater good of others. Nor, within inner circles of loyalty, to the equal good of others. Nor, within the inmost circles of affection, even to the lesser good of another. We should so live as to realise the greatest good we can, in our own lives, the lives of those we love, of our friends and of other members of any society or group of which we feel ourselves a loyal part.

All this in an ever-widening circle of diminishing emphasis, since love, and all the lesser loyalties, mean preferences.

To apply these rules aright in particular cases may, of course, be very difficult—involving both important value judgments and complicated arguments about consequences. But the right application of wrong rules, save in rare cases of good luck, would be worse!

As Keynes said: "The fundamental intuitions of *Principia Ethica* are too few and too narrow." I wrote, in 1950, to Ian Little, with whom I had started up a correspondence on these subjects: "I accept Moore's framework, but I have always thought he missed a lot in his infilling. He thought that much the best states of mind were those filled with love and with the appreciation of beauty. And this is probably true. But below this highest level he hadn't many examples to offer. I myself would add, at a pretty high level, a wide range of *tense experiences*, e.g. winning a keenly contested race (or election), making a very successful speech (or musical or dramatic performance), climbing a high mountain, piloting a plane in new or very difficult conditions, writing a good short poem, solving with a sudden flash of insight an intellectual problem which had got one stuck." Into many such examples being and doing good both enter.

Again, as a practical politician, when I see happy, healthy, well-dressed, well-fed people in my constituency, where a few years ago there was a quite different picture, I am proud and glad, especially in the knowledge that I have helped to make this change. And I judge that to be no bad state of mind. So, too, when I see a wide space of beautiful country, once fenced in for the enjoyment of a few, now thrown open, partly through my efforts, for the enjoyment of all.

Generally, it *is* good to see or know that one has *done* good.

So many bridges, even if at a relatively low level, link means and ends, within Moore's scheme of thought.

I am told by some philosophers that Moore's other philosophical writings are better than his ethics. I have no valuable opinion on this. Nor do I know which of his writings counted most with those who proposed him for the Order of Merit, rather late in his life, in 1951. Nor did I ever meet him. But I do know that he made an enormous difference to my way of thinking and feeling about the most important things in life.

I was much more interested, at Cambridge and since, in ethics than in metaphysics. I cared much more what was good than what was real. I heard, therefore, without dismay that Oxford philosophers have now abolished metaphysics.

In Christian metaphysics, as distinct from Christian ethics, I had ceased to believe at Eton. Nor, as I have said, did my father, though a Canon of the Church, take all the metaphysics of the Bible literally. In Christian ethics, on the other hand, I distinguished, more and more clearly as the years passed, between Christ's own teaching and that of many of His influential followers. Many of the latter repelled me. They seemed to narrow, coarsen and pervert the teachings of their Master. But I have always found deep wisdom and beauty and tenderness in Christ's own words and actions. "He that is without sin, let him cast the first stone." But many of his followers were professional stone-throwers.

Nor, since my political views took firm shape, did I ever recite the *Magnificat* without a thrill of pleasure. "He hath put down the mighty from their seat and hath exalted the humble and meek. He hath filled the hungry with good things, and the rich he hath sent empty away." But what humbug for defenders of our own unjust social order to join in! This is a Psalm for Christian Socialists only. In the Psalms of David and the Song of Solomon and the Poetry of the Prophets there is beauty that grows not old, for evermore.

In my time at King's most of the prominent Dons were agnostics. Oscar Browning, who was very kind and hospitable to me, as to so many others, kept a crucifix hanging on the wall in his outer room—"to fwighten the agnoggers", he told us.

The Don who had most influence on me was Lowes Dickinson. He lectured on political ideas, was a man of the Left and an anti-clerical. He was easily interested in young men and, from my first year, he took an interest in me which continued till his death in 1932. I owe him a great debt and I soon became one of his admirers.

He wrote beautifully clear and often very moving English. Of stylists in that generation I put him and Hilaire Belloc at the top. Nothing ugly, clumsy or obscure ever passed either of their pens.

Dickinson had an exceptional gift for seeing, and stating fairly and persuasively, conflicting views. In writing, he was a master of the symposium and the dialogue from *The Modern Symposium*, which made a great hit in 1907, down to *After Two Thousand Years, a Conversation between Plato and a Modern Young Man*, in 1930. In conversation he seldom expressed definite disagreement. He would say: "I think I see your point of view." When he was awarded the Kahn Travelling Fellowship, the avowed object of which was to widen the Fellow's mind, Rupert Brooke, like me a great admirer, said to me: "If they widen Goldie's mind any more, it'll break."

He had rooms on the top floor of Gibbs' Building in the front court. Late one night when, after a meeting of the Carbonari, Rupert and I were walking and talking below, a head, crowned with a nightcap, popped out of a top window, and said: "I wish you'd go to bed. I can't sleep." Next morning we went to apologise. "What were you talking about?" he asked. "Immortality," we replied. "Oh," he said, "if only I'd known that, I'd have come down and joined you." For this was a favourite subject of his and the theme of two of his small books. He published a large number of small books, and only one tome, *The International Anarchy*, his study of the causes of the First World War.

Rupert and I were invited by him, in our first year, to join what was known as "Dickinson's Society". This was a discussion society with not much more than a dozen members, half undergraduates and half Dons. It met in his rooms. Someone read a paper or opened a discussion, and others then spoke in an order determined by drawing lots, except that Dickinson himself always wound up, standing in front of the fireplace, moving his body up and down and rubbing his bottom with his hands. It was to this Society that Pigou, who was a regular member, read a paper in my time on "Recent Results in Psychical Research". He began: "The question 'Do men and women survive death?' contains three ambiguities. There is an ambiguity in the word 'survive'. When we ask 'Does a cat survive a drenching in a water-butt?' we may mean either . . . or . . . There is an ambiguity in the words 'men and women', for it might be that men survived death, but women did not." The third ambiguity I don't remember.

Less directly than Dickinson, for I never knew him well, Pigou influenced me greatly. Tall and handsome like a Viking, a mountaineer, already a strong intellectual and moral force in the College, he was only thirty-one years old when he was appointed to succeed Marshall in the Chair of Political Economy at the end of my third year.

He was shy in general intercourse, but he chose a series of young men as they passed through King's to whom he gave unwavering friendship and support. Good-looking, good on mountains, good moral tone. These, it seemed, were the gifts he most valued in them. Philip Noel-Baker, two years my junior, but my colleague first in the Carbonari, then in the Foreign Office and then in the Cabinet, was an outstanding member of this chosen band.

I confess that, though never intimate with Pigou, I became

one of his hero-worshippers. His mind, his presence, his personality, all attracted me. I regarded him, while I was studying economics at Cambridge and teaching it immediately after the war in London, as the most powerful brain among British economists.

His *Wealth and Welfare*, published in 1912, had on me something of the same effect as Moore's *Principia Ethica*. It changed old confusions into new clarity. It laid down sharper criteria for economic policy than I had found before. It brought out new conclusions, significant for practical action, from old generalities. It was a book that helped me, more than any other, to formulate my own approach from ethics, through politics, to economics. He was splendidly free from party or class prejudice, but he believed, as Marshall did before him, that great inequalities of wealth and opportunity are both unjust and wasteful of welfare. I have read most of his later writings and there is no doubt that his contribution to economics is conspicuously outstanding. But nothing later, in my view, has added so much to what went before as did *Wealth and Welfare*, his first large book. He had come to economics through the Moral Science Tripos, of which, before a separate Economics Tripos was instituted, economic studies were a part.

It was not clear at first whether he would become an economist. His first thesis for a King's Fellowship was on "Robert Browning as a Religious Teacher". When this failed, he changed, on Marshall's advice, to "Variations in the Price of Tinned Meat in the Nineteenth Century". This gave much scope for mathematical virtuosity, and he succeeded. His lectures, when I heard them, were, of their kind, perfect. An attractive presence; complete clarity; great precision of thought and definition; a little, but not too much, geometry and algebra on the blackboard; an occasional joke to illustrate some proposition; never a note.

He was very shy of women. Once, taken aback by an invitation from a Newnham girl at the end of a lecture, he promised to go to tea with her next Sunday, but wrote afterwards excusing himself, "I'm afraid I'm not very good at tea parties." Intellectually, he derived from Sidgwick almost as much as from Marshall. This is a clue to his incompatibility with

Keynes, who viewed Sidgwick in a very dim light. I myself got a good deal out of Sidgwick's writings, and gave him a high place among British economists.[1]

Pigou had been President of the Union and in his public speaking combined very clear exposition with impressive rhetoric—"a false rhetorician", Hubert Henderson once unkindly called him. In my first year Pigou spoke in one of our Union debates and thrilled me with his peroration. All I remember now is one sentence. "I often like to think that we here, with our greater opportunities, are trustees for the poor."

He often spoke on Free Trade and he wrote a perfect little book of its kind on *Protective and Preferential Import Duties*. Once, speaking at an election for Philip Noel-Baker's father, then Liberal M.P. for Finsbury, Pigou, with great persuasiveness and apparent conviction, developed the case for Tariff Reform. The platform and the audience grew restless. There were angry interruptions from the faithful. They thought he was a Tory speaker come to the wrong meeting. Then suddenly he stopped. "And what," he asked, "is the answer to that case?" And then he gave it, and swept the meeting off its feet.

There is a peroration too to *Wealth and Welfare*. It is characteristic of Pigou in his early prime. Later, I think, he became half ashamed of such creations.

"Whether man's life ends with his physical death, or is destined to pass unscathed through that gateway, the good and the evil which he experiences here are real; and to promote the one and restrain the other is a compelling duty. But . . . neither by the timidity that waits at a distance, nor by the wild rush of undisciplined ardour is the summit of great mountains attained. First we must understand our task and prepare for it; and then, in the glow of sunrise, by united effort, we shall at last, perhaps, achieve."[2]

Maynard Keynes came back to King's in my third year. He

---

[1] See my *Inequality of Incomes*, pp. 99–105.

[2] It was on this passage, in part, that I relied in a correspondence with Ian Little, arising out of his brilliant *Critique of Welfare Economics*, to show that Pigou held that welfare should, by definition, be maximised. Little argued in reply that *Wealth and Welfare*, which he admitted he had not previously read, was inconsistent on this point with the *Economics of Welfare* published eight years later. There is, I think, some force in this argument, though Pigou, to whom I referred the question, said that no change was intended. Anyhow, I prefer the sinewy youthful beauty of *Wealth and Welfare*—peroration and all—to its plumper, more middle-aged, successor.

preferred a Fellowship to going on at the India Office, where he had already warned those in authority that they were making a muddle of the rupee, and had been first ignored and then proved right.

I knew him better than Pigou, less well than Dickinson. He taught me economics in my fourth year. Thirty-five years later he was my economic adviser when I was Chancellor of the Exchequer. I met him only occasionally in this interval. The most important occasions were in the first post-war years, 1920–22, when I was living partly in Cambridge; and in 1931, at the time of the political crisis.

He too, in the year when he was teaching me, had formed a small society of undergraduates, where papers were read. We, in those pre-war years, made a corner in his brilliance, before it burst on the world in *The Economic Consequences of the Peace*.

His lectures on Money, I remember, were not only intellectually fascinating: "Money is that which one accepts only in order to get rid of it again"—on second thoughts, rather too wide a definition—but had an air about them of knowledge of the real world, the Stock Exchange and all that. In this he gave a different impression from Pigou. Keynes was a Man of the World, including the City, always on the move, with shining wings, from point to point, changing his opinions and prescriptions at short notice.

Pigou was a Man of the Temple of Truth, fixed in Cambridge. His system never greatly changed. He gave the impression of using *one* machine, most beautiful and powerful in its construction, to solve a series of problems, the solutions all tending, after he had settled down into middle age, to have a certain family likeness.

Keynes was always inventing new machines and new ways of using old machines. The solutions he produced were much more varied.

Cambridge was very fortunate to have two such great economists in one generation. Taking all in all, I judge that Pigou was great, but that Keynes was the greater.

Of other Dons I recall, above the rest, McTaggart of Trinity, the Hegelian philosopher, who, it was said, used every night to drink one bottle of port and read one new French novel before going to bed. He was the recognised adviser of the Union library on French novels. He gave an elementary course on philosophy every year for non-philosophers. I stuck it out till the last lecture. I heard him say: "We will now pass from a sheet of plate glass to the Absolute." Then, having been up late the night before, I fell asleep. I woke to hear him say: "We have now returned from the Absolute to a sheet of plate glass." He was a Tory in politics. He said: "People tell me that Ramsay MacDonald is not a manual worker. But his hands must be calloused with wire pulling."

And Bertrand Russell, only intermittently in Cambridge, joyfully good company, laughing at everyone's jokes, including his own. Most clear, most fearless, deepest thinker of them all. Now almost an immortal, mentally and physically still undaunted.

And Dent, of my own College, Professor of Music; writer on Mozart and Scarlatti; composer, on his own, of things, as some-one said, like "little far-off games of chess"; speaker of many languages, including quite a number of Italian dialects; a real internationalist; infinitely interested in the best of the young and, behind a slightly severe sardonic mask, infinitely helpful to all their enterprises, not only musical.

And Sheppard, also of my College, now Provost, then a classical Don, a most dramatic lecturer and talker, who made Greek amazingly exciting, trounced Gilbert Murray for mis-representing the Ancient Greeks as English Nonconformists, and held wide-open Sunday evenings for any undergraduates who cared to come.

Yes, there were Dons in those days!

In our fourth year, Rupert and I both went out of College in order to work; he to Grantchester to read and write on the Elizabethan dramatists, I to Newnham Croft to read economics. But he found time to be President of the Cambridge Fabians in succession to me, and took a lot of trouble over it.

We met one day after seeing some of the new freshmen. "Do these young men make you feel old?" I asked. "No," he said, "not old, only tremendous."

I got a II (1)—Class II Division 1—in Part II of the Economics Tripos. Maynard Keynes wrote to me: "You wobbled on the line of a First." Afterwards I heard that, of the examiners, C. P. Sanger had pressed for a First for me, but J. S. Nicholson, then Professor at Edinburgh, had pressed for a Second and prevailed. I was, for the moment, very disappointed not to have got a First. If I had taken my Mathematical Tripos at the end of my second year, when I could have got a Third as easily as I did a year later, and so given two years, instead of only one, to economics, I daresay I *should* have got a First.

But, looking back from years later and comparing myself with others, I think II (1) was just about my right academic assessment. In some aspects of my life I have been only Third Class; in others, perhaps, First Class. But I do not think those examiners at Cambridge were far wrong in 1910. And an academic II (1) is just about right for politics. In that world, where I was to spend so much time, men with academic Firsts are often most surprising failures. But there are some brilliant examples to the contrary, especially among that very fine body of young men who have come, as Socialists, to Westminster in 1945 and since. And most of that academic cluster, I must confess reluctantly, have come from Oxford!

So I went down from Cambridge after the best four years of my life thus far. Nor could I pick now on any later run of four that would outshine them.

I went down full of hope and eager interest in the future— my friends', my own, our country's and the world's. I had acquired, I believed, after much furious striving "to get things clear", a coherent philosophy of life and a true scale of values. I was immensely proud of my chosen contemporaries, ready to defend them against all attack. And their variety enormously increased their value. The variety within each of them, and their variety as between themselves. "A world containing you and me and Maynard Keynes", Rupert once said to me, "is obviously better than a world containing three people just like any one of us." We were as cocky as that! And, within the life of each of us, variety of experience and achievement was to be a prime aim always. The Principle of Organic Wholes stood forth, both in the group and in the individual.

Youth, and Death, and the Succession. "These high towers, in which, when some have fallen asleep, there shall still be laughter." That scrap comes back on the tide of memory from some paper I wrote, I think for the Carbonari.

I took a small part in both the General Elections of 1910. The Labour Party made no bid for my services. So in the January election I offered myself to Chiozza Money, whose *Riches and Poverty* was the first book I knew which had brought out, by a few simple figures, the stark inequality in the distribution of wealth and income in Britain. He was in name a Liberal, but in fact a Socialist. He did not need me, so I went to Nuneaton to help William Johnson, a Warwickshire Miners' Leader. All the miners' M.P.s then were Lib-Lab, but miners for all that! I stayed with him for the last ten days of the fight, speaking at meetings, canvassing and working in the Central Committee Room. When the result was announced, with a comfortable majority over the Tory, I telegraphed in keen delight to my father "Got the old man in!" My father, as I have already explained, did not like Liberals, but did like working men. So he was quite sympathetic.

Speaking in a scattered constituency is easier, as I was often to find later, than speaking in a compact urban area, because one can repeat the same speech, or, at any rate, the same illustrations and the same jokes and the same highlights, without much risk of many people in the audience having heard them before. And so I repeated, in Nuneaton itself and in several mining villages around it, a quotation from a poem, written in 1908 but not then published, of Rupert Brooke.

> *Exile of immortality, strongly wise,*
> *Strain through the dark, with undesirous eyes*
> *To what may lie beyond it. Sets your star,*
> *O heart, for ever! Yet behind the night,*
> *Waits for the great unborn, somewhere afar,*
> *Some white tremendous daybreak. And the light,*
> *Returning, shall give back the golden hours,*
> *Ocean a windless level, Earth a lawn*
> *Spacious and full of sunlit dancing-places,*
> *And laughter, and music, and, among the flowers,*
> *The gay child-hearts of men, and the child-faces,*
> *O heart, in the great dawn!*

This picture comes straight from William Morris's *News from Nowhere*. As a peroration to a spoken essay on the Fabian New World, it may have surprised the miners who heard it, but also, I hope, may have touched some of them a little.

I have quoted these lines, in whole or part, often since then. And once, in the Brangwyn Hall at Swansea, I remember they brought down the house.

In the December election of 1910 I spoke and worked in Devonshire for Charles Buxton, another Left Wing Liberal, who later joined the Labour Party, and then in Bristol for Charles Hobhouse. This contact nearly changed the whole course of my life, for Hobhouse recommended me to his brother-in-law, Sir John Fuller, who was just going out to Australia to be Governor of Victoria, and wanted an A.D.C. with an interest in politics. Had I gone, I am pretty sure I should have stayed and, after serving the Governor for a year or two, have become a Dinkum Aussie—and, perhaps, gone with the others to Gallipoli—for Australia, as I shall relate later, pulled me very hard when I did meet her. I was much excited by this possibility, and fixed the title of a book, or at least a short story, which I intended soon to write. It was to be called *Love under the Southern Cross*.

But this was to be neither written nor acted. Sir John Fuller had other names recommended to him, and chose another A.D.C.!

Over the next twenty years it gradually came about that I had more friends and contacts at Cambridge in other Colleges than in my own.

But when I was Parliamentary Under-Secretary of State for Foreign Affairs in 1929 I attended a Founder's Feast in King's. "A very happy binge," I recorded in my diary, "in the course of which, especially in the Junior Combination Room and afterwards, I wholly put off the responsibilities of office and joined in hunting Sheppard, our Vice Provost, all over the College, without finding him." I was later helped to bed by some of my companions. Next morning, emerging without much appetite from the guest-room, I met Nightingale, the Head Porter. He had been many years in the service of the College. He gave me a wise look. "Not much changed, sir," he said. The next time I was present, as a Minister, at a King's Founder's Feast was in 1946. I was then Chancellor of the Exchequer, and behaved with great decorum. I made a speech replying to the toast of His Majesty's Government. In that solemn context I made only a few jokes, but offered some quiet words of encouragement to the young.

CHAPTER IV

LONDON

WHEN I came down from Cambridge in 1910, I went in the autumn to live in the Temple. I shared residential chambers at 4 Brick Court with Billy Foss, whom I have mentioned in the last chapter as one of our Fabian Summer School party. I was already a member of the Middle Temple and beginning to read for the Bar. But I also made contact with the London School of Economics, which the Webbs had told me was a wonderful place, where one could learn much more about economics than at Cambridge. At Oxford, of course, at that time one couldn't learn economics at all. I went to lectures by Cannan on General Economics, and by L. T. Hobhouse and Graham Wallas. The quality and variety of the teaching staff at the School then, and for some time afterwards, was much better than that of the students, though some good post-graduates were beginning to arrive.

Pember Reeves, who had been a leading member of the Seddon Government in New Zealand and had put through some good social and agrarian legislation, was then Director of the School, and Sidney Webb was Chairman of the Governors. The staff included A. L. Bowley, the statistician; H. S. Foxwell, who had left Cambridge in disgust when Pigou, and not he, was appointed to succeed Marshall,[1] and was now Professor at University College, London; Lilian Knowles, a Tory Economic Historian and pupil of William Cunningham at Cambridge; A. J. Sargent, a handsome and typical son of Brasenose, later to be Professor of Commerce and, though no Socialist, a firm supporter of mine against would-be intruders on either my academic or political freedom; and H. B. Lees Smith, at that time Liberal M.P. for Northampton, and previously Professor of Economics and Public Administration at Bristol University. Hewins had been the first Director of the

---

[1] He was said to have taken his appointment so much for granted that he had already prepared both his Inaugural and his first course of lectures as Professor.

School, till Joe Chamberlain carried him off in 1903 to work
on Tariff Reform, Halford Mackinder was the Second Director,
from 1903 to 1908, until he entered Parliament as Tory M.P.
for the Camlachie Division of Glasgow. But he continued for
many years to hold his Readership in the University of London, and to go on teaching Economic Geography, with great
brilliance, in addition to his Parliamentary duties.

Thus at this time the School was by no means a Red hotbed.
Of its first three Directors two were notorious Tories, and the
third a New Zealand Radical. Two M.P.s, one Tory and one
Liberal, were among its most active teachers; two interesting
precedents for the combined operations, academic and political, which some of us conducted after the war.

In July 1911 I won a Hutchinson Research Studentship at
the School. I wanted to keep up my economics, and I was
taking my Bar exams rather slowly—not giving much of my
time to legal studies.

I began to work, under Cannan, on a thesis on the distribution of wealth, which was finally published in 1920 under
the title of *The Inequality of Incomes*. On this book—and on an
article on *The Measurement of the Inequality of Incomes*, published
in the *Economic Journal* in September, 1920, and later put into
the book as an Appendix—I was awarded my degree of
D.Sc.(Econ.) in the University of London. But, except in very
deep academic groves, where my Doctor's red and yellow
robes might suggest sunrise or sunset in the forest, I have always
discouraged the description of myself as "Dr. Dalton".

This Research Studentship led me to spend a good deal of
time at the School of Economics in the last three years before
the war. And it led me to meet Ruth Fox, whom, as I shall
relate, I married in 1914. In July 1911 Eileen Power of Girton
was awarded a Shaw Research Studentship at the School, so
Cambridge scored twice that year. The previous year a Shaw
Research Studentship had been awarded to William Kennedy,
an M.A. of Glasgow University, whom I came to know well.
He too worked under Cannan and in 1913 published his
thesis on *English Taxation 1640–1799, an Essay on Policy and
Opinion*. He was killed by the Germans on the Somme.

Living in the Temple was a great comedown after Cambridge. All my Cambridge friends were scattered. Some still at

Cambridge, others in different parts of London—in Hampstead, in Chelsea, at Toynbee Hall or in the Walworth Road. Meeting them was much more complicated, and took much more time, than when one had been able just to drop in on them in College or in lodgings. But, of course, life in London was freer in other ways than life at Cambridge.

Billy Foss, with whom I lived at very close quarters in the Temple for several years, had been at Cambridge with me, though not for long. He had come up to Emmanuel, from Eastbourne, in my third year. He was very gay and good-looking, small—he had been a good scrum half at school—and had a natural gift for acting. It was his acting which first caught Rupert's eye and mine, and brought him into our circle, including the Cambridge Fabians. Rupert and I had planned that he should become Secretary when Rupert succeeded me as President in 1909–10.

But his parents ran into financial trouble, and Billy Foss, to the great regret of us all, had to go down at the end of his first year and begin to earn a living in the City.

He and I not only shared rooms in the Temple, but spent several holidays together. We walked in Wales—long distances rather fast—and spent a night in the shack on top of Snowdon, sharing the limited accommodation and playing cards with a couple who were obviously eloping lovers. We went one summer to County Kerry and discovered a little hotel at Darrynane, to which I twice returned with other companions. There we combined sea-fishing with walks in the mountains, based on Glencar in the Macgillicuddy Reeks, and listening at night, in the kitchen of the hotel at Darrynane, to songs in Erse sung by the family and neighbours, and joining in the choruses of English versions of some of them.

We were both tremendous Belloc fans, and founded, between us, a Belloc Club. My copy of Belloc's *Verses*, published in 1910, is thus inscribed. "From the original member of the Belloc Club to the rest of the Club. H. D. from W. F." He was a perfect companion.

He was very attractive to women and when, in due course of fate, he married, I was his best man. He had several sons, who grew up to be as good-looking as their father. Him too the Germans killed—in an air raid.

Through him I met another great friend of mine, Douglas Rouquette. Two years junior to Billy Foss at Eastbourne, he went up to Sidney Sussex College, Cambridge, in October 1910, just after I had come down. He, indeed, excelled on a wide front. He won an open scholarship in Classics and took a Second, Division I, in Classics in 1913 and a Second in Economics Part II in 1914. It was on my advice that he followed Classics with Economics. Austin Robinson sends me this note of him from the College Annual of 1918:

"There was a certain distinction in everything he did, and he made his mark in the University at a time when there were many men of exceptional promise among us. He seemed to have a fine career before him. He was a good athlete, a high jumper and a President of the College Athletic Club, a useful forward in Rugby Football and Captain of the Lawn Tennis Six. In 1912 he was of the company which played *Oedipus Tyrannus*, and took the part of Leader of the Chorus with much dignity. Early in 1917 he married the sister of his friend J. E. Scott, of Emmanuel, whose brilliant interpretation of the Part of Oedipus is still remembered. Quite early in his University course he began to speak at the Union, and he was elected President at the end of the Michaelmas Term, 1913."

He spent a summer holiday with me in Kerry in 1912, seafishing at Darrynane, walking the hills I knew, and others which we discovered together.[1] When I married in 1914, he was my best man. He was a most delightful and sensitive companion. In September 1917 the Germans shot him down out of the sky in an air battle.

In 1910, after coming down from Cambridge, I thought I ought to see something of the North and of Industry, so I paid a visit, with suitable letters of introduction, to Tyneside, Teesside and County Durham. I visited shipyards in Newcastle, steelworks in Middlesbrough and a coal mine in Durham. The coal mine selected for me was Auckland Park, near Bishop

---

[1] I kept no diary in those days, but in a book, in which I wrote down phrases and sayings that pleased me, I find this:

"In the summer of 1912 I went to Kerry with D. R. Being interested in Mademoiselle C. de M., whom we found staying at Darrynane, he and she agreed to face the world as cousins. 'Ah!' cried Mrs. Keating, the wife of 'Himself', 'to think that you two should meet here like this at the back of Godspeed!'"

Auckland, and my official guide was Bill House, miners' agent and afterwards parliamentary candidate for the Bishop Auckland Division.

Eighteen years later I became the parliamentary candidate for Bishop Auckland. I had not been there in the interval. But the pit I had gone down was now closed, the workings flooded and most of the miners unemployed. Of all that waste and tragedy I shall have much more to say later.

From 1911 to 1914 I did no active politics. My mind and interests were elsewhere. There was not much to do in the Labour Party. There was no individual membership yet, and the Fabians, I thought, had become uninteresting. Nor was I then very keen on the I.L.P. Hilton Young, now Lord Kennet, who took a kindly interest in me at that time, asked me whether I would like to be the Liberal candidate for a Worcestershire constituency. But I wasn't attracted.

The Liberals, indeed, were making the running in those years. The Lloyd George Budget of 1909, and the fight with the Lords, and the Parliament Act, and the National Insurance Act; that was all good stuff, I thought, and my Cambridge Fabian friends thought, and we were hot in favour of it. But the Liberal Party as a whole, we felt, was not a good show; too many plutocrats in it, and snobs, and crashing bores. We did not want to get mixed up with all that lot.

But I went to Whitefields Tabernacle to hear Lloyd George speak on his Insurance Bill, and I was deeply moved. The climax came when he declared, in a ringing voice: "I will fight this through or I will fall." And men sprang to their feet, with tears streaming down their cheeks, crying: "Thank God for Lloyd George!" And I confess that I wept too, my Welsh blood stirred within me.

And I remember L. G. proposing the Royal Toast, I think at some public dinner to the Dominion Prime Ministers, in these words, "We are the descendants of the men who turned the Kings of England into Constitutional monarchs and, *therefore*, we are loyal to the Throne. The King!"

That gave me a thrill too.

My father told me that King George V, until he came to the throne, hadn't much liked Lloyd George. But, on the death of King Edward VII, when Ministers came to express their sorrow to the new Sovereign, Lloyd George, alone of them all, broke down and wept like a child. And this, King George said, made him think much better of Lloyd George, since he seemed to be both more loyal to the Throne and more sincere than the King had expected.

In 1913 a Lectureship was offered at the School of Economics in the Social Science Department. There were two candidates, C. R. Attlee and I. He had come down from Oxford in 1904, had been called to the Bar, and was now living at the Hailey-bury Mission. I was four and a half years younger than he was, was not yet called to the Bar and was living in the Temple. This was the first time our orbits crossed. Sidney Webb was Chairman of the Selection Committee. We were both inter-viewed and Attlee was appointed. Webb said to me after-wards, "Don't be discouraged. We thought that, if we ap-pointed him, he'd stick to it, but that, if we appointed you, you wouldn't." The war soon prevented either of us from "sticking to it". But after the war we became colleagues, first on the teach-ing staff of the School, then in Parliament in several periods of opposition, in more than one Government, including a Coalition Government in another war, and finally in a Cabinet over which he presided. All that, and especially the climax, would have sounded awfully unlikely to both of us in 1913!

Having finally passed my Bar exams, and having some time previously eaten the necessary dinners, I was called to the Bar early in 1914. I had already gone into chambers, as a pupil, with F. T. Barrington Ward, who had a large mixed Common Law practice. These were good chambers for learn-ing the craft. The latest arrival, after me, was a chubby-faced youth from Harrow and Balliol, named Walter Monckton. His strong combination of charm and brains was already obvious. We were a very happy family. But the war broke it up, and before the end of the year I had left those chambers, never to return to the law.

On May 26th, 1914, I married Ruth Fox. I had met her at the School of Economics, where she was taking a B.Sc.(Econ.) degree. In my first year as Hutchinson Research Student she was Joint Secretary of the Students' Union—there were always two secretaries, male and female. She and I and a few others formed a society which we called the Query Club, which met for discussions and social purposes. Other members included two eminent men now known as Lord Piercy and Sir Theodore Gregory, both likewise taking their first degrees, and William Kennedy and Eileen Power, whom I have mentioned already. Ruth Fox spoke French, Italian and German well, and read all three languages easily. She had a wide knowledge of the arts, to which I have never pretended. Like me she was a good walker. But she failed in arithmetic in the Newnham entrance exam. They were willing, all the same, to let her in to read Classics, but she changed her mind and came to the London School of Economics instead.

Her father, T. Hamilton Fox, who had retired from business, was a Conservative in politics, but, for this very reason, had been seized by Mrs. Webb to act as Treasurer of what we all, except the Treasurer, rather ribaldly called "the Break Up"— the Webbs' all-party "Society for Promoting the Break Up of the Poor Law".

Her mother, whose maiden name was Ogilvy, was a woman of very striking personality, half Scots and half Greek. Her father, Captain David Stuart Ogilvy, had been a regular soldier and served as a Sapper Officer in the Indian Mutiny and the Crimea. When he left the Army he became British Consul at Smyrna—the only case, it was said, when Gladstone, who was his cousin, ever made a job for a relative. At Smyrna he married a young Greek wife named Thalia Xanthopoulos. Ruth's mother was their only child. After the death of his first wife Captain Ogilvy married again, this time a Dutch woman. He was devoted to France, speaking and writing French perfectly, and, on the outbreak of the war of 1870, he joined the French Army as a volunteer and offered to Gambetta plans for the defence of Paris. He was killed in action by the Germans in November 1870.[1]

I have several times told Frenchmen this, desiring to establish, as it were, a family credential. And I remember a French Socialist Deputy, who stayed a night with us in the country, drawing himself up stiffly when my wife spoke to him of her grandfather's death, saying: "Madame, vous avez bien mérité

[1] Her grandfather's diaries of this period were published by my wife in the *Fortnightly Review* for June and July 1949.

de la France!" And she too, like her grandfather, has a deep love for France.

My wife, therefore, was half English, a quarter Scots and a quarter Greek. It was not the first time that I had felt the attraction of Anglo-Greek women, for I had been an admirer, several years before, of two of the daughters of Luke Ionides. But these were both married already.

My wife and I lived first in the smaller residential chambers in the Cloisters, Temple, to which I had moved from Brick Court when Billy Foss got married. Later we lived in Albert Bridge Road, overlooking Battersea Park.

We spent our honeymoon at Lockeridge, near Marlborough, in a house lent us by Mrs. Whitehead, wife of the Cambridge mathematician and philosopher. Thus began our intimacy with the Wiltshire Downs, on which sixteen years later we built a small house of our own, where after twenty-two more years I am now writing this account.

In that summer of 1914 I took my wife to Darrynane, where I had spent such happy days with two of my best men friends. But in August came war. We were at Darrynane in the early days of it. Ireland was on the brink of a civil war of her own, and that, no doubt, encouraged the Germans to have their go at Belgium, believing that we were too weak and preoccupied to intervene.

Redmond, it will be remembered, offered his Nationalist Volunteers to the British Army as readily as Carson offered his Ulster Volunteers. And on the sands close to our little hotel my wife and I saw drawn up, a day or two after our declaration of war, a company of Redmond's Volunteers, armed with rifles. They were addressed by the local priest, who told them there was war between France and Germany. Never a word about England, nor, that day indeed, about Home Rule. But "you know that France has always been a good friend to Ireland, and that Germany is the home of that accursed Higher Criticism of the Holy Scriptures. So, if you see a German warship rounding the corner of the bay, you will open fire."

When I came down from Cambridge, Rupert Brooke stayed up, living still at the Old Vicarage, Grantchester, working for a Fellowship. He won it in 1913 for a thesis on Webster, the

Elizabethan dramatist. We met fairly often, and wrote to each other a good deal. I have only one letter which I wrote to him, returned to me many years later by one of his literary executors. It was written on New Year's Eve of 1911, which I was spending at Windsor with my parents. The account is of a conversation in the smoke-room of the National Liberal Club, of which H. G. Wells and Rupert and I were all then members. The subject of jocund discussion was the Webbs' Break Up of the Poor Law, into the campaign for which both Rupert and I had been rather reluctantly pushed by the untiring Beatrice. (The dots do not signify omissions. They were part of Wells' style of writing, which Rupert and I often adopted.)

It will be 1911 before this is finished.

THE CLOISTERS,
WINDSOR CASTLE.

Yes, I'm afraid it will have to go—that true paragraph about the home. (My new style.) (It's like a monologue that begins a psychological novel.) There's a feeling in the air that *something* ought to be suppressed, isn't there? But they aren't quite sure what. Wells said so in the N.L.C. yesterday afternoon. I want to tell you about the Dramatisation of the Minority Report. *He* talked about it for three hours. He and Chesterton did it one Sunday. It's an admirable thing, but they say Granville Barker's very angry, and says it's not the sort of thing he meant when he advocated the "presentation on the stage of urgent social problems".

The first curtain rises on a workhouse ward. "Pauper imbecile nursing pauper child (upside down)." A notice is displayed over the window "Paupers are forbidden to look out of this window," and over the door "Visitors are earnestly requested not to give tobacco or buns to the paupers."

The ultimate curtain falls on a scene strangely similar. Belloc nursing a child ("still upside down, but not quite so upside down"). Over the window and the door the same two notices, only that "Paupers" is crossed out and "Workers (No. 3 grade) under disciplinary training" is written over the top. . . . Between every two scenes there's an interlude, and Belloc and Chesterton are shown drinking, the number of empty bottles

increasing gradually through the play. . . . There's a great
scene on the Death of Bumble. The murder takes place off the
stage, and then leading Fabians come on dancing to triumphal
music, James and Dr. Dodd, Pease and Mrs. Hylton-Dale,
Tina and Ben and Jesse Holiday, each carrying on a pitchfork
a piece of Bumble. . . . These are put into a boiling cauldron,
and clouds of steam rise. . . . On the clouds are discovered
sitting the Gods of the English, Mill and Bentham and
Herbert Spencer, throned and crowned, and . . . S. and B.
Webb.

. . . .

And I want to tell you about the Webb Diaries. We all come
into them. They will be published twenty-five years after she
dies. When do you go to Poland? I shall be delighted to give
you some hints on how to treat the inhabitants. I shall be in
town almost continuously, almost forever, from next Wednesday morning. You might have a bed . . . and a little soda . . .
and eggs. Beds! There'll be a spare bed in My Menage next
week. Or there's a sofa. Poor Mr. X has been sleeping there
lately, whispering through his dreams about the Dead Lives of
his Old Schoolfellows, and Your Dead Life. . . . Then there's
a bed, where the Lord Chief Justice sometimes sleeps, but
which I control, a bed where my more eminent friends sleep,
Privy Councillors, and Judges of the Court of Appeal, and
Australasian Professors, a bed in Devereux Court. You might
sleep there. . . .

There's some story about Alfred, and Mr. X lending him
money at $15\frac{1}{2}\%$, and high finance, and a key of the Solicitor-
General's door, and an unpleasant scene on a platform at
Euston. Do you know anything about it? . . .

Well, well! You must come and see me, for I can't just go on
writing. And I want to know about Democracy and the Arts, and
Mr. Allen and his father. And I want you to see my new head-
dress which is symbolic of the Celtic Renaissance. You saw it,
years since, at Portmadoc but you will not remember! . . .
It had other uses in those days! . . .

HUGH.

Of Rupert's letters to me in this period here is a Fabian
one.

24, BILTON ROAD,   *July 5th, 1910.*
    RUGBY.

Where are you? I sit here and prepare stirring harangues for the People of South England on Poor Law. I go there at the end of next week. On Saturday Messrs. Allen, Paget and self attended the Fabian Conference. It was great fun. Dear Ensor in the chair. The Northern delegates were superb men. They lashed the women with unconquerable logic and gross words. There were most frightful scenes, and the women gibbered with rage. Mabel was almost beyond herself with purple-faced hatred. They were quieted by Sidney, with an evasive speech. But they *were* devils, running "The Cause" for all they were worth—against Socialism. The Executive were, I gathered, better than last year: though they still shirked the populace a bit. Old Shaw popped up and down; and a man from Manchester and I conspired democratically in a corner. But vainly. What I want is *Local Government* (isn't it?); anyhow one of the Webbs' books. Can you let me have it? Young men in London kept coming up and telling me that Winston or Lord Wolverhampton was goin' to write a preface to your novel about your parents. I affirmed the report. A postcard from you to my brother was hurled in here the other day. I just rescued it before my mother got hold of it. I shall send it to him sometime. Don't know where he is. I have not seen him since May.

You might let me know sometime when it is you are coming to Clevedon; and I'll try to fit the dates.

I suppose you talk in nominatives absolute now: God help you!

                                 RUPERT.

And here, nearly two years later, is a letter in reply to one from me, sympathising that he had not got his Fellowship that year. He had been near death.

BEACH SHADE,   *Easter 1912.*
    BANK,
       LYNDHURST.

Dear Hugh,

You were good to write to me. It doesn't matter about the scientist who got a fellowship for two reasons

(1) Nothing matters.

(2) They will give me a fellowship next year.
The electors seem agreed upon that.

The scientist, you see, had no more shots. I have one more. Both our dissertations were extremely good. He discovered a very important thing about the Blood of Coal Miners. It needs far less Oxygen than you think. And, it follows, they can live for longer and far oftener when the Worst happens, than you suppose.

Friend of my laughing careless youth, where are those golden hours now? Where now the shrill mirth of our burgeoning intellects? and by what doubtful and deleterious ways am I come down to this place of shadows and eyeless pain? In truth, I have been for some months in Hell. I have been very ill. I am very ill. In all probability I shall be very ill. It is thought by those that know me best (viz. myself) that I shall die. Nor do I greatly want to live, the savour of life having oddly left it, and my mind being worn and flabby, a tenth of anything it used to be.

I do nothing. I eat and sleep and rest. My thoughts buzz drearily in a vacuum. I went in January to a slightly American nerve-specialist who said I was deplorably unwell. He made me drink stout and swallow the compressed blood of bullocks. In consequence I am now enormously fat. Boys laugh at me in the street. But that is partly, also, on account of my manner. For I am more than a little gone in my head, since my collapse.

I go back to Germany soon. They are a slow race and will not know I am stupid. I shall never appear in England again. I shall never write poetry or limpid prose again. I may ultimately become sub-reader of English Philology in the Johns Hopkins University, Wa. (or Ma. or Ra. . . .).

I am a despicable, toothless creature and I mock at the Spring.

I salute you from these depths. Give my love to the Middle Temple.

Ever

RUPERT.

But a few months later he wrote to me, much less sadly, from Berlin.

BEI D. WARD,   *August 7th, 1912.*
    CHARLOTTENBURG,
        BERLINERSTRASSE 100,
            BERLIN.

I gather from postmarks that Frau Neeve kept your card for four days and my mother for two.

I am, as you say, dead. Further processes even have set in.

> *Though one be mild as Moses*
> *His meekness clouds and closes;*
> *In the end he decomposes;*
> *And he is sure to smell.*

As Swinburne or you or some one of the romantics puts it.

I am under pretext of doing my dissertation here. Actually I have not done a word.

I spend my time in making love to female dancers. They pirouette scornfully away. . . .

After the 10th of December I shall come to London. Then I shall sit one night and repeat poetry to you, and you will repeat dirty stories to me; till 8.30 a.m. Then I shall go to bed. In January I go to America for 3 years.

Cambridge must be full of people one knows. Perhaps it is nicer not to be there. But I am sorry not to see them capering in the Greek Play.

I have discovered the real division of mankind; into the Petrine and the Jesuine; those who are crucified head downwards and those who are crucified right way up. It is immensely important. Perhaps the greatest discovery of the Twentieth Century. Beyond that I have done nothing; written but one line, but that a good one.

> *Ah, love, there is no something in the sun!*

It ends a sonnet (—but what sonnet?).

It is the truest line in English except Meredith's "And Life, some say, is worthy of the Mews."

Be in London in December.

                                                    RUPERT.

Next year he went on a voyage to the South Seas, crossing America on the way. On this journey and on the Pacific Islands he wrote some of his best poems and prose.

He came back to England in June 1914. The last time I saw him was early in July. Here is the last letter I had from him. The fifth of July seems a recurrent date.

off to   *5th July, 1914.*
    24, BILTON ROAD,
        RUGBY.

My dear Hugh,

I find I can't get back in time for Tuesday night. I'm sorry. I am free as the wind on *Thursday* night. Are you? You can shelve your wife. Nothing shall occupy me on Thursday night till I hear from you. Write immediately to Rugby. All other times I am dining with E. Gosse, or H. James, or S. Olivier, and others of my contemporaries.

How horrible it is to be a bachelor.

RUPERT.

He picked me up at my chambers in the Temple and we dined alone together.

Three weeks later the war came. He wrote his famous sonnets, joined the Royal Naval Division, retreated from Antwerp, and died in the Aegean.

CHAPTER V

WAR

I was deeply shaken and sharply astonished by the outbreak of war. I was intellectually aware of the tensions in Europe, and particularly of the threat to Britain of the ever-growing and highly efficient German fleet. But I was not emotionally aware of any close risk of catastrophe.

And I was very angry. "I do not believe", I wrote in a book I published fourteen years later,[1] "that I was alone in feeling passionately in August, 1914, that the young generation in all the belligerent lands had been collectively betrayed." I had little doubt that the Germans bore an overwhelming burden of responsibility. They had built this great fleet; they had been threatening and trying to bully everybody for years; they could obviously have pulled Austria-Hungary up short, if they had chosen; and finally, and clearest evidence of guilt, they had violated Belgium. But why, I demanded, had not the rest of us somehow stopped them? Surely a warning that *we* should come in against them, would have done that.

I was, however, a very civilian person. I did not think I should make a good soldier. I had not been outstanding in the Eton College Volunteers—the dog-potters, as we used to call them—though I did my drills and field days and camp with the rest, and quite enjoyed camp. I had no keen appreciation at that time of the soldierly virtues. That came later, keenest of all when I was a Minister of the Crown from 1940 to 1945. On the other hand, I had not the faintest glimmer of conscientious objection to military service. We were all in this together, and most of my friends were joining up. I did not want to lag behind them. Being at the Bar, the most natural way seemed to be through the Inns of Court O.T.C., which I joined in the autumn.

My military career was not distinguished. After obtaining my commission I served first in the Army Service Corps, and

[1] *Towards the Peace of Nations*, p. 309.

then in the Artillery. But I never rose higher than Brigade Supply Officer in the one case, and Acting Second-in-command of a six-inch howitzer battery in the other.

My emotional approach to casualties illustrated my mood. I was deeply shocked at first when young men, fresh from civil life, were killed in action. I had supposed that the old Regulars would go down first—Colonels and Sergeant-Majors and the like. After all, it was *their* trade. These youngsters were only coming in to help them out.

But gradually, as the young died, and many of my dearest friends among them, I grew callous, and passed through bitter early grief and many tears to a cold, silent, repressed acceptance of whatever fate might hold in store for any of us.

In the Inns of Court O.T.C., after a few weeks of drilling and preliminaries in London, I went to train at Berkhamsted. Early in 1915 I was commissioned. How I came to join the Army Service Corps I do not clearly remember, except that one day I was summoned, with another cadet, to go to the War Office from Berkhamsted to see General Sir Bindon Blood, who received us very kindly, asked us whether we could ride a horse, to which we both said yes, and then told us that good officers were wanted for Divisional Trains and that he thought we should both fill that bill. I was posted to the 35th Divisional Train, and did the first part of my training at Darley Dale, near Matlock, in very agreeable open country, now nearly all built over. Our train was horse-drawn, both then and all our time in France, though served, when the whole Division was assembled, by a Mechanical Transport Supply Column.

The 35th Division was known as the Bantam Division. Apart from a Pioneer Battalion of the Northumberland Fusiliers, all the infantry (other ranks) were bantams, men too undersized to be accepted in ordinary units. But their officers, and the Artillery and Engineers and the Divisional Train were men of normal, or, as in my case, more than normal height.

This experiment, as experience in France showed, was not a military success. Many of the bantams were slum-dwellers, undernourished from birth, from Glasgow, Manchester and other big cities. Their average level of endurance and achievement was bound to be lower than with the general run of other units.

It took a long time to collect and train the various elements
of the Division. We completed our full Divisional Training on
Salisbury Plain at the beginning of 1916. On January 22nd
I was warned that Brigade Supply Officers were to leave for
France next day, via Southampton, as part of an advance
party. Ruth was staying with me at Ludgershall, and at 3.30
a.m. on January 23rd I left our lodgings and walked in half an
hour to Tidworth. A full moon was shining wonderfully down
through a belt of mist. I wrote letters and packed, and at 8.45
a.m. our party started, in four cars, from Tidworth.

These are the first entries in a diary I kept while in France.
It is, for the most part, a very dull diary, written up daily—I
had never kept one before—about R.P.s (Refilling Points) and
Dumps and Billeting, with comments, some friendly and some
not, on individuals with whom I served, or whom I met in the
course of my duties. Our Senior Supply Officer, a Lowland
Scot and a Temporary, was not a favourite of mine, nor of the
other Brigade Supply Officers. I much preferred serving under
Regulars.

In France, after a period behind the front, the Bantams took
over a section of the line near Armentières. That day the Germans hoisted above their own trenches notices inscribed
"Cock-a-doodle-do". Their intelligence was pretty good!

The Australians had now come on to France from Gallipoli
and Egypt. On April 7th my diary records: "Ride into Armentières eight miles . . . I pass lots of Australians. Very attractive!
It's not only their sombrero hats, or their sunburnt and mostly
cleanshaven faces—so much more becoming than our foolish
'military moustache'—or their casualness about saluting, or
their obvious utter lack of the barrack-square stamp, that
endears them to me. Not even the knowledge that in their
country, as one of them said to me, 'the sun shines every day
and every man has a chance'; nor even, as another added,
'and a Labour Government is in power'. It is their litheness,
and looseness of limb, and self-assurance, and clean-cut
features, and their jolly way with one another, and with small
children and with women—not mere leching. They are a
splendid band of brothers. All this of the N.C.O.s and men. I
see hardly any of their officers. Those I do see look rather
ordinary."

Two names which often recur in my diary are Fawcett and Nicholls. Colonel Fawcett, the famous explorer, over whose death in the Brazilian forests mystery still hangs, was in command of the 158th Brigade, R.F.A. I was his Supply Officer. He was a "dug out", a Regular returning to the Army from his explorations, and longing to go back to them when the war was over. I saw a lot of him and we liked each other. I used to go with him, and some of his officers, to their O.P.s. As early as April I was thinking of a transfer to the Gunners, though I did not finally manage this, in spite of repeated efforts, till the following January. On April 29th, my diary records: "Dine with H.Q. 158. Fawcett is a splendid chap—an explorer. Some day he's going back to find a city built of stone in the unexplored heart of Peru, to which an aboriginal white race withdrew when the Incas came. It is screened from the world by savage tribes, man-monkeys and impenetrable forest. There is strong evidence, he says, that this race still exists. Once he was within forty miles of their territory with three companions. But one went mad and the other two went sick. So he had to come back, 'because there was no one to carry the instruments'. Another time he went six weeks without food, living only on brackish water. He photographed himself at various stages and at the end was mere skin and bone."

And on May 10th: "Great activity over sanitation. Flies to be exterminated. Busy with model latrines, urinals, etc. Dine with 158. Fawcett in very good form. Childishly greedy about jam. Delightfully radical. Denounces primogeniture, entail, etc.; also hereditary titles. Says that, after the war, 'you'll *have* to divide up the money'. Arrange to witness some interesting operations on Saturday night. A lovely ride home. Chilly, and starlight, with spring night smells in the air."

And on June 27th, on the way to the Somme: "Fawcett gives interesting account of artillery action down south. We shall be in the thick of it. Tra-la-la! All our supply work is to be done at night."

Then on the Somme, July 8th. "Visit 158 with Nicholls in evening. Fawcett in a very cheery mood. Thinks we may well break through about the end of July. Expects disease on a great scale if really hot weather comes. Germans will suffer worst from this because worse fed, and civilians worse than military, because less sanitary. This might finish the war."

But there was no break through.

On August 18th: "Talk to Fawcett. Hearing I'm trying to transfer, he says he'd like to have me in his brigade. That would be my mark. He'd be a glorious chap to serve under. He's fed up with things at the front, and very down on the staff, both Corps and Divisional. They've thrown away 23,000 men at Guillemont, and simply committed wholesale murder. And the men are so splendid! They'd go anywhere and do anything. And the Artillery has been bitched up too. The Corps people want too much shooting at front-line trenches, and much too little counter-battery work. The staff live way back in Chateaux, and plaster each other's breasts with decorations, and never go near the trenches or gun positions. Our Staff are either miserable old dug-outs, with influential pals in military clubs in London, or young fellows without much experience, whose heads have been turned by rapid promotion. The Germans were quite right, in their initial comment on our possibilities, that you can improvise an Army and make it as large as you like, but you can't improvise a Staff. The Somme has proved this."

On November 3rd: "Visit Arras. See Fawcett, for the first time since leaving the Somme. He is being sent home on a course, because he is the junior Brigade Commander. Furious! Says the war will be over by next October. He has a vision of open fighting once again, and a battle being decided in three days. It would be like a Wells' romance! The Anglo-French Army will reach, but not cross, the Rhine. A British general of genius may yet be thrown up."

While in England on his course, he pulled some strings for me, and my transfer, after delay and obstruction at every level, including the War Office itself, finally went through. On January 25th, 1917, I was "notified to proceed to England to train for transfer to Royal Artillery".

I never saw Fawcett again. After the war he went back to the Brazilian forests, in which he finally disappeared in 1925.

Captain Leslie Nicholls was a young Regular, eight years younger than I was, who succeeded in June 1916 to the command of No. 3 Company of the Divisional Train, the Company with which I worked. He was good at the piano, very good on a horse, and had great charm. Our friendship ripened steadily. We both got thoroughly sick of our immediate superiors, and we both plotted to transfer to other arms of the service. Soon after I switched to the Gunners he became airborne and served with the R.F.C. till the end of the war. Then he came back to earth with the Sappers, and served in India. After January 1917, when we had some drinks together on my transfer, I did not see him again till 1941, when he walked in on me one day at the Ministry of Economic Warfare. He was now a General and I was a Minister of the Crown. But we began just where we had left off twenty-four years before. He was still a most amusing companion and seemed to be quite good at his job. I hope he felt the same about me! He had become a great expert on communications and wireless, and was the first British general to be attached to Eisenhower's H.Q. in North Africa. This relationship was not, from the start, quite easy. Some Americans were jealous and mistrustful of him— but his competence and his social gifts got him through, with Eisenhower's insistence on teamwork and "integration".

From then on we kept in touch. I asked him to take notice of various young officers, who were personal friends of mine and serving near him, in North Africa, in Italy and in Western Europe. He told me that, if Patton had been in command at Anzio, we should have taken Rome in forty-eight hours.

In 1945, when it fell to me as Chancellor of the Exchequer to carry through the nationalisation of Cables and Wireless, I picked Leslie Nicholls as a member of the new Board. He was first class, both as a technician and a diplomat, very energetic, very keen on all forms of national service, and very anxious to make this particular show succeed. He has done a fine job at Electra House, and is now Chairman of the Board.

In the first days of July 1916 the 35th Division had moved down to the Somme. It was on that battlefield that those sacrificial armies, the best that Britain had ever put forth, entered the fiery furnace. British losses in France in the three months following the first day of that offensive were greater than all the British losses of the Second World War—Army, Navy, Air Force, Merchant Navy and civilians killed in air raids, all added together. Our Division was not in at the start, but before the end of the third week we had suffered very heavily in all our brigades.

Last words? How about these? A mortally wounded private of the K.R.R. brought in to the Main Dressing Station. "Oh, Padre, you *should* have been with us this morning to see the King's go over!"

Our poor little Bantams couldn't make it. They were too small to be able to jump the German trenches. And they hadn't the stamina, any more than the stature, for the jobs they were ordered to do. In my diary for July and August I have some grim entries. Here is one.

"August 16th . . . The discipline of some of the Bantams may have been undermined by this recent incident, which thus will have defeated its purpose. A corporal and a private were in an advance post. They were left there thirty hours without food (except presumably an iron ration, which is not supposed to be eaten without the authority of a general!). Corporal then came back to ask if they could be relieved. He was told no, and sent back to the post. They remained there ten more hours, still without food. Then they came back. For this they were tried by court martial. Our Divisional General took the view that the strain had been more than they could reasonably be expected to bear and urged leniency. But the court martial sentenced the corporal to death and the private to five years' penal servitude. The corporal was shot in Happy Valley. For discipline's sake his whole battalion was paraded to witness the execution. Other battalions of the brigade were close by, within sight and hearing. The battalion was called to attention and the firing-party was ordered to fire. They all deliberately fired wide, but one, not firing quite wide enough, wounded the corporal in the shoulder. It then became the duty of the officer in charge of the firing-party to advance and finish off the corporal with his revolver. This duty was faultlessly performed, except that this officer wept. Most of the other officers and many of the men of the battalion on parade were guilty of the same weakness. It is said that this man had been a very good corporal and that he faced death at the hands of his friends quite heroically. In such an incident there is far more of the horror of war than in most of the real fighting."

"August 26th. I believe I am correct in saying that *officers* are not shot for cowardice—except in the Australian Expeditionary Force, where it is done by their own men after one minute's grace and opportunity given to go on. Officers in the B.E.F. are, I believe, sent home. With men it is otherwise. This may be a grave charge hereafter. It will be impossible to hide all these things when the New Armies are disbanded."

So I imagined. But, when armies are disbanded, they dissolve and scatter. Apart from individual pride and occasional formal reunions, growing fainter year by year, the corporate spirit soon fades. So, nearly thirty years later, the great Eighth Army of the desert, which some had thought would be a significant political force after the war, was first diluted with drafts, and then dispersed into its elements. When peace came, of that great soul of glory no solid body remained.

We left the Somme at the end of August, and trekked five days by road to the Arras sector, where we stayed, in comparative quiet, for some time. From September 14th to October 6th I was Town Major of Agnez, a little township near Arras, a relief from the monotony of the daily dump. There I had quite amusing, and I hope helpful, relations with the Mayor and other local notables, trying to smooth out problems of billeting, sanitation, etc.

At the end of October I had some leave, and then returned to my routine in France, still in the Arras sector, till my transfer went through.

I left for England, for transfer to the Gunners, on January 25th, 1917. I had been just twelve months in France. I trained at Horsham, then on Salisbury Plain, then at Lydd for shooting, and finally at Prees Heath, Shropshire. Ruth stayed near by on Salisbury Plain and at Prees Heath.

In June I was ordered to proceed to France, in charge of a draft of "reinforcements for Siege Artillery Batteries in Italy". On July 6th I crossed the Channel.

I wrote the story of my service in Italy in a book I called *With British Guns in Italy*. I wrote this up from the diaries I kept in Italy—one was destroyed by shellfire—and from my recollections while still fresh. It was all done in the first two months of my civilian life. But, being thus hurriedly written, it is full of banalities, and I had no time to polish it all, though I took trouble over some passages which pleased me. It contains, I think, some good accounts, especially of our part in the retreat from Caporetto, and of the final advance across the Piave. But, apart from the style which is uneven, it seems to me now to be very immature and sentimental. Much of it, at this distance of time, reads rather schoolboyishly. But it got some favourable reviews. The *Times Literary Supplement* called me "a reliable witness", and declared that my "descriptions of . . . operations exhibit the writer as a keen, scientific and practical gunner".

And the *New Statesman* thought that I had "composed a narrative curiously unaffected by pre-conceived ideas, curiously clear-headed and curiously level in tone. Very nearly a model of what such a book should be . . . Were the world to hold an enquiry into the war, and were this book a deposition" I "would be reckoned a good witness. And here and there he is something more; in his feeling for landscapes and men (notably in his description of an army in retreat) he approaches the poetic."

In what follows I make some quotations from this book. But these form, not a narrative, but only scraps of a narrative, picked out here and there from what I felt and saw.

After the Somme and Arras, I fell in love with the Italian front at first sight.

The Isonzo front, I wrote, "is not like the front in the High Alps, where, as on the Adamello, trenches are cut in the solid ice, where the firing of a single gun may precipitate an avalanche, where more Italians are killed by avalanches than by Austrians, where food, ammunition, reinforcements, wounded and sick have all to travel in small cages attached to wire ropes, slung from peak to peak above sheer drops of many thousand feet, where sentries have to be changed every ten minutes owing to the intense cold, where battalions of Alpini charge down snow slopes on skis at thirty miles an hour, where refraction and the deceiving glare of the snow make accurate rifle-fire impossible even for crack shots—the Isonzo front is not so astounding and impossible a front as this, yet it is very different from any on which British troops are elsewhere fighting in this war.

"It is a country with a strange beauty of its own; in its own

measure rough and mountainous, and within sight of loftier
mountains to the north-west. At my first view of it I remembered a speech of Carlo, the hero of Meredith's *Vittoria*, con-
cerning Lombard cities away on the other side of the Trentino:
'Brescia under the big eastern hill which throws a cloak on it
at sunrise! Brescia is always the eagle's nest that looks over
Lombardy! And Bergamo! You know the terraces of Bergamo.
Aren't they like a morning sky? Dying there is not death; it's
flying into the dawn. You Romans envy us. You have no Alps,
no crimson hills, nothing but old walls to look on while you
fight.' To me those words were always recurring on the Italian
Front. 'Dying here is not death; it's flying into the dawn.' I
would have liked them engraved on my tombstone, if Fate had
set one up for me in this land, whose beauty casts a spell on all
one's senses.

"Observation was unbelievably easy on these high hills, in
this clear air. What worlds away from the dismal flat lands of
the Western Front! Said one enthusiast of ours, 'This is a gunner's heaven!' "

I was posted in August, after a spell at the base, to 302 Siege
Battery, commanded by Major Graham, a Regular who had
served with mountain batteries in India. I stayed with that
battery, and with him, for seventeen months, till after the war
was won. "He had the reputation," I wrote, "of being the most
efficient British Battery Commander in Italy and, so far as my
experience of others went, he deserved it. . . .

"Personally he was a most delightful man, a very amusing
talker, a pleasant companion and an excellent C.O. . . . He
had been twice wounded already, once on the Somme and
again in the Italian May offensive. In 1918 he was wounded a
third time." He and I liked each other from the start, and
always got on very well together.

One day one of our sergeants saw a little man in Italian
uniform trying to photograph our guns. This was contrary to
orders and the sergeant instantly placed him, and a young
Italian officer accompanying him, under arrest, and sent off a
bombardier to report to the Command Post. The little man
protested, in rather bad English, that he was the King of Italy
and the young officer seemed to be backing him up. The sergeant told them not to try to spin that sort of yarn. But it was

true! Major Graham apologised to the King, but commended the sergeant.

Ours had been the first British battery to come into action in Italy and had fired the first British shell against Austria. "And," I wrote, "as my story will show, it was either the first or among the first on most other important occasions, except in the Caporetto retreat, and then it was the last."

Our battery position was up on the rocky Carso, and in the early days I did a number of front-line reconnaissances, to get to know the ground, and the Italians, especially their infantry, and to help to give them confidence in our support. I joined just in time to take part in the big Italian summer offensive, when the Italian Second Army captured the Bainsizza plateau beyond the Isonzo and, but for a shortage of ammunition, might have broken through the Ljubliana gap, taken Trieste from the rear and even gone right through to Vienna.

We may still speculate on what might have happened if we had pushed really hard, with all available forces and supplies, on the Italian front in 1917, and not so hard in France. Lloyd George was for it, but he allowed Haig and Robertson to over-rule him. This is one of the most disappointing chapters in Lloyd George's *War Memoirs*. He could quarrel with his generals, feel no confidence in them, and tell them so. But he never seems to have felt enough confidence in himself to fire them. Churchill, in this respect, when his turn came, was a much stronger war leader than Lloyd George.

Meanwhile in August 1917 the offensive of the Italian Third Army, commanded by the Duke of Aosta, of which we formed part, was checked, with very heavy losses, on the Carso. So our guns were switched northward in support of the Second Army, which was doing so well. I shared an O.P., in a ruined farmhouse a few miles south of Gorizia, with a young Italian artillery officer, Antonio Frongia, a Sardinian. "He and I spent many hours together, watching those bloody, memorable hills. I think of him often with affection, and with an eager hope that he passed unharmed through all the vicissitudes which were to follow." Seven years later, Ruth and I, on one of our Italian summer holidays, went to Desulo, near Cagliari, where his home had been. But all the family were gone, and it seemed that he had not returned after the war.

At the end of August the Italians took Monte Santo. This was a famous high place, where a convent had stood. It was one of the pillars of the Austrian defensive system on the Middle Isonzo. On August 24th Frongia had told me that it was reported taken, but the news was not yet sure.

"I saw him again three days later and by then all the world knew that Monte Santo had fallen. For Cadorna in his communiqué of the 25th had cried: 'Since yesterday our tricolour has been waving from the summit of Monte Santo!' Already we could see the flashes of Italian field-guns in action near the summit. All day I was buoyant, exhilarated, and as absorbed in the war as any journalist.

"Victory has an intoxicating quality in this bright clear atmosphere and among these mountains which it has, perhaps, nowhere else. All day there seemed to be in the air a strange thrill, which at evening seemed to grow into a great throbbing Triumph Song of the Heroes—incomparable Italians, living and dead. The emotion of it became almost unbearable.

" 'Our tricolour is waving from the summit of Monte Santo!'

"Here on the night of the 26th there occurred a scene wonderfully, almost incredibly, dramatic. The moon was rising. Shells passed whistling overhead, some coming from beyond the Isonzo toward the Ternova Plateau, others in the opposite direction from Ternova. Rifle shots rang out from beneath Monte Santo, along the slopes of San Gabriele, where the Italian and Austrian lines were very close together, where no word on either side might be spoken above a whisper. Suddenly there crashed out into the night the opening bars of the 'Marcia Reale' played with tremendous *élan* by a military band. The music came from Monte Santo. On the summit of the conquered mountain an Italian band was playing amid the broken ruins of the convent, standing around the firmly planted Italian flag. It was the Divisional Band of the four brigades which had stormed these heights. On the flanks of the mountain, along the new lines in the valley beneath, along the trenches half-way up San Gabriele, Italian soldiers raised a cry of startled joy.

"The Austrians opened fire on Monte Santo. But the music still went on. The 'Marcia Reale' was finished, but now in turn the 'Hymn of Garibaldi' and the 'Hymn of Mameli', historic battle-songs of Italian liberty, pealed forth to the stars, loud above the bursting of shells. And as the last notes died away upon the night air, a great storm of cheers broke forth afresh from the Italian lines. The moon was now riding high in the heavens, and every mountain top, seen from below, was outlined with a sharp-cut edge against the sky.

"Four days after, not far from this place, General Capello, the Commander of the Italian Second Army, decorated with the Silver Medal for Valour some of the heroes of the great victory. Among these was a civilian, a man over military age. It was Toscanini, Italy's most famous musical conductor. Charged with the organisation of concerts for the troops, he had found himself in this sector of the front when Monte Santo fell and, hearing the news, had demanded and obtained permission to climb the conquered mountain. He reached the summit on the evening of the 26th and found his way among the rocks and the ruins of the convent to where the band was playing. His presence had upon the musicians the same effect which the presence of a great general has upon faithful troops. They crowded round him, fired with a wild enthusiasm. Then Toscanini took command of what surely was one of the strangest concerts in the world, played in the moonlight, in an hour of glory, on a mountain-top, which to the Italians had become an almost legendary name, to an audience of two contending armies, amid the rattle of machine-guns, the rumble of cannon, and the crashes of exploding shells.

" 'Our tricolour is waving from the summit of Monte Santo!'

"If the souls of poets be immortal and know what still passes in this world, be sure that the soul of Swinburne sings again today, from hell or heaven, the 'Song of the Standard':

This is thy banner, thy gonfalon, fair in the front of thy fight,
Red from the hearts that were pierced for thee, white as thy mountains
    are white,
Green as the spring of thy soul everlasting, whose life-blood is light."

In September the Italian offensive petered out. They had no more shells. If only we had had even half a dozen of the first tanks, I thought, while these were still a fantastic new weapon, we could have gone right down the valley of the Vippacco, demoralised the enemy and made the hell of a mess of his supply lines!

Early in October we started digging—and blasting—in for the winter in our existing positions on the Carso. I was now acting Second-in-Command of the battery. But the Russian front had collapsed and on the 19th the Intelligence Report stated that a number of German Divisions had been detraining at Ljubliana and that a thousand Austrian guns had been moved across from the Russian to the Isonzo front in the last few weeks. And we were disagreeably conscious of an increase in the number of their heavy howitzers.

The Italian High Command meanwhile had been caught in two minds. Up till the middle of the month they had been planning a new offensive—they had accumulated some more ammunition during the past few weeks—on the Second Army front. Then they had changed their minds. But they had concentrated an abnormal number of batteries on this front, and pushed most of the guns much farther forward—to suit their own offensive plans—than could be justified if an enemy offensive was coming.

And on October 23rd and 24th it came, along both the Second and Third Army fronts. German divisions, following a long bombardment with gas shell, broke the Second Army line at Caporetto. Great numbers of guns, much too far forward, were lost and the whole Second Army line gave way. The Third Army, though violently attacked all along its front, stood firm. But, with the Second Army front in ruins, we had to retreat, or we should have been encircled from the north.

In that retreat, and in the fine resistance it put up before and during and after it, when we halted on the Piave, the Italian Third Army won the name of "L'Armata Invinta"—the Unconquered Army. Fifteen years later, when I met Mussolini, this enabled our conversation to start well. I addressed him in Italian and he asked me where I had learnt it. "At the front," I replied ("nella Zona di guerra"), "I am a soldier of the Unconquered Army."

We had been furiously attacked for three days and nights, and had replied strongly. Then "on the 27th the rumours became bad. . . . Orders came that all British batteries were to pull out and park that night at Villa Viola, behind Gradisca, 'for duty on another part of the front'.

"That day the sun was shining, and the Italian planes in this sector seemed to have regained command of the air. For the moment there was a little lull in the firing, but we felt that some big fate was looming over us. I went away to my hut for five minutes and wrote in my diary, 'I here put it on record once more that I am proud to fight in and for Italy. I repeat that dying here is not death, it is flying into the dawn! If I die in and for Italy, I would like to think that my death would do something for Anglo-Italian sympathy and understanding.' "

We pulled out that evening, having fired away all our ammunition. We had sent off all the guns, drawn by Italian tractors. In transport the Italians did us very handsomely, at the cost of losing some bigger guns of their own. The War Office had called *our* transport home a month before!

The Major and I and about forty men marched back to Gradisca, which was "blazing in the night. It began to rain, but that made no difference to the burning. Burning petrol was running about the streets. Earlier in the evening there had been a queer scene here. The headquarters of the British Staff had been at Gradisca, and the Camp Commandant had made a hobby of fattening rabbits for the General's Mess. When the time had come that day to pack up and go, it was found that the lorries provided were fully loaded with office stores, staff officers' bulky kit and 20,000 cigarettes, which the general was specially proud of having saved from his canteen. There was no room for the Camp Commandant's rabbit hutches, so these were opened and the fat inmates released, to the delight of the civilians and Italian soldiery, who knocked them over or shot them as they ran.

"A few miles away, at the Ordnance depot at Villa Freifeldt, thousands of pounds' worth of gun stores stood ready, packed in crates, to be removed. But no transport came for them, and they were abandoned and fell into Austrian hands. Whoever ordered these things seems to have thought it more important to save the staff's kit and the general's cigarettes.

"Just before we entered Gradisca, we passed a battalion of the Granatieri, the Italian Grenadiers, all six feet tall, with collar badges of crimson and white, coming up from reserve to fight a rearguard action. I had seen them a few days before in rest billets and admired their appearance. And in their march that night and in their faces was scorn for fugitives and contempt for death. The major said to me, as they swung past us, that *that* battalion could be trusted to fight to the end."

We reached Villa Viola at 11.30. It was to have been a rendezvous, but there was no one there. "We marched off again through pouring rain, our path lit up by the flames, which in places thrust their long tongues right across the road. The wind blew clouds of smoke in our faces. The air was full of the roaring of the fires, the crackle of blazing woodwork, the crash of houses falling in, the loud explosions of ammunition dumps and petrol stores, which now and again for a few seconds lighted up the whole night sky for miles around with a terrific glare, and then died down again. Everywhere behind the front of the retreating Third Army a systematic destruction was being carried out. The Third Army was retreating in good order, unbroken and undefeated, retreating only because its northern flank was in danger of being turned.

"I seemed to hear in the air the music of '1812' and the bells of burning Moscow ringing out loud and clear above the triumph song of the invader."

Later, near San Giorgio di Nogara, I found myself in command of the last three British guns on the road, a post of honour which I continued to hold. Two were our own, and the third belonged to another British battery, which we had picked up a long way back with only three gunners in charge of it, and which would certainly have been lost if we had not taken it in tow, behind our much-overworked tractor. This in the end finally and irremediably broke down. We were fairly stuck now, half blocking the road. Great excitement, as was only natural, developed among those behind us.

"I saw, a little distance in front, an Italian field artillery colonel in a state of wild excitement. He was rushing about with an unopened bottle of red wine in his hand, waving it ferociously at the heads of refugees, and driving them and their carts off the road down a side track. A queer pathetic freight some of these carts carried, marble clocks and blankets, big wine flasks and canaries in cages. The colonel had also driven off the road a certain Captain Medola, who was sitting sulkily on his horse among the civilian carts. The colonel's object, it appeared, was to get a number of field batteries through. He had cleared a gap in the blocked traffic and his field-guns were now streaming past at a sharp trot. But he was an extraordinary spectacle and made me laugh. Treading very delicately, I approached this infuriated man and explained the helpless situation of our guns, pointing out that we were also unwillingly impeding the movements of his own. I asked if he could order any transport to be provided for us. He waved his bottle at me, showed no sign of either civility or comprehension, only screaming at the top of his voice, 'Va via, va via!'[1]

"I gave him up as hopeless, and went back to my guns. But the Latin mind often follows a thread of order through what an Anglo-Saxon is apt to mistake for a mere hurricane of confused commotion. Within five minutes Captain Medola came up to me and said that the colonel had ordered him to drag our tractor and guns."

And so at last we came to Latisana and the bridge over the Tagliamento. General Pettiti, our Corps Commander, had given orders to blow up the bridge, but not until the British guns were all across. He sent a special orderly to ask me if mine were the last. I told him yes. Our tractor broke down three times on the bridge itself. One of our gunners waved a small Italian flag. But at last we were over. And a few minutes later the bridge went up with an explosion that could be heard for miles.

Finally we reached Treviso, and ate enormous quantities of polenta. That was the end of *our* retreat.[2]

We rested and refitted at Ferrara, and fraternised with the Italian gunners, who had a barracks and a depot there.

We left on December 12th, with a tremendous send-off from both the military and the civilians, and were for some time in strategic reserve at San Martino di Lupari, a little village near Bassano, on the river Brenta.

It was here that I heard that I was a father. Our little daughter Helen had been born on December 17th, 1917.

---

[1] "Go away! Go away!"

[2] I was awarded, soon after, the Italian Medaglia di Bronzo al Valor Militare, with this citation,

"In sette mesi di servizio prestati in Italia diede sempre belle prove di coraggio e sangue freddo, eseguendo ricognizioni ardite e pericolose; durante la ritirata della terza armata, 27–31 Ottobre, si distinse moltissimo per operosità e sprezzo del pericolo, concorrendo a portare in salvo i pezzi della sua batteria. Strada di Palmanova Latisana 27–31 Ottobre 1917."

This made me feel both very proud and very humble.

IN THE ARMY, 1915

In January 1918, we were the first British battery up the mountains, on the Asiago Plateau. The physical discomfort of the early days was great, but we were full of buoyancy and health. In the middle of March the British divisions, which had come out after Caporetto, all moved up to the plateau, and all the British heavy artillery was concentrated in the Asiago sector. My battery stayed up here, with two short interludes, for seven months. I had an O.P. up a pine tree on a hill-top, with a superb view.

On June 15th the Austrians made their last serious effort at an offensive. Our battery had a heavy time and a lot of casualties, but our line held.

"The Austrian gunners had a fine sense of discrimination in their targets. The wooden hut, in which I and two of my brother officers used to sleep, had been hit two or three times that day, and much of our kit had been destroyed. So had both volumes of Morley's *Rousseau*, which were on a shelf over my bed, leaving behind only a few torn and scattered pages. Much damage had also been done to a collection of Pompeian photographs of great historical and scientific interest. But Baedeker's *Northern Italy*, which lay alongside, had not been touched!"

In July we and two other batteries were sent up into the Trentino above Bezzecca, where Garibaldi obeyed the order to come back in 1866, below the Cima D'Oro. In such country, and at such altitudes, there were many difficult gunnery problems on which I expatiated in my book.

In August we returned to the Asiago Plateau, and in October we moved down to the Piave, in readiness for the final battle. I had just taken a week's Italian leave in Naples, on Capri and in eastern Sicily. From Taormina I had seen and heard Etna in eruption, red-hot lava, like golden snakes, sliding down the mountainside in the dark, and the distant boom, as of guns firing at the front. "Up there is the artillery of heaven", said an Italian, as we stood on the high terrace looking down on the Greek temple and the sea.

On the Piave we were to be a silent battery until the start of the offensive, the time of which was to depend on the height of the river.

"By the night of October 24th the river had fallen a few inches, and British infantry crossed in small boats to the Grave di Papadopoli, a long island of sand in the middle of the stream. On the right a battalion of the Gordons crossed, rowed over by Venetian boatmen. I met one of their officers afterwards. 'Every one of those boatmen deserved a decoration,' he said. 'They were as cool under heavy shellfire as if they had been rowing on the Grand Canal.'

"On the night of October 26th, half an hour before midnight, the big bombardment opened and our guns spoke again. It was to be their last great oration. It was, of its kind, a fine, thunderous performance, and the Austrian reply, in our own neighbourhood, was feeble. Our targets were enemy batteries and brigade headquarters. We fired continuously for hours, first high-explosive, then gas shells, switching from one target to another, until a strong wind got up. Then we got orders to change back to high-explosive.

"On the morning of the 27th, just before 7 o'clock, our infantry attacked, crossing from the island to the farther bank of the river. There were no bridges, and the water was breast-high in some places. Sometimes it came right over the heads of the smaller men, but their taller comrades pulled them through. Where the current was strongest, cables were thrown across and firmly secured, and to these men held on, as they forced their passage through the water.

"Next day I went over the river and right on, one of the two forward observation officers from our brigade who were to keep contact with the advancing infantry. Three signallers and a runner came with me, carrying rifles, bayonets and ammunition, a day's rations and much signalling gear.

"I passed and identified from the map one of the targets of my battery in the preliminary bombardment, an Austrian battery position, which we had shelled with gas and high-explosive alternately. Our shooting had been accurate and deadly. The position was a mass of shellholes. One of the guns had been blown up, a second badly damaged. A third had been pulled out of its pit and halfway up a bank by a team of horses. The enemy had made a desperate effort to get it away. But horses and men and fragments of men lay dead around it. It was a well-prepared position, and well concealed by trees. But Italian airmen had spotted it, and marked it down with precision on the map, marked it down for destruction. The enemy had done much work here. There were fine, deep dug-outs, well timbered and weatherproof, comfortable dwelling-places in quiet times and strong enough to resist shell splinters and even direct hits by guns of smaller calibre. But we had got a direct hit on one dug-out and killed half a dozen occupants. And the others had not been proof against our gas. They were full of corpses, mostly victims of gas. Some were wearing their gas masks, but our gas had gone through them. Some had apparently been gassed outside, some with masks on and some without, and had crawled dying into the dug-outs in the vain hope of finding protection there. However hardened one may grow, by usage, to the common facts of war, few can look on such a sight as this without feeling a queer thrill of very mixed emotion. My men looked with solemn faces at the work they had helped to do. One said, 'Poor chaps, *they* were pretty well done in!' And then we turned and went on.

"That night I made my headquarters in a wrecked church, from the tower of which I sent back signals in morse by means of a lamp. I slept for an hour or two under an Austrian blanket, none too clean, as it afterwards appeared, and drank Austrian coffee and ate Austrian biscuits. . . .

"British cavalry went through in the dawn, spectral, artistically perfect, aiming at ambitious, distant objectives, Northamptonshire Yeomanry who had come from France to Italy a year ago and had been kept behind the lines all through the war and were having their first show at last. Next day they suffered many casualties, but they did damned well. Their reconnaissance officer came into the church soon after midnight and asked me if the Austrians still held any part of the village. I told him no, not since yesterday morning.

"When I was relieved, I tramped back to the Piave, many miles now, and wading channels that were still unbridged returned, tired and footsore but with a song in my heart, to my battery."

In the next few days our attack developed along the whole Italian front, from the sea to the heights of the Stelvio, amid the glaciers on the Swiss frontier. And on November 1st I went on a wide reconnaissance by car, through newly liberated country. The last phase had come, and the completeness of victory. On November 3rd an armistice was signed, and on November 4th at 3 p.m. all fighting ceased. That day Trento, Trieste and Udine fell. Old Natale's message to the enemy, chalked in German on our hut beside the Vippacco before the retreat, "You German pigs, we shall soon come back", had come true. It was only one year and one week ago!

"The fighting was over! That night of the 4th of November all the sky was lit up with bonfires and the firing of coloured rockets and white Very lights. One could hear bells ringing in the distance, back toward Treviso, and singing and cheering everywhere. It was an hour of perfection and of accomplishment; it was the ending of a story.

"It is all over. For a few days it seemed possible that we might be sent northward, through redeemed Trento and over the Brenner and the crest of the Alps and down through Innsbruck, to open a new front against Germany along the frontier of Bavaria. But that will not be necessary now. It is all over."

The battery rested near Padua among the Euganean Hills, where Shelley wrote a famous and beautiful poem.

"Our guns, which will never fire any more, sit in a neat row, 'dressed by the right', along the garden path outside the Villa, their noses pointing across a grass lawn. Their names, which are the battery's Italian history, are painted on their muzzles and their trails in large white letters, picked out with red upon a dark green ground: Carso, Piave, Altipiano and Trentino. They look very ornamental in their new coats of paint, and with a high polish on their unpainted metal parts. It is an hour of anticlimax."

I said my Nunc Dimittis and went home on leave.

On December 3rd, 1918, I left Italy. I had now spent more than four years of my life in the Army. I had got some good out of it, though I did not think so at the time. And I was soon going back to civilian life with no very clear idea of what to do next. But one thought was firm within me. I badly wanted to go into politics, to help put right what my elders had put wrong. Just nine years later, when I had become a Member of Parliament, I thus began the Preface to my book *Towards the Peace of Nations:* "I am of that generation which during the Great War was massacred in droves upon the battlefields. Like

many millions of others, I served in the Army and, unlike most
of the best friends of my youth, I survived the war. It was the
belief that politics, rightly handled, can put an end to war,
which, more than anything else, drew me into the life of active
politics when the war was over."

Death had made almost a clean sweep of those of my own
age who had meant most to me at Cambridge. The first Carbonaro casualty was Kenneth Elmslie. He was a handsome,
upstanding cavalryman, a Conservative in politics, but
cherished in our society partly for this eccentricity, as most of us
thought it, but still more for his good looks and his charm. He
had a commission in the Reserve of Officers, joined his unit the
day war was declared, and was killed in the retreat from Mons.
This hit me hard. But a much harder blow came when Rupert
Brooke died, not in battle, but in a hospital ship off Skyros. Had
he not died then, the odds would have been heavy against him
on Gallipoli. With his passing, a bright light seemed to go out
of my life, and a bright hope out of the future, for I had confidently expected that he would write prose and plays, and
more poems too, which would be wonderful and deathless, and
that through long years the influence of his unique personality
would run wide and deep among those lucky enough to meet it.
When the news came, I repeated Walter Headlam's lines:

> *Ne'er again*
> *Death may bring such burning pain*
> *As devoured my brain,*
> *When they told me you had died,*
> *You so young and morning-eyed.*

A few months later, still in 1915, a third Carbonaro died.
Nigel Crompton was killed in France, repairing wire between
the lines. He was a Sapper Officer, the son of Colonel Crompton, also R.E., an amazing old character, and one of those who
share the credit for the invention of the tank. I knew that
family well. They treated me almost as though I were Nigel's
brother and I often stayed with them both in London and in
Yorkshire. With Nigel I was as intimate as with any of my
Cambridge friends. He was not much of an intellectual—he
was an Harrovian—but he inherited great vitality. He had a
genius for friendship and for enjoyment, and he paid me the

great compliment of sharing with me some of the secrets of his private life, both gay and sad. When he died too, I became almost indifferent to what might come after.

But much more came after.

Alfred Brooke, Rupert's younger brother, equally good-looking, though in a more obvious way; not a poet, but full of the joy of life and intending to make his career in the City; Alec Ramsay of Caius, Scots Liberal Presbyterian and President of the Union; Ben Keeling of Trinity, my first Socialist leader; Bill Hubback, also of Trinity—these last two members of the Fish and Chimney—whose widow in later years was a great campaigner for Family Allowances; Douglas Rouquette, best man at my wedding, of whom I have written already; William Kennedy, Research Student with me at the School of Economics, who was a Company Commander in one of the Highland Light Infantry bantam battalions of the 35th Division; these and many more of my friends never came back.

Cambridge for me, for some years after the war, was a place too full of the dead to give me either happiness or peace. Dons there were, of course, most of them too old or too expert in something else, to have been in the Army. But, of my close undergraduate friends at King's, Gerald Shove and Philip Noel-Baker were almost the only survivors.

People have sometimes asked, since then, why I had so few men friends of my own age. The answer is the war. Before that, I was very rich in friendships. But I have become rich for the second time, as the years have passed and as younger people, some much younger, have honoured me, across a wide gap in age, with their friendship and their confidence. In politics, particularly, to which since 1918 I have given so much of my effort, I have done my best to help on younger people who seemed to me to have quality and promise, and I have enjoyed exceedingly the friendship and companionship of many of them. And I have stood obstinately through my own decades for youth against age, and for the premature against the post-mature.

CHAPTER VI

L. S. E.

WHEN I arrived in England on December 7th, 1918, I was only on a fortnight's leave from Italy. But, after a few days of intense activity and wirepulling, an arrangement was made between the Ministry of Labour and the War Office whereby I should be seconded to the former for work in the Whitley Councils Department and, until the necessary formalities were completed, my leave should be extended from week to week indefinitely. Pretty disgraceful! Wirepulling counted for much more then than after the Second World War. There was no formula of just priority then, based on age and length of service. It was catch-as-catch-can, with threats of mutiny in the background if things did not go quick enough.

I was demobilised, without regret, on February 7th, 1919. At the Ministry of Labour I shared a room with my immediate chief, Robert Wilson, a quiet Scot. It was not very exciting.

I decided not to go back to the Bar. I had lost my barrister's wig and forgotten nearly all my law. It would have taken a lot of working up again, and it would, I thought, be a slow and speculative business to build up a practice and a decent income. I was much more attracted by the prospect of teaching economics, and completing some economic research. And, as I have already said, I was sure now that I wanted to go into politics. But to have learned even as little law as I had, helped me both as an economist and a politician.

Nearly thirty years later, in 1946, the Middle Temple made me an Honorary Bencher, an honour which I much appreciated.

I went to Cambridge early in 1919 to address the University Labour Club, and denounced all who had had any responsibility, however remote, for the war. With an echo of Woodrow Wilson in my mind, I declared that: "We want a holocaust of elder statesmen everywhere." I overheard a young man at the back of the hall ask: "How old is he?" Not quite 32!

Meanwhile I had published my first book, *With British Guns in Italy*. I signed the preface and handed over the typescript to Methuen's in February and they got it out in May.

"May 5th. My author's copies arrive. Very elevating to the morale to be the author of a published book, on which one stands to lose no money!"

In January 1919 I visited the School for the first time since the war, and saw Cannan and others. He wanted me to come on to the Staff in the autumn as his Assistant in the Economics Department. He said it should not be difficult to make a reputation there, once I got my foot in.

But we quickened this programme. It was arranged that in the Easter term I should take over Cannan's Public Finance lectures and also give an elementary course on Economic Theory. So I left the Ministry of Labour at the end of April, and on April 29th I gave my first lecture at the School. I had returned to academic life. It was partly the chance that my first post-war lectures were on Public Finance, though I had been interested in the subject before the war, that led me to continue to make a special study of this branch of economics. I was to talk and write about it for many years afterwards, and to introduce four Budgets as Chancellor of the Exchequer.

I was now very eager to finish my book on the *Inequality of Incomes*, on which, when war broke out, I had accumulated a great mass of notes and a certain amount of semi-finished writing. If there had been no war, it might have grown into a frightful tome—perhaps into two fat volumes.

But I was now determined to cut my coat according to my time. I tried to finish it that summer, which Ruth and Helen and I spent at Treknow, on the North Cornish coast. I made good progress, but did not quite manage it. I finally signed the preface in March 1920, and it was published in August.

This was the most ambitious book I ever wrote as an academic economist. It has continued to sell steadily for thirty-two years[1] and has never gone out of print, though I have never revised it.

Part I deals very briefly with Some Ethical Aspects of the Inequality of Incomes. There are some good quotations here

---

[1] On an average, about a hundred copies a year over the whole period, and more than this since 1945.

and some discussion of inequality in relation to economic welfare on the one hand, and justice on the other. I argue that bringing in considerations of justice gets us no further.

Part II, influenced by Cannan's approach, discusses the Historical Development of the Theory of Distribution. I make the point, with much supporting evidence, that economists have ignored, to an almost incredible degree, the importance of inherited wealth as a prime cause of the inequality of personal incomes; also that much of their theories consisted of doubtful answers to the wrong questions.

In Part III I consider the Division of Income between Categories, including the traditional "factors of production", and also two categories which I bring into sharper relief than other writers have done, namely, income from civil rights and from private gifts. By "income from civil rights" I mean that species of income, created by Statute, much more important in 1952 than 1920, which includes what we now call social service benefits.

I say in my preface that "the theory developed in Part III is very much a skeleton, but even a skeleton is easier to clothe than a ghost, and there is only the ghost of a theory on this subject that can be discovered in existing textbooks. I shall watch carefully for later writers, who will clothe my skeleton with flesh, or even perhaps rearrange its bones." Although some progress has been made, I am still watching.

In Part IV I discuss directly the Division of Income between Persons, and the causes of the great inequalities which are still a crude feature of modern economic landscapes. In this part there is a discussion of the comparative law of property, and in particular of inheritance, and of the operation of custom within the limits of the law. Cannan emphasised what the Cambridge economists of my undergraduate days had not—the great importance of social and legal institutions. The borderland between law and economics was then, I thought, too little cultivated, either by economists or lawyers. And I think so still.

Toward the end of Part IV I bring together a number of proposals for diminishing inequality without loss, and if possible with gain, to productive power. For this was the combined operation I was always planning.

I make the distinctly original proposal that the Public

Trustee should take over (1) all intestate estates, in excess of a low minimum, and (2) "subject to certain exceptions, the legal ownership of all property passing under a will, the income from such property being paid, of course, to the beneficiaries named in the will".

I argue that "the advantages of such an arrangement would be two. First, the accumulation of capital would be assisted by the prevention of *de*cumulation", or, as we say now, of dissaving. "An inheritor would no longer be able, as he is now, to sell inherited property and spend the proceeds. Second, effective machinery would be provided for the application of the Rignano principle to the taxation of inherited wealth, and for further developments which may be thought desirable in the future."[1]

This bright idea was not pursued, either by me or by others. But it is, I think, still worth considering. The Rignano principle, named after the Italian economist who propounded it, is that wealth inherited for the first time should be taxed less heavily than an equal amount of wealth inherited for the second time. The third time, the State might take all. This, Rignano argued, and Pigou and I and others agreed, would be both just and a stimulus to work and saving. Later, in my *Public Finance*, I propose a simpler way of doing this, not involving the compulsory use of the Public Trustee.

Turning to monetary policy, I urge that the best arrangement is that the general level of prices should slowly fall. This, I argue, would have many advantages and would, on balance, diminish the inequality of incomes. With the growth since then of income from civil rights, this argument is greatly strengthened. I set against it, however, in 1920 the consideration that large war debts obstruct and might even reverse this tendency, since falling prices would enrich the rentier, to whom the general community is so heavily indebted. I therefore conclude that "if, as a result of deliberate deflation or otherwise, prices are brought down, and a tendency to reduce inequality thus set up, a tendency in the contrary direction will also be set up, unless a large part of the debt is redeemed by means of a capital levy or other emergency device".

I find it very remarkable, looking back to this book, that I

[1] *Inequality of Incomes*, p. 337.

had then no apprehension of mass unemployment. This plague did not hit us till 1921, a year after my book was published. I had supposed in 1920 that a *slow* fall in prices need have no effect upon employment, and I took the same line in a number of memoranda referred to in the next chapter, which I wrote at this time for the Labour Party.

I had planned, as the final part of my *Inequality of Incomes*, a pretty full discussion of the measurement of the inequality of incomes and of the application of various rival measures to the available statistics. But this wide project, which no one even yet has carried out, shrank under the pressure of my timetable to a short article on the "Measurement of the Inequality of Incomes", published in the *Economic Journal* for September 1920. Rather an ingenious piece of writing, I still think, with some algebraical and differential decorations and drawing attention to some elegant theorems of little-known Italian economists, in whom, owing to my knowledge of the language, I made a temporary corner, reviewing a series of them in the *Economic Journal*. But it was based on hypotheses which were a bit unreal.

If I had remained an academic economist, and not gone into politics, I should have done more work on a number of questions raised in this, my first and major economic treatise.

The book suffered from a quick post-war compression of a half-matured pre-war plan. Pigou wrote to me that much of it "gives rather the impression of heads of discussion than of a full discussion. You often lead up to something and then dismiss it as too large. It creates an impression that, if it had been twice as long, it would have been more than twice as good." But he found some of Part III "confused and confusing". An anonymous reviewer in the *Oxford Magazine*—I guessed from style and sentiment that it was L. L. Price—wrote: "We can imagine Professor Cannan's quizzing look of grim recognition at the high elevation on which, in almost solitary grandeur, he has been set by the clever author of this bold, though unfinished, essay. . . . Yet, with the deference due to the positive, caustic reasoning we know so well in Oxford, and with proper recognition of the creditable piety of a grateful disciple to his master, we must doubt whether Dr. Cannan alone, or with a very small group of choice companions, is felicitously right, and the great bulk of economists, past and present, have been, and are, perversely or unfortunately wrong."

R. H. Tawney thought that I had "written an extremely important book, the significance" of which was that I had "sailed into an almost uncharted sea—the influence of legal institutions and, in particular, of the law of inheritance upon the distribution of wealth". Some respectable reviewers half detected a political wolf in economist's sheep's clothing. But the *Observer* spoke of a "lucid and deliberative treatise" and the *Times Literary Supplement* testified that I wrote "as a scientific student, not as a political partisan". A reviewer in the *Fabian News* thought that "the book is an extraordinarily dangerous one . . . to the possessors of large incomes from inherited or un-earned property. The attack is delightfully insidious; each step proposed is so gentle, so plausible, so eminently reasonable, that few could take offence; but the cumulative effect is immense." But Emil Davies stated in the *Daily Herald* that "Mr. Dalton is a lecturer at the London School of Economics, and his geniality and humour confer upon him a popularity that is the object of despairing envy on the part of some of his colleagues. These attributes do not, however, make themselves evident in the work under discussion, which is inclined to be dull and cautious."

Meanwhile Beveridge had succeeded Pember Reeves as Director of the School, and brought a strong dynamic urge to its expansion. He set to work, most ardently and successfully, to collect money from the Government, the L.C.C. and other local authorities, from the Cassel Trust, from the City of London and from the business world. To encourage *them* a new degree of Bachelor of Commerce was invented. He also collected large sums in dollars from the Rockefeller Foundation. New buildings sprang up, new teaching posts were created, new subjects were brought within the scope of the School. There was a surging growth in numbers, in accommodation—serviceable rather than beautiful—in scholarships, exhibitions and bursaries, and in range of studies. The quality of the student body improved greatly and showed much wider variety, as compared with pre-war.

Sir William, now Lord, Beveridge, has done a lot of first-class jobs in his life, but none better, nor with more energy, resourcefulness and determination, than the expansion of the London School of Economics in the earlier years of his Directorship. He held this office from 1919 to 1937, when he became Master of University College, Oxford.

With a humdrum successor to Pember Reeves, we should have made very little progress. We should have gone on living insignificantly in a quiet backwater leading out of the busy Strand.

Beveridge and I had an amusing succession of relationships. He was my academic chief from 1919 till 1935, when I resigned from the teaching staff of the School. I was his political chief for a few months in 1942, when I was President of the Board of Trade in the War Coalition government, and he produced for me a theoretically perfect plan for rationing coal, electricity and gas. But this plan roused the united opposition of the leaders of the National Union of Mineworkers and of the 1922 Committee of Tory Back Benchers. I did not, therefore, proceed with it!

I was his political chief again in 1950–51, when he was Chairman of two New Town Corporations in County Durham, Peterlee and Aycliffe, and I was Minister, first of Town and Country Planning and then, with added functions, of Local Government and Planning. His old gifts were still there, and these two most promising new communities, one on the borders of my own constituency, owe much to his untiring guidance in their early days.

In 1919 Halford Mackinder was still a Conservative M.P. as well as Reader in Geography in the University of London. Lees-Smith was no longer an M.P. He had lost his seat as a Liberal in 1918 and was now, in June 1919, just joining the Labour Party and the I.L.P. after six months' intensive study of these organisations. He was a methodical man, and still taught Public Administration.

Sargent was now Professor of Commerce, and Graham Wallas Professor of Political Science. T. E. Gregory, later Sir Theodore Gregory, was Foxwell's assistant. Later he became a Cassel Reader and then succeeded Foxwell as Professor of Banking.

In the Ratan Tata Department of Social Science and Administration one of the Senior Tutors was C. R. Attlee. He

lectured on Industrial Conditions and on Outlines of English
Local Government. He also took, jointly with others, a class
for students interested in welfare work. Of nine Lecturers and
Tutors in the Ratan Tata Department, he and Tawney, who
also taught Economic History for the B.Sc.(Econ.) degree,
were the only men. The other seven were women. All these
interesting particulars I have extracted from the School
Calendar for 1919–20.

Harold Laski came to the School from Harvard in 1920. He
succeeded Graham Wallas as Professor in 1923. He and I saw
much of each other in the years that followed, both at the
School and in politics.

I became a Lecturer in 1919, and was appointed in 1922 to
one of the newly created Cassel Readerships in Commerce.
In 1925, having been elected to Parliament, I became a part-
time Reader in Economics. I held this post till 1935, with un-
paid leave of absence during the period from 1929 to 1931
when I was Under-Secretary at the Foreign Office in the
Second Labour Government.

In addition to lecturing on Public Finance, I took over from
Cannan the course in Elements of Economics for the Inter-
mediate, both B.Sc.(Econ.) and B.Com. These lectures were
delivered in the largest hall in the building to an audience of
several hundred. They were repeated in the evenings to an
audience of like size. I lectured for an hour. Then I answered
questions for a second hour. This was first-class training for
public meetings.

In the first post-war years we had a large entry of ex-Service
students, very lively and, some found, difficult to control.
Having just come out of the Army myself, I found them easy
and agreeable to handle. But on the day of my first lecture on
Elements in the autumn in 1920, a number of these young
men, now in their second year, waylaid me in my room on
the second floor and plied me with most persistent and innocent questions about their studies. So I entered the great
lecture-room, crowded with freshmen and freshwomen, a few
minutes late. I was greeted with tremendous laughter and
cheering. I was pleased at this, thinking that my reputation
and my popularity were already well established, even with
new arrivals. The demonstration continued uproariously while

I made some introductory remarks and began to give out a list of books to be read in connection with the course. I discovered afterwards that, while on the second floor I was being deliberately delayed, on the ground floor I was being impersonated. Most of those present would not, of course, know me by sight. But Mark Abrams, one of the bright lads of the previous year, wearing a gown, had mounted the platform and had spent some minutes introducing the subject and giving out a reading list. "Finally," he had said, "for up-to-date economic information always read my paper *Dalton's Weekly*." Then, hearing me approaching, he had disappeared through a window at the back of the platform!

I also lectured, for the B.Com. degree, on industrial questions, and supervised a number of research students working for higher degrees. I tried to make my lectures on Elements at once clear, stimulating and amusing. I quoted, in my opening lecture, Winston Churchill's good advice to Shane Leslie, while at Eton, "Don't turn your mind into a damned ammunition wagon. Turn it into a rifle for firing off other people's ammunition."

The School was at this time, and has since remained, a great international meeting-place. Students came to us from almost every country in the world, the majority to work for higher degrees, but some, better still, to take their first degrees, the B.Sc.(Econ.) or B.Com., with us. They came from all the countries of the Commonwealth, from the United States, from most of the countries of Europe, from China and Japan. A surprisingly large number, considering its small population, came from Palestine. When some thirty years later I visited what was now the State of Israel, I found old students of mine occupying many key positions. Moshe Sharett, who had taken the B.Sc.(Econ.) at the School, was now Foreign Minister of Israel; David Hacohen, who had taken the B.Com., was managing director of Solel Boneh (one of the many offshoots of the Histadrut), the biggest road building and constructional undertaking in Israel; Ascher Levitsky, who had also taken the B.Sc. (Econ.), was one of the leading lawyers in Israel. At a party given for me by Mr. Sharett at Tel Aviv no fewer than eight of my old students turned up and presented me with a most eloquent and flattering address of welcome.

"The London School of Economics," they wrote, "immediately after the first great war became a great workshop and centre of learning for the forging out of economic problems and for the development of all other main branches of social science and political thought. As the first students in England from Israel (then Palestine) we remember with reverence our years of study in this great School, in which you, Sir, distinguished yourself as a brilliant lecturer and a great friend of the student whether he hailed from some part of England, the Empire, or from foreign shores. We can state with pride that the London School of Economics was a great factor in founding the character of many an active worker in the management of the affairs of our young State of Israel."

In my first post-war years I also took two Tutorial Classes in Economics for the Workers' Educational Association, one at the Battersea Polytechnic and one at Morley College. From such classes an academically trained economist learns quite as much as he teaches. He learns, in particular, how to minimise jargon. It is a test of how much that is important in our rather elaborate theories can be put into simple and intelligible English. Not all, but much. Some of the adult students attending W.E.A. classes had minds fixed in Marxist or other predetermined moulds. Debate with these was often even better exercise than with the more open-minded. I formed the view that every young University teacher, of economics certainly and of some other subjects too, should take his turn in this Extra-Mural teaching. It would be as good for him as for his students.

When I went into Parliament I vowed that I would never make a speech in the House that would sound like the speech of a University Don. I hope I succeeded.

From the time when I first came to the School before the war, I was, I know, one of Cannan's favourite pupils and, first as his Assistant in the Economics Department after the war and then as his colleague as Reader, I enjoyed to the full his friendship and his stimulus. He never discouraged me from going into politics, but, if I had chosen to remain an academic economist, he would have thought of me, I know, as a likely successor when he resigned his Chair. Ruth, who confessed that she got little from his lectures, thought the real reason why he liked me was because I laughed so loudly at his many jokes.

RUTH DALTON, 1929

He was twenty-seven years older than I was. When at mid-summer in 1926 he retired at 65, I was 38. It is not easy to bridge so wide a gap with a real friendship, but I believe we did. He gave me what many older people soon lose the power to give to the younger, a relationship, if I chose to take it, based on complete personal and moral equality. He encouraged me always to speak to him quite frankly on all subjects, and to be disrespectful, whenever I felt like it, just as he was disrespectful to his elders, as well as to his contemporaries—most disrespectful of all, as his writings show, to "those whom, when we were young, we called 'the old economists' ". He and I often laughed not only at the same jokes but at the same people, both dead and living. Yet his laughter never carried malice and I never remember him unreasonably angry.

But he had a great twinkle. Some of the best things he said to me are, I fear, by our conventions unprintable. In my first term at the School after the war, he showed me in the Common Room some examination questions he proposed to set. I said of one of them: "That's an awfully bad question. You ought to cut that out and think of something better." He said he'd think about it. When I had gone, Foxwell, who had overheard our conversation but did not then know me by sight, asked who I was. Cannan replied: "That's Hugh Dalton, my new Assistant." "What!" cried Foxwell, "Your Assistant! I would never allow any Assistant of mine to speak to me like that." Cannan repeated this to me with great delight. Foxwell was a considerable authority on money and banking and was said, unlike most economists, to know his way about Bank Parlours in the City. But he seemed solemn and self-important. His best piece of writing, in my view, is his Introduction to the English translation of Menger's *Right to the Whole Produce of Labour*, with its wholesome emphasis on the need for economists to know some law and take account in particular of the economic effects of variations in the law of property and contract. This was also a favourite theme of Cannan's.

And I have this note, dated June 1919, of Cannan's views on giving evidence before Royal Commissions. He had just performed before the Sankey Commission on the Coal Mines. "You must make up your mind whether you're going to talk for the public, or for the Bluebook. If the latter, you must be prepared to make an apparently poor show, e.g. Pigou, who made things worse by smiling at the Commissioners all the time. If the former, you should aim at saying smart things, and making cheap scores. When in a hole, and asked a question you can't immediately think of a good answer to, begin talking at the same time as your questioner. Then the shorthand reporter will get confused and take it down wrong, and you'll be able to correct the proofs and think out the best answer at leisure."

Of Cannan as an economist I have written in my *Inequality of Incomes*, and in the opening essay in *London Essays in Economics: In Honour of Edwin Cannan*, published in 1927 to commemorate his retirement. I pay tribute there both to his critical and his constructive work, and to the large influence he had on me and, both directly and indirectly, on many others. He and Pigou—of whom he thought highly, though towards Marshall he was more iconoclastic—were the two economists who influenced me most in the years just before and just after the First World War. Keynes' influence increased later, but in these two periods it was less pervasive.

I must take some responsibility for the academic birth and childhood of Lionel Robbins. I needed an Assistant, to deal in particular with the mass of essays written by members of my First Year Class on Elements. So I was keeping my eyes open for suitable talent. They lighted on a young man who had come out of the Army—he too had been a gunner—and was outstanding among those taking the B.Sc.(Econ.) degree in style, appearance, intelligence and personality. Both Cannan and I were well aware of him, but what finally tipped my judgment in his favour was this incident. I was lecturing on Public Finance and explaining that the effect of a given tax on a person's willingness to work, or save, depended on his temperament. Thus some would work harder, others less hard, if income tax went up. To illustrate this I invented some figures and took a vote in the class to see who would work more, and who less, in consequence of some tax change. We took a show of hands. Some voted one way and some the other. I noticed that Robbins did not vote at all. After the lecture I asked him why. He said: "You put the question so imprecisely that it seemed to me to have no meaning." I gave him full marks for this and, soon after he had taken a First in his Finals, we brought him on to the staff. He has had a distinguished career since then both in the academic world and, during the war, in Government service. Although he and I do not agree on some important questions in economics and politics, I have never regretted giving him an initial push along the road of academic advancement. But I do regret that, whereas Cannan and I both believed in creating a deliberate variety of approach and outlook among teachers of economics at the School, and appointed Robbins partly with this in mind, knowing him to be a stronger individualist than either of us, there has been a tendency since then for this variety to disappear and for the School to teach a much more uniform brand of right-wing economics—and politics too.

Robbins served on the staff as Assistant, and then as Lecturer, in Economics from 1925 to 1927; then went to Oxford for two years as Fellow of New College, where he was a great success. Cambridge had also thrown a fly over him. But I advised him to go to Oxford, partly because Oxford offered him a Fellowship and Cambridge did not, and I advised him to go where he would sit above the salt, partly because at Oxford at that time there were fewer good economists than at Cambridge. In that dusk his star would shine more brightly.

In 1929 he came back to the School as Professor. Allyn Young of Harvard had succeeded Cannan in 1927, but had died suddenly in his first year. I had acted, though now in Parliament, as head of the Economics Department for the following year. I urged Robbins' appointment as Professor. Some said he was too young. I was irritated by this, and replied that all the older people, who would be willing to take the job, were too dreary.[1] Finally it was decided to create two Professorial Chairs in Economics, one Senior and one Junior, and to give Robbins the Junior, leaving the Senior unfilled for the moment. It was never filled!

He can write and speak, at his best, with great distinction and persuasiveness. But he is apt to hold intellectual opinions with an excess of emotional fervour. He has a phobia about State action, except in wartime. He is apt to ignore the realities of

[1] I find this note in my diary, regarding an election to a University Readership. "The majority voted for A, though Cannan and I wanted B. Much younger and more brilliant. Beveridge, as Cannan once said to me, always prefers middle-aged failures to young men of promise."

politics and public opinion. And he sometimes uses too many, too long, words to express his meaning. "You suffer", I said to him once, "from terminological elephantiasis." This comes, perhaps, from reading too much German. He became an addict of the Mises-Hayek anti-Socialist theme. Socialism, they said, was not so much bad as impossible; so "irrational" that there was nothing to discuss; under socialism there could be no "calculation". I could not succeed in persuading Robbins that it was even interesting to enquire how the Planned Economy of the Soviet Union actually worked. But he has what few economists have—a true appreciation and wide knowledge of the arts. He is entitled to be proud of his appointment in 1952 to be a Trustee of the National Gallery.

In these post-war years I was a good deal in Cambridge. For some time, as I relate in the next chapter, while I was prospective Parliamentary candidate for the Borough, Ruth and I had a house in Cambridge. I spent part of the week there and part in London.

In 1922 and 1923 I examined for Part II of the Economics Tripos and invented a number of ingenious questions. Among those to whom we gave Firsts in those years were Austin Robinson and Maurice Dobb, both still teaching at Cambridge today.

In 1923 I was appointed a member of the Cambridge University Statutory Commission. Our function was to pass statutes for the University and for the Colleges, in accordance with the recommendations of the Royal Commission on the Universities of Oxford and Cambridge, over which Asquith had presided, and before which I, with others, had given evidence on behalf of the Labour Party. There was a separate Statutory Commission for Oxford. The Chairman of the Cambridge Commission was Lord Ullswater, who, as James Lowther, had been Speaker of the House of Commons. I thought he was dreadfully slow in the Chair. Other members were Anderson, the Master of Caius, Giles, the Master of Emmanuel, Dame Bertha Philpotts, the Mistress of Girton, and Will Spens, who in 1927 became Master of Corpus and retired in 1952, under the College Statutes we made, at the age of 70. Out of eight Commissioners, I was the only one under 40 and the only member of the Labour Party.

My name had been suggested to Edward Wood—now Lord Halifax—then President of the Board of Education, by Ramsay MacDonald, on the prompting of Arthur Henderson. When the Bill setting us up was in Committee of the House of Commons, Rawlinson, Tory M.P. for Cambridge University, and Somerville, Tory M.P. for Windsor, had tried unsuccessfully to get my name struck out. As I have related earlier, this infuriated my father and finally decided him to vote Labour, against Somerville, at the next general election. My diary records: "October 3rd, 1923. First meeting of Cambridge Statutory Commission at Emmanuel Lodge. Only discuss procedure. I hear from Arnold McNair that my fellow commissioners expect me to be very troublesome and do most of the talking! I disappoint these expectations today."

Among our most difficult problems were the fixing of retiring ages, combined with a pension scheme, for all future holders of University and College appointments, and for such present holders as chose to come under the new Statutes. There was a Master of a Cambridge College in my time who was over 100 years old. If he retired, he would have no pension. Some fifty years before he had voted for himself for Master, having broken a compact with his rival that each would vote for the other. He had been elected by one vote.

The Royal Commission had firmly recommended fixed retiring ages for all. But most of my colleagues wanted to go back on this, and I had to dig my toes in. I said that, if I was outvoted, I should appeal to Mr. Asquith. Finally I won. Sixty-five was to be the retiring age for all University teachers and Fellows of Colleges, except that Heads of Houses might go on to 70. As I was the youngest of the party, and the Chairman and some others were already either over 65, or very near it, I was conscious of the delicacy of my position. But also of the importance of my victory. Remembering Jackie Fisher's famous injunction, I composed for myself this Alexandrine epitaph,

He sacked the lot at sixty-five and helped the young to climb.

And this fragment of an uncompleted sonnet,

Suburbs of superannuated Dons.

Then there was a fight on scholarships.

"December 11th, 1923. I want the Asquith Report carried out. Free rooms or equivalent without proof of need, but all additional money payments only on proof of need. This is opposed by Spens and by most of the others. Even Anderson wants to slide back towards the *status quo*. Arguments as to prestige of scholarships being endangered, 'thin-skinned men' who won't plead need, danger to small colleges, etc. I am practically alone and not much encouraged by Ullswater. I stress importance of outside opinion, and refer gingerly to 'recent political events'." These were the heavy Conservative losses and Labour gains in the general election which had just taken place, leading to the formation of the First Labour Government.

"December 13th, 1923. To Cambridge, for joint meeting with Oxford Commissioners, a majority of whom are with me on scholarships. Chelmsford, their Chairman, makes an excellent speech. Refers to basic principles in the Asquith Report, the diversion in the past of endowments intended for the poor (scowls from my colleagues)—he had got this from Albert Mansbridge—and the importance of outside opinion. Quite a Labour speech! (None of us suspected today that, though not a member of the Labour Party, he was about to enter a Labour Cabinet as First Lord of the Admiralty.) I agree cordially with him in discussion. As we separate there is the following exchange between the Chairmen.

CHELMSFORD: 'We are less insensitive than you to outside opinion.'

ULLSWATER: 'We are more academic and less political.'

But scholarship policy is an acid test for outside opinion. I contemplate the possibility of a public and reasoned resignation.

"January 22nd, 1924. Scholarships postponed. Dine in Corpus. A very good dinner, but Geoffrey Morris gives me some bad brandy afterwards which makes me ill.

"January 24th, 1924. Recovered and again attend the Commission. Settle retiring ages.

"February 6th, 1924. Cambridge Commission in London. Victory on the scholarships question. Opposition to the Oxford proposal collapses in the most surprising way. Agree to £30 without proof of need, plus £10 for the Long Vacation Term. Joint sitting with Oxford Commissioners in the afternoon, when this decision is communicated. Mansbridge brings a carefully prepared speech, which he has now no occasion to deliver. Spens gives in, he tells me, because I assure him that it is necessary in order to satisfy public opinion. But he urges me, and I promise, to do my best with Charles Trevelyan, the new President of the Board of Education, and others to get the Government grant increased."

I did. And twenty-one years later, when I was Chancellor of the Exchequer, I put up the grants to the Universities to a higher figure than ever before. And I am sure I was right. The Government grant to Oxford and Cambridge in 1923 went, among other purposes, to create new pension funds, and to increase the number of University teaching posts, and thus indirectly to relieve the Colleges, since more of their Fellows would now be drawing salaries as University teachers. On this Spens and the Mistress of Girton—she had been threatening to resign on the Women's question—reached an admirable *modus vivendi*, which the Commission adopted. He had been pressing on behalf of the younger Dons that, if they had been lecturing for more than a certain period, they should be entitled to be appointed University Lecturers. He got this through, with additional backing on the ground that it would bring in a certain number of Women Dons under an automatic rule, and so avoid any risk of a fight over the appointment of the first one or two women to University teaching posts.

I heard afterwards that, though the Oxford Commission gave the impression of being more advanced and sensitive to outside opinion than were we, there was more evasion in the Oxford Statutes than in ours.

On June 19th, 1922, our little daughter Helen died. She had been for more than a month in the Chelsea Children's Hospital. She had nephritis, with many other "complications" towards the end. Happily she had not much pain, but increasing discomfort and fear of the unknown. She was only four and a half years old. She was cremated at Golder's Green, and we scattered her ashes on a bed of roses. Only Ruth and I and my father were there for this last act. We had asked all others to go away. My father had read the few prayers very beautifully. I wrote that day: "She is safe anyhow now. Safe from disappointment and disillusion, misusage and a broken heart and the next war and growing old. Safe, too, from love and beauty and the sunshine."

Both for Ruth and for me this was a very hard blow, leaving a deep bruise. We had no other child. But this loss made us both care even more, as the years passed, about younger people.

That summer I finished my book on *The Principles of Public Finance*. I wrote the preface in September and the first edition came out in December 1922. Since then it has reached its third edition and its nineteenth impression and has been translated into eight foreign languages. It has had a very good run as a textbook, and it has gone on selling surprisingly well, particularly in recent years.[1]

The book, in its first edition, contained the substance of my lectures on the Theory of Public Finance delivered at the School. I tried to keep it short and clear and readable. I aimed, quoting Bacon, "to excite the judgment briefly, rather than to inform it tediously".

The reviewers, on the whole, took it well. *The Economist*, not always on my side in later fights, testified now that "Mr. Dalton is a profound student of economic theory, and has succeeded in expressing general economic concepts in simple language, without being 'tendencious'. He does not give judgments; he suggests to the reader the lines upon which they can be correctly formed."

Sir Josiah Stamp, however, let it be known in high quarters that, in his opinion, my book would "do harm to the School" and was unsuitable for use as a textbook. He wondered whether all the views expressed formed part of the "officially accredited teaching" of the School, or were my own "personal adventures in political thought". I was very vexed at this, and particularly by the phrase "officially accredited teaching", which seemed to put in doubt our academic freedom. I took this up at once both with Beveridge and Sidney Webb, warning them

[1] On an average, more than 1,700 copies a year since publication, and just 4,000 copies a year since 1946.

that I had another little book coming out soon in support of a Capital Levy. Both assured me that they would defend my academic freedom, and that of any other teacher, against attacks from the City of London or any other quarter.

Webb had, indeed, foreseen the possibility of such a threat when he put into the Constitution of the School a provision that no member of the staff should be penalised in any way for his political opinions or activities. But, so long as those members of the staff who were most active in politics were Conservatives, or even Liberals, no dog barked.

Webb now told me that he had expected for some time that this sort of trouble would arise, that, if it became acute, he would be prepared to take action, that it would be easy if necessary to blow the City people out of the water, but that meanwhile we should move cautiously and make it as easy as possible for Beveridge.

I also knew that, if any attack was made on me personally, I could count on firm support from Cannan and Sargent. My personal position was, therefore, pretty strong.

None the less there were mutterings among some of the business men who had lately become Governors of the School. I was invited, a month or two after this brush, to meet one of these gentlemen at a tea-party in Beveridge's room. He wondered, he said, whether a rule could not be made forbidding all members of the staff to take any part in politics. "No doubt", he added, "we should lose one or two members of the staff if we did that, but I think it would be a good rule." I listened, but said little, knowing that a rule in any such wide terms would have raised a magnificent storm. That fight would have been great fun!

Since those days early in 1923 the City and the Business World have gradually come to think better of the London School of Economics. For the centre of gravity of its political and economic thought has moved steadily from Left to Right, and is now well to the Right of either Oxford or Cambridge. The proportion of the staff of the School who were actively associated with the Left in politics was never high, though some of us—Laski and Tawney and I in particular—enjoyed some notoriety as bogymen. But now most of the leading figures and the best-known teachers are highly respectable.

My little book, *The Capital Levy Explained*, came out in March 1923. It reached a tenth impression in April 1925, but most of its sales were in 1923. It ceased to be topical when Snowden, in his first term as Chancellor of the Exchequer, referred this project to the Colwyn Committee on the National Debt and Taxation in the hope that they would bury it.

But the Capital Levy, it is interesting now to recall, was the main issue of public debate at two successive general elections, in 1922 and 1923. It was certainly the most exciting item in the Labour Party's programme. I not only wrote this little book in explanation and defence of it, but I had a good deal to do with its official adoption by the Party, as I shall relate in the next chapter. I spoke and lectured about it all over the country, and also did a good deal of journalism in support of it. It was by the association of my name with the Capital Levy that I first became widely known in the Labour Movement and came to be regarded as one of the Labour Party's financial pundits.

I was, indeed, extremely keen on the Capital Levy. I was convinced that it was perfectly practicable and greatly in the public interest. It had behind it high economic authority: Ricardo after the Napoleonic War, Pigou and Keynes and Hobson after this one, with Edgeworth and Stamp saying there were good arguments on both sides, and only W. R. Scott, not quite a heavyweight among certified economists, openly against it.

But, as the war receded and the thing was not done, the case for doing it grew less impressive and less urgent, though the loss through not having done it was still quite clear to me. Thirty years later, after another war and many other big changes, the whole idea must, I think, be approached somewhat differently, with less exclusive emphasis on the burden of the national debt and more on other burdens which such a levy might lighten, and on the need for greater economic equality.

In 1923, in just over four years since the end of the war, I had published four books, one on War and three on Economics. Even if I was not soon to feel the Parliamentary pull away from serious authorship, clearly this pace was too hot to last. It was not till 1928 that I published my next book, this time on Peace.

CHAPTER VII

FIVE QUICK ELECTIONS

I WAS now setting an even hotter pace in fighting Parliamentary elections. There were three General Elections in successive years, 1922, 1923 and 1924. I fought all three and two by-elections as well, five elections in thirty months, each time in a different constituency. I think this must just about give me the record for rapid fire on this particular range. I lost the first four and won the fifth—much the most fortunate arrangement if I was to win only one of the five. My first Parliament lasted for five years, 1924–9, and I started in Opposition, which is a great advantage for a new member. If I had been beaten a fifth time in 1924, I doubt if I should have stood again. Five defeats running would have ruined my political reputation, and my patience was becoming exhausted. I think I should have gone back to being a full-time academic economist, and turned very theoretical and "pure" and unworldly.

If, on the other hand, I had won any of the first four seats I fought, I should almost certainly have lost it in 1924. And that would have meant being out of the 1924–9 Parliament and out of the 1929–31 Government.

My series of electoral adventures shows what uncertainty attaches to political life. "Young man," said Bertie Lees-Smith to me, when I first became a prospective candidate, "you have chosen one of the most cruel and speculative professions in the world. Today on the pedestal, tomorrow in the dust, and no credit or discredit to you for either."

Since winning Peckham in 1924, I have fought six Parliamentary elections between 1929 and 1951, all in Bishop Auckland, and won five and lost one. In all, therefore, I have fought eleven, won six and lost five. And my wife, in addition, won a Parliamentary by-election at Bishop Auckland in conditions which I shall relate in due course.

As I have said, there were several precedents at the School

of Economics for members of the staff both running for, and sitting in, Parliament. There was also Webb's declaration of political rights in the School's Constitution. No official objection was raised at the School to any of my Parliamentary candidatures. When in 1924 I was elected to Parliament, I became a part-time, instead of a full-time, Reader in the University; when in 1929 I became a Minister, I was granted leave of absence; when in 1931 I ceased to be a Minister and also lost my seat, I resumed my part-time Readership, which I finally resigned just after the 1935 election, and before entering on my duties, which I foresaw would be heavy, as Chairman of the National Executive of the Labour Party in 1936. I was treated throughout with the greatest consideration by the School authorities.

There is, I think, much to be said in the case of the School, since it is within a quarter of an hour's walk of Westminster and Whitehall, for having some part-time members of the teaching staff who are actually engaged in politics. This can bring a touch of actuality to their teaching which might otherwise be missing. Lees-Smith's lectures on Public Administration certainly gained in this way; and mine on the practice, if not on the theory, of Public Finance likewise gained something from my membership of the Estimates Committee of the House of Commons, as well as from my Parliamentary work generally.

So too, since the School is also within a quarter of an hour's walk of the City and of various business headquarters, I would think it useful to have a few part-time members of the teaching staff working in the City or as business executives. Best, in all these cases, if they begin as full-time teachers, and then, as I did, become part-time when they take on other relevant work. No British University except London is physically so close to so much relevant reality, in economics and politics, and a complete company of full-time academic hermits seems out of place in the Strand!

In July 1919 I was adopted as prospective Labour candidate for the Abbey Division of Westminster, where it was then thought there might be a by-election. I was to be bound for a by-election only, and free to go elsewhere at a General Election. My name had been suggested by my friend J. T. Houlihan, of the Union of Post Office Workers, a handsome, humorous, self-confident Irishman, full of energy and initiative. The General Commitee of the Party met on July 16th at 25, Tothill Street. No other name was before them. Webb was in the chair and he and Beatrice were both a bit annoyed because neither of them had been consulted, either by Houlihan or by me, about my candidature. But I noted that this "will probably make them run after me all the more later on", since they will realise that I am not too much dependent on their support, but have other allies. After Webb had said some kind words about me, everyone present—there were about a dozen—except one man, was willing to adopt me without more ado, I having said nothing. But he said, not unnaturally, that he would like to hear something more of my past history and present opinions, though apparently he was willing to vote for my adoption first and to get his information afterwards. At this point I made a short speech, stressing the importance of the so-called "middle class" coming into the Labour Party and doing their share of the work. This quite satisfied the man who had wanted to know more about me. He said that what the Labour Party in the House of Commons most needed was men like me who could talk to the Chancellor of the Exchequer about finance on a footing of equal knowledge—and that he would have much pleasure in moving my adoption.

In the evening the Party held an At Home, attended by about seventy people, including both the Webbs. I made a speech on the political situation, in which I said a little about many subjects, but more about foreign policy and public finance than about the rest. These were already, and over many years remained, the two subjects on which I most specialised in politics. Even then, as twenty-six years later, my ambition lay, without much preference, either towards the Foreign Office or the Treasury, but never, with any intensity, towards No. 10, Downing Street.

My candidature for the Abbey went no further. There was no immediate by-election, and I was soon drawn into other negotiations.

It was decided that the Labour Party should give evidence before the Royal Commission on the affairs of the Universities of Oxford and Cambridge. I was one of those—and the only

Cambridge man—brought into the discussion of this evidence. The others were all Oxford: Tawney and J. L. Stocks, and Bob Young, who had been at Ruskin and sat for many years in Parliament, finally becoming Sir Robert Young and Deputy Chairman of Ways and Means.

I wrote a memorandum as the basis for our evidence. This was the first job of written work I did for the Labour Party and it led to my first meeting with Arthur Henderson. He had been appointed a member of the Royal Commission, but could not give the time, so was replaced by Willy Graham, who had just got into the House and was already making a reputation.

On November 26th, 1919, Tawney and I lunched with Henderson at the House of Commons. I thought him rather slow, pompous and self-important, but very much a politician. We had a heavy lunch—soup, fish, roast beef, Yorkshire pudding, two vegetables and apple dumpling—but no alcohol! Ten years later I succeeded in doing something which I think nobody else ever did. I persuaded him once at Geneva to drink some white wine with his lunch.

He told us that day the story of the Russian whom he met in the train during his mission to Petrograd just after the first Russian Revolution in 1917.

Henderson: "You say you have self-determination now. What does that mean?"

Russian: "It means that now we have won the right to say what we like, and go where we like, and take what we like."

I did not see him again till the end of 1921, but then I found him very friendly and communicative. The pomposity of our first meeting had quite fallen away. Someone had been praising me to him—I think his son Arthur, whom I had been seeing a good deal at Cambridge; he went up to Trinity Hall immediately after the war—and also Arthur Greenwood, then in charge of the Research Department at Labour Party Headquarters. It seemed that at this time Henderson, in the light of what he had heard, thought well of me as an economist, particularly on financial questions.

In 1920 and 1921 I wrote a number of memoranda for Labour Party Headquarters. Arthur Greenwood encouraged me to do this. He was not only a most popular, but a most efficient, officer; very good at producing drafts, after confused discussions in Committees, so as both to carry out the general intention of those present and to state a sensible and coherent case. And he stood well with most of those who mattered in the leadership of the Party at that time. Henderson, as Secretary of the Party and his immediate chief, had great confidence in his judgment and ability. And the Trade Union leaders liked and trusted him. The I.L.P. leaders, MacDonald, Snowden and the rest, stood a little apart, particularly before the 1922 election when they came back to Parliament. They wrote their own books, ran their own weekly paper—*The Labour Leader*, later the *New Leader*—held their own conferences, declared their own policy and carried on their own propaganda, all this though affiliated to the Labour Party. But I think they distrusted Greenwood less than anyone else in the official machine. The Party, and many of us individually, owe him a big debt for his work in this period—and indeed for a long time after. As I write this, in 1952, his son Tony is showing good promise and should make an effective Minister in the next Labour Government, if put in charge of a department which suits his talents. He has personal charm and distinction, works hard and speaks well.

I wrote several memoranda for Arthur Greenwood and his Committees on Taxation and the Cost of Living. These were joint committees of the National Executive and the General Council of the T.U.C.

In 1920 I find I recommended:

(1) Repeal of food taxes on sugar, tea, cocoa, coffee and dried fruits, and halving of tobacco duty.

(2) Raising of exemption limits of income tax to £250 (single) and £350 (married).

(3) Loss of revenue under these heads to be set against reduction of public expenditure through Government's abolition of subsidies on bread, railway transport and postal services.

(4) "The excess profits duty is a bad tax, but, if remitted, should be replaced by increased super-tax on large incomes, increased death duties on large estates, the taxation of land values, or a higher corporation profits tax, from which co-operative societies should be entirely exempt."

(5) "Without prejudice to larger reforms in local finance,

new houses should be exempt from local rates for twenty years."

(6) "A capital levy should be imposed, to pay off at least half the national debt within the next few years, before any great fall takes place in either the general level of prices or the rate of interest."

My mind and that of many of my colleagues, including economists both inside and outside the Labour Party, at this time was on the price-level. We wanted to bring it down. "Labour unrest" before the war, and since, was due to rising prices much more than to unemployment. I was in favour, as were many other economists, of a slowly falling price-level. And I wanted, as I had stated in my *Inequality of Incomes*, a Capital Levy, among other reasons, to offset the effect of falling prices on the distribution of wealth.

I wanted deflation, and was not afraid to call it by that name, and was quite prepared to use part of the proceeds of the Capital Levy to bring in and cancel currency notes. And this aim, though not this method, was in line with the Report of the Committee on Foreign Exchange, of which Pigou, along with some bankers, was a member. Keynes' criticism of this Report, when mass unemployment had struck us—we had more than a million unemployed in 1921—first shook my faith, till then almost absolute, in Pigou's economic judgment: of the bankers I was never so confident. But of mass unemployment we had no fear in 1920, and my proposals were fairly acceptable to Arthur Greenwood's Committee of Wise Elders of the Labour Party.

Looking forward from 1920 to much later years, I retained my disapproval of excess profits taxes in peacetime, preferring straightforward taxes on profits. I got rid as soon as I could, when Chancellor of the Exchequer, of the E.P.T. of the Second World War, and imposed instead a Profits Tax, differential as between distributed and non-distributed profits. And I opposed Mr. Butler's Excess Profits Levy in 1952, describing it as a "disincentive demagogic device", fathered on the Tories by Mr. Churchill, anxious to make it seem that Tories were against excessive profits.

Likewise in 1920 I was against the War Wealth Tax, to be based on the excess of post-war over pre-war wealth, much preferring the straightforward Capital Levy. And in the last year or two I have been very lukewarm about a Capital Gains Tax, plausible though it sounds, unless as part of a much wider tax, for which there is much to be said, on expenditure as distinct from income.

It is interesting how fashions change. In 1931, when we had had mass unemployment and falling prices and cost of living for years, the rentier, the man with a fixed income from investments, seemed the profiteer. And, in that year of crisis and crash, many of us wanted a special additional tax, to help balance the budget, on rentier income.

In 1920 the Wise Elders did not like my rate exemption on new houses (borrowed from Marshall), and asked me to work out more details of a tax, or rate, on land values, and also of a Capital Levy. This I did. I was in favour of a tax, or rate, or both, on land values, but always subject to steady progress in increasing public ownership of land in various forms. Some years later I pleased Jos Wedgwood by drafting a plan for a national tax on land values, the proceeds of which should be used to buy private land for the nation. Nothing came of any of this except Snowden's land-value taxation in 1931, which, like Lloyd George's in 1909, never got going and was repealed by the next Government.

On the Capital Levy I elaborated details, including a proposed graduated scale, running from nothing on the first £5,000, and 5% on the next £1,000, up to 60% on all above £1 million. This was adopted by the Party and published early in 1922 with the title *Labour and the War Debt; a statement of policy for the redemption of War Debt by a levy on accumulated wealth*. This was, apart from minor amendments made by others, my composition.

I went on steadily writing memoranda on various economic questions for the Party until I got into the House in 1924, and on to the National Executive in 1926. Then other people began to write memoranda for me!

Sidney Webb once said that, until you are forty—or was it fifty?—other people get most of the credit for the work you do, but afterwards you get most of the credit for work that others do.

Mrs. Rackham and Susan Lawrence first thought of me as Parliamentary Candidate for Cambridge. They thought that, in a straight fight, many Liberals would vote for me against Sir Eric Geddes, the sitting member and, if I was adopted soon, it might be straight. And the fact that I was a Cambridge man, and was still remembered as a leading Fabian and speaker at the Union when an undergraduate, would be in my favour.

I was adopted, I recorded, "without opposition and with a moderate degree of enthusiasm" on February 18th, 1920; at the adoption meeting "very direct, sane and friendly speeches. Cambridge has good types of Labour men," and women too.

For just over two years I was their candidate. Part of the time Ruth and I took E. J. Dent's house at 77, Panton Street with his faithful cook-housekeeper, whom he had trained to cook the most admirable Italian dishes. I travelled up and down to London for my work at the L.S.E. We had very happy relationships in Cambridge during this time, with the University, both Dons and undergraduates, and with a great number of workers in the Cambridge Borough Labour Party. Of the latter, many of the leaders were railwaymen and building-trade workers. There were strong personal loyalties among them, and good fellowship. W. L. Briggs, railway clerk and first Labour Mayor of the Borough; Bill Few, a stalwart engine-driver; Jim Overton, secretary of the Trades Council and Borough Labour Party, an I.L.P.-er from Bradford, a skilled watchmaker; Arthur Cross of the building trades; Albert Stubbs, who organised the agricultural workers and sat as M.P. for Cambridge County in the historic Parliament of 1945–50. These, among many others, stand clear in my memory. Of women, four stand out. Leah Manning, then at the Homerton Women's Training College, a fiery orator, later, like Stubbs, a member of the 1945 Parliament and M.P. before that, for a short time, for Islington. She and I have campaigned together in many places over the years.

Then three other women, all Dons' wives, with whom Ruth's relations and mine were very close, all three of whom showed us great hospitality. Petica Robertson, a most charming and understanding person, with a genius for friendship, wife of Donald Robertson, later Regius Professor of Greek. She was killed by the Germans in an air raid on Cambridge. Agnes Ramsey, a very enthusiastic and cheerful companion, wife of the Vice-President of Magdalene, and mother of the highly gifted Frank Ramsey, mathematician, philosopher and economist, who died much too young. She was killed in a motor accident. Finally Mrs. Rackham, whose husband Harris Rackham, Classical Tutor at Christ's, died some years ago. She has given over the years, and is still giving, as much voluntary service to the Labour Movement as anyone I know. She has served on the County Council, the Borough Council and the Bench, and has spoken at innumerable political meetings, attended innumerable political committees, and cycled innumerable miles in the doing of it. Happy is a Constituency Labour Party which has such workers, both men and women, as these!

The Liberals adopted a candidate, Cope Morgan, a barrister, and I directed much of my fire on him and his party. It was clear we could not win Cambridge next time, but we must run a good second and put the Liberals at the bottom.

I have many gay memories of that campaign. Here is one: July 1921, an open-air meeting at Milton Road Corner in Chesterton. I am standing on a chair, near a pub. It is a hot day. While I am speaking, a man, not quite sober, approaches from the pub holding up a pint of beer. He says he's brought it for a bet, that *he* wouldn't dare and that *I* wouldn't drink it in one go. I tell him to hand it up, and win both his bets for him! A cheer from the now growing crowd.

And now, by a deviation, to the Cambridge by-election. "February 11th, 1922. To Dunford House for the weekend." A mixed party, led by the Webbs. "Not very exciting. Too much 'functional organisation' and 'efficiency audit'. Beatrice's admiration for the Japanese is becoming a joke. She disliked in the Chinese 'their devastating common sense'. She admired in the Japanese their 'reverence'. 'Reverence for what?' I asked. She replied, 'For their ancestors, for the Emperor and for scientific method.'

"February 13th. Lunch at the Webbs'. Henderson, Clynes, Snowden—who hasn't met Henderson for three years; what need for 'social liaison' in the Labour Movement!—Graham, Morgan Jones and I. Conversation moved to the Capital Levy. I defended it, supported by Webb. Snowden opposed, rather ignorantly, not really understanding what is proposed, dwelling on 'bad trade', 'reserve funds of companies would be reduced', etc. Henderson said it was an important question. We must have a policy on this and push it. We had better form ourselves into a Committee on it and meet again at the House of Commons. (Some day, when they form a Cabinet, it will just depend on who is there at the moment. *They* will get the jobs!) I walk back with Henderson to the House and offer to draft a memorandum. He agrees.

"February 23rd. Meeting at House of Commons to discuss my draft for Debt Redemption Levy. Present: Webb, Snowden, Graham, Pethick Lawrence, J. A. Hobson and I. Not much opposition, except on details. Snowden won over. In middle of discussion Henderson comes in, taps me on the shoulder and says: 'You've got an election on!' 'What?' says I. 'Geddes has resigned,' says he. (Sensation.) Henderson promises me 'full support'."

I got it too, in speakers, organisers and finance. Sir Douglas Newton was the new Tory candidate.

I wrote afterwards: "I have never had three happier weeks. Enthusiasm mounts daily. We have wonderful meetings (how little they signify!). A fine array of national speakers, Henderson, Clynes, Wedgwood, Thomas, Margaret Bondfield, Lansbury, Tawney, Jack Mills, Graham, Morgan Jones, F. O. Roberts. . . . Neither of my opponents have anything like this. Buckmaster and Simon come down for the Liberals. Tryon, Parliamentary Secretary to the Ministry of Pensions, is the best the Tories can do. I refuse to speak in the open till the last four days. But my voice, and my physical strength, last well. Ewen Montagu gives very valuable help with his car. Runs me round for the last few days all day long. Car decked with red streamers and ribbons, a photograph of me and exhortations to vote for me. We tour the wards all day with a man ringing a muffin bell. The people come out of their houses and I shake them all by the hand and ask for their votes. Children swarm all over and round the car. We give them joy rides by dozens at a time.

"Maurice Dobb and other undergraduates also very useful. Dobb quite good as an open-air speaker, and also as a bell-ringer.

"Cope Morgan has an appeal to University voters issued on his behalf signed by Bond, Berry, Benson, Clapham, Holland, Keynes senior, Keynes junior, Laffan, Salter, etc., claiming to

represent both wings of the Progressive Party, urging people to
vote for him simply on the ground that he has a better chance
than I. They are very bad judges. And it is pretty stiff that this
list should include so many Fellows of King's, including one
who taught me mathematics and another who taught me
economics. With my father's best man, now Master of Magdalene, thrown in! But I deal with this at a packed meeting in the
Guildhall. My Liberal opponent, I say, draws class distinctions.
He has one appeal for the University, another for the rest. But
I send the same election address to Romsey Town (where the
railwaymen live) and to Trinity College.

"We keep fairly clear of personalities, and this election is a
good deal below the average in scurrility. The worst single
item is a Liberal document issued on the eve of the poll,
suggesting that, if I am elected, co-operative societies will be
extinguished, Trade Unions done away with, houses owned
by the workers and all their savings confiscated. I get many
questions on the Capital Levy, mostly from people who are
genuinely interested in the proposal.

"A great scene on the eve of the poll. I return to my committee
rooms after four indoor and three outdoor meetings. It is
suggested that I shall go on to the Market Square, but I say no.
The Tories have the Guildhall and outside will be a knock-
about show. But after a few minutes B. K. Martin", later to
become famous as Kingsley Martin, Editor of the *New Statesman*, "arrives at the double from the Market Square. He says
both Newton and Morgan have been trying to speak there and
have been howled down and the crowd, which is largely mine,
is shouting for me. So I go, in Montagu's bedizened car, with
red streamers flying and Dobb ringing the muffin bell like hell!
It is 11 p.m.

"Coming down Regent Street and Petty Cury, we run into
part of the crowd pouring away from the Market Square. Turning
round out of the back of the car, I wave to them and shout 'Come
back!' And so they pour back and swell the crowd, still large,
that is still on the Square.

"We halt opposite the Guildhall and I get up in the front of
the car. My supporters are cheering like mad and a large hostile section is shouting 'Newton! Newton!' It is some minutes
before I can make myself heard. I can only get out a few

sentences, occasionally, shouting through the din. I tell them that this has become a fight between Truth on the one side and Falsehood on the other; that Truth will win tomorrow; that the two other parties between them have just about ruined the country. And so back to my committee rooms, still great cheering crowds outside and a tight pack of enthusiasts within. And so to bed.

"March 16th, 1922. Polling day. Tories have 82 cars, Liberals 40, we six. Our organisation is, on the whole, very good, thanks to outside assistance. Polling is heavy and exuberant enthusiasm mounts as the day goes on. In the evening most of my workers are confident that I am in. 'Going in like an aeroplane!' is a phrase that catches on. A big crowd at East Road (our central committee rooms) at the close of the poll. I speak from an upper window, but make no prophecy.

"March 17th. Ruth and I agree that we shall have done well if we get within 2,000 of Newton, badly if the Tory majority is much above this. We are confident of having beaten Morgan pretty easily. At the Count the Liberals rather visibly depressed, everyone else looking fairly cheerful. Newton and I make small talk, but Morgan *will* argue about 'splitting the Progressive vote' even *in mediis*! I say that the conclusion will be drawn that, if *we* can do so well *here* in a three-cornered fight, we can win three-cornered fights in most other constituencies. This, he thinks, will be 'disastrous'. 'Not for us,' I reply. The final figures, received just after noon, are:

NEWTON	10,897
DALTON	6,954
MORGAN	4,529
Tory majority over Labour	3,943

"I congratulate Newton, who says he feels 'too much overcome by the whole situation' to be able to say much. After the vote of thanks to the Mayor, we go to an upper window, facing the Market Square. The Mayor leads, Newton follows, then I. I confess to a sense of triumphant pleasure in leaving Morgan in the rear and again, at the window, in coming up on the Mayor's left, Newton on his right, both of us in full view of the crowd, Morgan invisible behind us. A huge crowd, the majority Tory, a strong minority mine and hardly a Liberal favour to be seen. Newton speaks through a megaphone. A few halting sentences. The effects of this victory will be felt, even in South Africa. Lady Newton kisses him on the back of the neck in view of the crowd. Then I monopolise the window, with Ruth. I reject the megaphone and shout that we have put up a magnificent fight; we have shaken up this old town as it has never been shaken up before; we have beaten the Liberals (tremendous cheering) and next time we'll beat the lot. Morgan then asks, through the megaphone, 'Are we downhearted?' There is not much reply. Then, after more cheers, salutations and scuffles in the street, I am carried some distance on the shoulders of two—fortunately sober—supporters, to the singing of 'For he's a jolly good fellow'. Ruth and I then take three or four of our undergraduate helpers back to lunch. Following suddenly upon the end of the fight, during which I was hardly tired at all, I now feel in a state of physical collapse. I had put everything in. And the result, frankly, is rather disappointing, though the outside world will think I did very well."

Such was my first experience as a Parliamentary Candidate. I soon became accustomed to fighting elections and found that, in many of their features, they repeated themselves. But I was very eager during these three weeks of my initiation, and deeply moved by all the personal devotion and loyalty of my supporters. I felt that I had learned and experienced something very vital and important.

But I decide not to fight Cambridge again. 4,000 is too big a majority. If it had been 2,000, it would have seemed different. At the General Election we shall have a less good organisation, and very little outside help, and probably shan't do so well. But Ruth and I are torn with pangs at the thought of leaving all our workers and friends and Cambridge itself.

Our Local Executive "are awfully nice about it, and obviously don't expect to keep me. *They* think I ought to be given the best Labour seat in the country! They say that, when I get in, I shall represent *them*, as much as if I sat for Cambridge." But this Parliament is far spent, and there are not many constituencies, with even an outside chance of winning, still vacant.

I was adopted in May for the Maidstone Division of Kent, which seemed as hopeful as any other still available, and reasonably near London. Before leaving our house in Cambridge I gave a party to a number of undergraduates from the University Labour Club. I wrote: "They *are* a jolly crowd. They matter tremendously to the world, the first of the new generation unscarred by the war. Politics, if it means dedicating oneself to their happiness and opportunities, is a trade well worth following."

Maidstone was a constituency part urban, part rural. Close on half the electors lived in the rural districts. This, I think, is the most satisfying type of constituency to represent. I campaigned all August and addressed nearly forty village meetings and one or two in Maidstone itself. I touched every polling district. During this campaign Ruth became quite a practised speaker. She and I stayed in a succession of small country pubs. Many of the publicans were Labour, especially in the hop-growing districts. I spoke in favour of reducing indirect taxes, including the beer duty. Also of restoring the National Agricultural Wages Board, which the Lloyd George-Tory Government, when they broke all their promises both to farmers and farm workers, had done away with. This was a big issue in all the villages.

In October the Tories did away with Lloyd George, Bonar Law became Prime Minister and an election quickly followed. In Maidstone we had a three-cornered fight. In addition to Commander Bellairs, the sitting Tory M.P., and myself, Mr. Foster Clark, a well-known local manufacturer of jellies and custards, came in at the eleventh hour as an Independent with much Tory and Liberal support. He spent a lot of money on advertising. His programme was Economy and anti-Socialism. His style and addresses were rather academic, potted economic history and statistics from the point of view of the entrepreneur.

In the election campaign "the Capital Levy was, here as elsewhere, the most obvious issue, which suited me all right. I also spoke much of the price of beer and, I think, carried most of the brewery workers, who are numerous in Maidstone. In the villages this and the Wages Board were the chief topics. Nationalisation of mines and railways was quite in the background."[1]

---

[1] I recorded a call on a leading Liberal in Maidstone, soon after my adoption. "He said he didn't want everything nationalised. I said I limited myself, in this campaign, to coal, railways, land, drink and armaments. He said he was willing to go that far, but he still wore a hostile look." Our short list is subject to change!

In my friend Walter Hunt I had an admirable agent, who had already proved himself an excellent organiser, though the constituency was too wide, and in parts too difficult, to be completely covered.

"Towards the end it looks as though anything might happen and both *The Times* and the *Morning Post* say that I might win. The latter has a poster 'Labour Menace at Maidstone'. A wonderful series of Ward meetings in the town on the eve of the poll. We have thoroughly stirred the place up! On Polling Day Clark has 250 cars, Bellairs 130 and I two. In the morning a thick fog. Ruth and I, touring the polling stations in a taxi, nearly run into a Bellairs car near Stockbury. Said I, 'The Lord hath delivered them into my hand!' All cars will be either colliding or crawling. But about 11 a.m. the fog lifted. Great scenes in the North Ward (our surest stronghold) in the evening. Cheering crowds till long after the close of the poll.

"At the count the general expectation is that Clark is in, I a close second, Bellairs bottom. The latter comes late, looking like a beaten man, and his agent's face is gloomy.

"The result surprises everyone, most of all Bellairs.

BELLAIRS	8,928
CLARK	8,895
DALTON	8,004

Conservative majority over Independent 33
Conservative majority over Labour   924

"I won in the town and in the Western rural strip. Yalding, Nettlestead and Leeds did specially well for me. But I came down very badly in Lenham, Staplehurst and Headcorn, at the eastern end of the Division, where we had no organisation. These three polling districts did me in." These were corn villages, not hop villages, and feudalism was still strong.

"But our people were very rightly proud of our fight. It was the nearest approach to a Labour victory in Kent, Surrey, Sussex and Hants. And I mustn't forget the little boy on polling day who sat in front of my taxi and monotoned 'Vote for Dalton. 'E's the man. 'E knows what e's doin'. If you vote for 'im, you won't 'ave to work so 'ard; you'll be able to save some money; you'll get your breakfast all right. We don't want no Tory lies. We don't want no sticky jelly merchants, do we, lidy?' I gave him half a crown and told him he'd be a Labour leader one day."

After this election, which gave the Tories a comfortable Parliamentary majority of 89 over Labour and both Liberal factions combined, the Labour Party became the official Opposition and MacDonald its leader. Snowden, who, like MacDonald had been re-elected after four years out of Parliament, said to me when I next saw him, a fortnight later, "Well, your Capital Levy got some of us into trouble." I assumed that this Parliament would last for years. So I decided to give constituencies a rest and returned with renewed academic ardour to the School. Greeted with applause on mounting the platform to give my first lecture after the election, I exclaimed: "What shadows we are and what shifting shadows we pursue!"

But, when the new Parliament was barely one year old, Baldwin who, following the resignation through illness of Bonar Law, had been Prime Minister for less than six months, suddenly on November 10th asked for a dissolution. He said that Protection was the only cure for unemployment, and he must have a mandate to apply it. He took everyone, including most of his own colleagues, by surprise. And he certainly surprised the Labour Party. We had several hundred constituencies, where no candidate had yet been selected. All these had to be fixed up within a fortnight. The strain and effort of all this pressed very hard on Egerton Wake, our National Agent. But I wish to put it on record that he, like his chief, Arthur Henderson, always showed great kindness towards me and great confidence in me.

I was uncommitted to any constituency, but had been carrying on a mild flirtation for some months with Chesterfield. This was a predominantly mining division, then represented by Barnet Kenyon, an old Derbyshire Miners' Agent, but a Lib-Lab, and so not a member of the Parliamentary Labour Party. It was uncertain whether he would stand again or not.

"November 11th. To Chesterfield. Spend the night with Frank Hall", an old friend, secretary of Derbyshire Miners. "He advises me against calling on Kenyon at his house, since Mrs. K. will be there and will make trouble. He suggests I should see K. at House of Commons which reassembles (for the last time before its dissolution) on Tuesday the 13th.

"November 12th. See Wake in afternoon. Horrified at news from Chesterfield. Says: 'We are running straight into a cul-de-sac.' Arrange to lunch with Wedgwood at the House next day, and ask him to find out K.'s intentions, if he can.

"November 13th. Ruth and I lunch with Wedgwood, Leach, Greenwood and Bob Richards. A jovial meal. We settle Compromise Land Report, based on my memorandum of the summer. Wedgwood says he has spoken to K., who intends to stand again. Someone says West Leicester is still without a Labour Candidate. This is a Labour seat. Winston Churchill is the Liberal candidate. This sounds very attractive.

"I decide that Chesterfield is off, and begin to look elsewhere. Wake has six or seven seats that look hopeful, but doesn't know in how many cases H.Q. will be asked to recommend. Brockway at I.L.P. Head Office gets on to W. Leicester. The next three days, 14th, 15th and 16th, are full of furious activity. Brockway arranges a meeting for me at his office with Banton and Borrett of Leicester and I get an I.L.P. nomination for W. Leicester. Mrs. Webb puts up £250 towards my expenses from Sir Arthur Acland, who wishes his son, Sir Francis, had gone Labour[1] and makes this gift for 'a young University man standing for Labour'. This makes it possible to say that I can guarantee expenses anywhere. It is said that J. R. M. is trying to push his son Malcolm, still up at Oxford, into W. Leicester. I gather from Brockway that this plan is not being persevered with. But Pethick is in the running and so is a Boot and Shoe Union nominee, in succession to Hill the retiring Member. Unfortunately there is no time for a Selection Conference, at which I should be pretty confident of winning, and a vote will have to be taken in our absence. I get Greenwood to write to Leicester on my behalf. I am receiving telephone messages from a number of constituencies, all pretty hopeless, which have made no preparations and have no money, but to whom my name has been circulated with others as 'available'.

"November 17th. I hear this morning that Pethick has got W. Leicester by a narrow vote at 1 a.m. after a prolonged sitting of their Executive. It appears that the vote went in his

---

[1] His grandson, Sir Richard Acland, did.

favour owing to a recommendation which he asked for, and obtained, from J. R. M.[1] It is not clear whether the latter knew that I was in the field."

Pethick Lawrence won West Leicester, beating Winston Churchill and a Tory, and held it till 1931.

Meanwhile on November 6th I had been invited to meet MacDonald at Eccleston Square. A conference of our "financial experts", mainly on the Capital Levy. Also present Henderson, Webb, Lees-Smith, Greenwood, Sydney Arnold and Pethick Lawrence. But not Snowden!

MacDonald wants to drop the Capital Levy at the coming election. He says he has received many letters urging him to do this. What about the yield? Would it not be less than we thought a little while ago? He is not, of course, going to drop it, just because some of our people are frightened. But he wants us to be quite frank. Pethick Lawrence, Arnold, I, Webb, Lees-Smith and Greenwood successively advise to keep it in. Most of us think that the yield would be greater now, none that it would be less. Most of us think it good electioneering, as well as good economics. Webb thinks it would look very bad to drop it now.

MacDonald accepts our advice, saying: "Very well, the flag is up." Henderson, who has expressed no view on the merits, says that we should now organise conferences in order to instruct M.P.s and candidates on the subject.

Having missed West Leicester, and the opportunity of beating Winston Churchill, I decided on the morning of November 17th to go to Cardiff. Wake had been holding up two Cardiff seats, East and South, which had asked Headquarters for candidates, at great inconvenience, until West Leicester had been settled. On November 16th I had got a letter of invitation from Cardiff East. Uncle and Wake both said that, so far as they knew, there was nothing to choose between the two Cardiff seats, and a sporting chance of lifting them both. I, therefore, since Cardiff East had invited me, wired acceptance. Little Arthur—Arthur Henderson, junior—with whom I was on most friendly terms, took Cardiff South. Later it became clear that he had got the better of the two constituencies. But that was luck, not plotting.

---

[1] MacDonald had sat for Leicester, then an undivided borough, together with a Liberal, from 1906, when he first entered the House, till 1918.

Ruth and I went down to Cardiff on November 18th. The next two and a half weeks were spent electioneering. I had the most amazing platform successes, both in Cardiff and in the Welsh valleys. I remember, in particular, a glorious meeting at Pontypridd. Next to J. R. M. at Aberavon, I was more fully reported and more violently attacked by the South Wales Press than any other candidate. Our meetings in Cardiff surpassed all my previous experiences for enthusiasm. But it gradually appeared that there was no organisation. Bert Collins, of the N.U.R., a good friend of mine with whom I have kept in touch through the long years since, acted as agent and did all a man could do, with no machine to help him.

The Capital Levy was the chief issue at all meetings.

I form the opinion, as the fight goes on, that Lougher, the Tory sitting member, is out of it. Protection makes very little appeal in Cardiff, and he is a weak candidate with a poor organisation. It lies between Sir Harry Webb, the Liberal, and myself. He issues a violent anti-German[1] and anti-Labour leaflet on the eve of the poll. He has swarms of cars and a good organisation.

The count on December 6th is at the City Hall for all three Divisions.

The final result is:

WEBB	8,536
DALTON	7,812
LOUGHER	7,513

Liberal majority over Labour 724

Lougher's poll is larger than I had expected, a tribute to the solid, silent, unseen Tory strength. I had not expected, at the last, to win, but had put my chances at anything between a majority of 700 in my favour, and a majority of 1,500 against me. So the result is nearer my lower level!

"Outside the scene is very dramatic. A crowd of thousands waiting in the large open space outside the City Hall, a sea of dark faces. We climb up a ladder to a broad platform, high above them and illuminated by arc lights. The Lord Mayor and Webb go first. Terrific booing from the great majority of

[1] I am accused of belonging to a Party which is too pro-German!

the crowd below, our people and the Tories. Liberals never seem to show up in force on such occasions.

"I follow, and receive a wonderful greeting. Webb tries to speak, but his voice is completely drowned by his opponents. He turns to me and says, 'Do you think it would help if we shook hands publicly?' So we shake, in view of them all. Loud cheers, but still louder babel when he tries again.

"Then I go forward to the edge of the platform, in front of him, and sign to them with my hands to be still. The tumult dies down a little and, shouting, I appeal to my supporters in the crowd to let Webb speak. He succeeds in getting out a few words. And then Ruth, who has been sent for, comes forward beside me and waves her bouquet, in our colours, presented by our supporters, at the crowd. At once there is a renewed roar of cheers and Webb is drowned again. She had thought that he had finished by now, and that I was speaking. I go forward once more and sign to them to be still. He struggles on a little longer, and then gives up. I then address them and just make myself heard. I end by appealing for silence for Lougher, who speaks a few sentences amid rising din. Then we all go down the ladder and wait in the City Hall. The other two divisions are recounting.

"News comes through that Mond is out in Swansea. This is compensation. I call out 'Three cheers! Mond is in the pond!' Liberals are furious, our people radiant. Then comes the Cardiff South result. Little Arthur is in by 400! He is dragged down by his supporters, a rather too large bowler hat pushed over his eyes, looking rather alarmed by their enthusiasm, heartily smacked on the back and vigorously wrenched by the hand. The 'Red Flag' is sung in the Great Hall as he comes out, and there is a tremendous cheer as he mounts the ladder. Later comes the Central, Gould (Tory) returned with a slightly reduced majority and Jimmy Edmunds, our candidate, second.

"Then we drive back to the Labour Hall in Cardiff East and speak of our moral victory, and the reduced majority, and how we will win next time. And so to bed in the small hours!"

Next day, December 7th, newspapers in bed. Big Labour and Liberal gains. Will Henderson is in at Enfield, but Uncle Arthur is out at Newcastle. Father out—for the moment—but two sons in. When he got in at a by-election at Burnley, his two sons introduced him. No precedent for that.

"In the evening I give my supporters a straight talk at the Labour Hall on the need for organisation, propaganda and money-raising. Then we are dragged by ropes in a car to the Centre in Charles Street. A great crowd singing and cheering, with a few drunks. J. R. M. has been and gone. I am very voiceless, but manage to whisper a peroration. The South are blaming the East for letting me down. The Chairman, from the South, says that Headquarters placed at the disposal of the East one of the finest candidates in the country, a star shining in the firmament, and they had failed to get him in. I have once more to praise my workers in reply to this.

"Then on by car to the station to see Little Arthur off. I speak to a great crowd outside, my voice and fight returning. I tell them that news has just come in that Baldwin has resigned, and the King has sent for J. R. M. A bit premature! So back to bed.

"On December 8th, 1923, I leave Cardiff by a morning train. Ruth and I travel in the same carriage as MacDonald and his secretary, Miss Rosenberg. At Newport Dick Wallhead gets in with his daughter, Mrs. Muriel Wallhead Nichol, and another woman relative.

"A cheering crowd sees us off at Cardiff. Two Tories call, 'Good-bye, Bolshie!' I reply, 'Good-bye, you dirty dogs!' This shocks J. R. M. Our supporters sing the 'Red Flag' as we go out. J. R. M. says 'Ah! That is the funeral dirge of our Movement!'

"I am too tired to talk much or argue. J. R. M. says he thinks the Capital Levy has lost us fifty seats. I say that, if they hadn't attacked us on that, they would have attacked us on 'socialism' and 'nationalisation', which would have been worse. He thinks that would have been 'vaguer' and less damaging. He thinks a large section of opinion would have been willing to back us but for the Capital Levy. He was dining a few weeks ago with a lady, very famous in her day, but now leading a very quiet life. She had told him that she sympathised with Labour very much, and agreed with all our policy except the Capital Levy. But she didn't want to lose half her fortune. . . . A pause. . . . 'You would be very interested if I told you who that lady was,' said J. R. M. . . . A long silence. . . . At last he says, 'It was the Honourable Mrs. George Keppel.' . . . A longer silence and Dick Wallhead looking down his nose."

I met Mrs. Keppel some years later at a dinner party, I think in Rome at our Embassy. She said to me, "Are you still a Socialist?" "Yes," I said, "and are you?" "I never was," she said. "I remember Mr. MacDonald telling me," I replied, "that you told him that, if he dropped the Capital Levy, you would be in favour of everything else." "I never told him anything of the kind," she said.

This morning there were more cheering crowds at Paddington. J. R. M. asked me to come along to the 1917 Club that evening. There I found him talking to Ernest Hunter; shutting up like an oyster on his own intentions; cursing Egerton Wake who had made a statement to the Press that there would be no coalition; wishing to keep silence while leaders of other parties spoke; resenting speech by other members of his own party; fearing that, "if indiscretions continue", his game will be spoilt; anxious that the I.L.P. should make no pronouncement.

When he has gone, Hunter asks me if I can gather his purpose. "Surely," I say, "to form a purely Labour Government." Hunter isn't sure.

With all the results before me, it is much more annoying than it was in the first hours of defeat not to be in the House. This will be a critical Parliament, in which new reputations will be made. Many people have passed me on this lap, and many seats have been won that I might have had if I had foreseen events. But this Parliament may not last long.

The Tories had lost 88 seats, we had gained 47 and the Liberals 41. The Tories had 258 seats in the new House, we 191 and the Liberals 158.

Four days later to a squash at the Webbs', candidates victorious and vanquished. Congratulations and condolences. Short speeches by J. R. M., Webb, who tells us all to be discreet and not ask for jobs, Uncle Arthur and Wake.

Back by bus with Wedgwood and his wife. He wants the Colonial Office, he says. I tell him J. R. M.'s story about Mrs. Keppel. We agree that only a few types among us are proof against the blandishments of Court and Society. He says "and J. R. M. has no woman, which makes it all the more dangerous".

After my defeat at Cardiff, I spent Christmas with my parents at Windsor. The first Minority Labour Government was imminent. On Boxing Day Lord Stamfordham, the King's Private Secretary, invited me to come and see him. He asked me many questions about Labour policy. The King, he said, had been very much disturbed by the speeches of some of the Glasgow Labour M.P.s, especially one by Rev. Campbell Stephen, who had declared that, if MacDonald asked for a dissolution and was refused, that would be the end of the Monarchy. The King had rung up Stamfordham from Sandringham about this speech.

Stamfordham blamed Asquith for having raised in a recent speech the constitutional aspects of the right of a Prime Minister to obtain a dissolution. Stamfordham said he would have liked the King to refuse Baldwin's demand for a dissolution last month. He had thought this demand was political madness anyhow, but Baldwin had told him on the eve of the poll that they had been through all the constituencies with a toothcomb, and were sure of a majority of at least thirty over Labour and Liberals combined. Stamfordham said he took the view that the King always had the right to refuse a dissolution. I thought this was pretty reckless doctrine and remembered that he had advised the King in 1910 not to accept Asquith's advice on the creation of peers, but, fortunately for the Monarchy, the King had been guided by Knollys' opinion and not Stamfordham's.

Stamfordham told me that he would like to see a stronger foreign policy, *vis-à-vis* France, and hoped for this from a Labour Government.

He then spoke at some length about clothes. Will Labour Ministers wear Court dress, and frock coats at Privy Councils? The King, it seems, is very touchy about all this. He once refused to take John Burns in his carriage to some function, where Burns was to be Minister in Attendance, because he appeared in a bowler instead of a top hat. When the King wanted to invite J. R. M., who had recently become Leader of the Opposition, to dine at Buckingham Palace, Stamfordham was sent to see him to ask whether, if invited, he would come and whether he would wear the right clothes. This was the only time Stamfordham had met J. R. M., who had been "very courteous" and struck him as being "quite a gentleman". He had, indeed, made Stamfordham feel very awkward, for he had said that, of course, if he was invited to dine at the Palace, he would accept and wear the right clothes. Stamfordham had made a joke about frock coats, saying that he knew that J. R. M.'s colleague, Arthur Henderson, had a beautiful frock coat. J. R. M. had replied: "Yes, but don't imagine he bought that in order to go to the Palace as a Privy Councillor. He bought it because he is a Methodist preacher. I am a Scots Presbyterian and in my Church we pay professional preachers."[1]

I told Stamfordham that I looked forward to the extinction of the Liberals and a return to a two-party system. He said he hoped it wouldn't be rich against poor. He dreaded that. He said that "a Liberal financier" had told the King that "the day Ramsay MacDonald kisses hands three hundred million pounds will leave this country". Stamfordham doubted whether this was physically possible. I said such talk was all nonsense anyhow, and very unpatriotic as well.

I sent an account of this conversation to J. R. M. on New Year's Eve. Stamfordham also wrote an account of it and sent it to the King, who read it aloud to the Queen, and both were slightly reassured. So, at least, Stamfordham told my father.

Labour Ministers are now quite used to taking office, and there are enough old hands to give hints to new hands. But in

[1] The Duke of Windsor (A King's Story, p. 187) also relates that at this time: "My father . . . was in considerable doubt as to how the Socialist leaders would conduct themselves towards him in their new role of Ministers of the Crown. Many of them, in their youth, had publicly scoffed at the Monarchy. And my father was not only apprehensive that some of his new Ministers might refuse to participate in the State ceremonies, but he also had some grounds for believing that they might even refuse to wear Court uniforms. Fortunately Mr. MacDonald proved to be a reasonable man; the new Prime Minister and his Cabinet in due course made their debut at Court colourfully clad in the uniform of Ministers of the Crown—a blue, gold-braided tail-coat and white knee-breeches with sword —a courtesy that went far to reassure my father." J. R. M., of course, loved dressing up, so as to show off his good-looks. That was human enough! But some others appeared very ridiculous, even in black knee-breeches with evening dress. I remember a devastating photograph of Sidney Webb and Noel Buxton, the dwarf and the stork, side by side in this get-up, crowned with opera hats, outside the Palace. This photograph was circulated in Glasgow by the I.L.P., over the caption "Was this what you voted for?" The wearing by Labour Ministers of Court dress, and even of black knee-breeches, and of frock coats at Privy Councils, went out after the Second Labour Government. Clem Attlee deserves the credit for this, and it was accepted on his suggestion, almost as a matter of course, by the Palace.

the early days there was a wealth of good stories, some of which were true. Way back at the end of 1905 John Burns, when invited by Campbell-Bannerman to be President of the Local Government Board, had grasped the Prime Minister by the hand and exclaimed: "Well done, Sir 'Enry! That's the most popular thing you've done yet." And next day, entering his office for the first time and being received with an air of grave respect by the Permanent Secretary, he said: "So you're the Permanent Secretary. Can you do short'and and type-writin'?"

Mrs. Webb told me that, a week after Arthur Henderson had entered the Asquith Coalition Cabinet in 1915—he had never held office before—she asked him what most impressed him about being a Cabinet Minister. He answered: "The number of things I used to have to do for myself, which other people now do for me." This was a shrewd reply.

Of the many stories told of Labour Ministers taking office for the first time in 1924, I offer these few.

Jimmy Thomas, arriving at the Colonial Office before the official announcement of his appointment and telling the messenger that he was going to be the new Secretary of State, and the messenger saying to his mate, in a sympathetic under-tone, "Another shell-shock case, I'm afraid."

Jimmy Thomas's Private Secretary, inherited from his pre-decessor, asked how he liked his new chief. "Very much indeed. It's much more intimate. My old chief used to ring the bell for me. My new chief puts his head round the door of my room, and says: 'Come 'ere, you b——!'"

Stephen Walsh, the little Lancashire miner, as Secretary of State for War, opening the first meeting of the Army Council, remembering the troubles in the Curragh in 1914,

"Gentlemen, always remember that we must all be loyal to the King."

John Wheatley's account of his first conversation with the King. "Your Majesty, I would never lift a finger to change this country from a capitalist Monarchy into a capitalist Republic. Of course, when capitalism goes, the Monarchy will go too. But I hope there'll be no ill-feeling on either side."

In January 1924, at Brailsford's invitation, I joined the *New Leader* lunches, on Mondays at the 1917 Club. I was writing notes for the paper at this time. The company at lunch varied from week to week, and included Arthur Ponsonby, Margaret Bondfield, Nevinson, Bertie Russell, Clifford Allen and Norman Angell.

On February 4th MacDonald turned up at the lunch. We had had no notice to expect the Prime Minister and Foreign Secretary. He said he had come to speak seriously to Brailsford, whose line in recent issues had been unhelpful. Brailsford was in France, so Angell, who was acting editor, came in for the scolding, and did not scold back, as Brailsford would have done.

J. R. M. deplores all strikes. Strikes by the dockers and the miners are threatened. This sort of thing will "knock us out" if it goes on. What is wanted is to "preach Socialism" in the country and the importance of political action. "Some reductions" of wages may be justifiable. Strikes may prevent trade revival. The military may have to be used to run lorries. "The complexities of the situation" may even become such as to compel us to have "a national Government", "nearly a Coalition but not quite". We may have "to bring in some people from the other parties and to bring some of ours out". Men never want to strike, unless they are instigated by their leaders. The dockers can't get an advance at the present time. He could not ask for a dissolution in any case for the next few months. Within a year he might be able to bring about a revolutionary change in the European situation.

I had a very nasty taste in my mouth at the end of all this. I intervened once or twice, but Allen, Angell and others sat round like a kindergarten. Some of the liveliest lunchers were absent. As for the "national government", we had been warned—seven years warning![1]

I was readopted for Cardiff East on two conditions: that I was free to take a by-election, and that they would build up a better organisation and fighting fund. I was with them at the

[1] Sir Norman Angell, in his autobiography *After All* (pp. 243–4), gives an account of this same lunch on this same date. Our accounts agree broadly, though each brings out some points not in the other. He makes MacDonald say: "I want the I.L.P. to carry on a socialist propaganda, instead of which everybody wants to be a Cabinet Minister, or . . . to make a Cabinet of their own." And again "The dockers do not want to strike. It comes from Bevin. They . . . are earning ten to eleven shillings a day. That was not, of course, enough, but it was ridiculous to pretend that it was starvation wages and that they could not postpone things."

end of June. I recorded: "I am angry with the local people for muddling my engagements and losing the Roath by-election (for the City Council). It wouldn't take much to make me chuck this constituency! And indeed politics altogether. I am wasting the energies of the best years of my life."

And then:

"July 4th. Oddly enough, just after my last entry, comes an invitation to stand in the Holland-with-Boston by-election! The death of Royce" (Labour M.P. who had just been appointed Governor of Tasmania, born in the constituency, the son of an agricultural worker, went to South Africa, married an Afrikaner wife, made money as a contractor, came home and bought a large house and estate, including the cottage where he was born) "puts us in a quandary. At first I refuse, on the ground that it was a personal vote, not Labour at all. Then say I'll give a reply tomorrow. I take advice," lots of it; most advise me to go.

"July 5th. Having slept on it, I decide to go. 'The old war horse and all that!' Wake is delighted. But I insist on the writ being held up to allow me to get all round."

From July 7th to 31st, Ruth and I were hard at it. "Physically a healthy election, motoring in open car between villages. A huge constituency, 43,000 electors of whom 11,000 in Boston, 5,000 in Spalding, the rest agricultural. A rich country, flat as your hand, largely reclaimed. Potatoes, fruit and corn. No gentry and no sport. We fight on Agricultural Wages Board, Pensions (old age, widows and ex-service), Houses and Snowden's Budget, but some prices have gone up since it was introduced, so gilt is wearing off the gingerbread!" I also promised guaranteed prices for agricultural produce, which led the Tories in the House to demand whether this was yet official Government policy. It wasn't! I was ahead of Snowden, who was angry. But my friend Walter Smith, Parliamentary Secretary at Agriculture, gave a good reply. "Spirit in the villages very fine and fearless. Splendid young men leading the agricultural workers here." But Boston and Spalding, the two market towns, were the weak spots. With the Tories our relations were quite good, with the Liberals very strained. Sir Richard and Lady Winfrey, parents of the amiable young Liberal candidate, who had just come down from

Cambridge, were very active. It was put about that I had written an anti-religious book, which was used as a textbook in Communist Sunday schools; also that I was a foreigner. Lady Winfrey issued an "Appeal to the Electors" in which she said that, if the people voted for the Socialists, "the children would be told that there is no God, that Bibles, Chapels and Churches should be burned, that the story of Jesus is a legend and that they would pour ridicule upon the sacrifice of Christ upon the cross. For the sake of the children have nothing to do with the Socialist Party."

We hit back in the Spalding Free Press. Ruth published a sharp reply to Lady Winfrey. Six local clergy wrote a protest against her Appeal. My father, as a Canon of the Church, wrote, for publication, a letter to me in which he said: "I see you have gone down to do battle against the Philistines once again. . . . Ramsay MacDonald is working like a hero, and I trust he will bring the London Conference of the Allies to a satisfactory conclusion. Hoping you will be victorious at the end of the month."

At the count on August 1st, Dean, the Tory, established a lead early and kept it. The result was

DEAN	12,907
DALTON	12,101
WINFREY	7,594

Conservative majority over Labour 806

My reaction to this fourth defeat in twenty-eight months was sheer weariness and anger. I was utterly sick of politics, and felt a fool to have come on this adventure. My friends spoke of a "fine fight" and assured me that no one else could have done so well. Wake and Henderson were both very complimentary. But what was the good of it?

Ruth and I went off, ten days later, for a holiday in Sicily and Sardinia. We rightly judged that in August the English visitor would think this part of the world too hot. We met no compatriots on either island. But we rode up on mules to the highest point on each, Etna and Gennargentu. We slept in the *rifugio* just below the top of Etna, under blankets, with a brazier burning. Down at sea-level at Catania it was the hottest night ever recorded. And we heard that Sir Eric Geddes—who had caused my Cambridge by-election—had camped out a few months before on the slopes of Gennargentu on a shooting expedition, but couldn't sleep all night. "He was a very fat man," said our Sardinian guide, "and it was very hot, and he had no clothes on."

"Hardly were we back from the South, and the L.S.E. term just begun, when the political storm broke. I had to piece together, on my return, the displeasing story of J. R. M.'s car—given him with an allowance for upkeep by a biscuit manufacturer whom he had put in the Honours List. That and the Campbell Case, which did no one in any Party any credit, but was made the excuse for the General Election, are now part of the trivialities of history. The final crash of thunder came in the first week in October at the Queen's Hall, where we were holding the Annual Conference of the Labour Party, when J. R. M. announced an immediate dissolution. I was there and had seen Wake in a back room about constituencies. I was stiff against standing again, except for an A1 seat. I was feeling very fit after my holiday, but a bit above the battle. I hadn't been in the First Labour Government, and I was sure we were going to lose the next election. So what did it all matter to me personally? Wake swore to do his best to get me Hanley, and Wedgwood and Tawney, both with local influence, tried to help. But this move came to nothing. So I said, 'I won't stand anywhere', and stuck to it for several days, refusing many invitations and arranging to speak for a number of my friends.

"Then suddenly, a few days before nominations, Peckham came loose. Wake sent for me very urgently and explained that the Tory majority over Labour was only 156 last time. 'It'll be a lot bigger this time,' I said grimly. He went on to argue that the local circumstances were very exceptional, and very much in our favour. Collingwood Hughes, the retiring Tory M.P., was not standing again. He voted with us, and against his party, on the Campbell Case, and justified his vote vigorously in a letter to the Press. So the local Tories were all at sixes and sevens, and had had to bring in a new candidate at the last moment, a Colonel Sir Martin Archer Shee, ex-M.P. for Finsbury. The Labour candidate last time, who was to have fought again, had just had a stroke, and was out of it. But he was elderly and had spent many years in India. I should be a much stronger candidate, and poll many votes he wouldn't have got.

" 'No,' I said, 'I'll only stand for an A1 seat, and Peckham isn't that.' He said he quite understood how I felt, but wouldn't I at least meet a deputation from the Peckham Party and hear what they had to say? They were coming up that afternoon to the London Labour Party Office, and he had mentioned my name to them on the telephone, without, of course, committing me, and they had been so delighted, and would be so disappointed if I wasn't there. Of course, I should be perfectly free to turn them down at the end of the interview. 'All right,' I said, 'I'll see them. But I shan't accept. I'm not standing this time.'

"Then I went back to the L.S.E. and gave a lecture and had lunch and rang up Ruth. 'Don't take it,' she said. 'Don't let them fool you again.' I said I wholly agreed with her, and we arranged that she should come with me to strengthen my hand. We drove in a taxi from the School. She said, 'Now don't give way to them.' 'No,' I said, 'I won't.' But, just as we were getting out, the thought crossed my mind, 'Only 156. And what a bloody fool I should feel if I refused this, and then someone else took it and won it!'

"In addition to the London Labour Party officers and the deputation from Peckham, Wake was there too. The Peckhamites, particularly an old Irishman called O'Bolger, who kept a tailor's shop in the High Street, painted a bright picture. They were sure that, with me as candidate, they could win. But I soon disposed of all this by asking a few pertinent questions. They had to admit that they had no organisation, and a very small individual membership, and hadn't a seat on the L.C.C., and very few on the Borough Council. And finally, to end the interview, I said to them, 'And of course, you have no agent to run the election.' 'No,' they said sadly. And I shook my head sadly too, and was on the point of rising from my seat, to wish them good luck, but to say, quite firmly, that I was not their man, when Wake intervened. 'You are quite right', he said to me, 'to attach so much importance to having a good agent. In this constituency I think that will just make the difference between defeat and victory. I have waiting in the next room a most capable and experienced agent, who has already conducted several Parliamentary elections. He happens to be free and I want to use him to the best advantage of the Party. I am prepared to put him at your disposal and that of the Peckham Party, if you will accept the candidature. He can start work today.' So I fell for it!"

It was a very strenuous contest, but a compact area. I canvassed vigorously every afternoon and spoke at night. One woman whom I canvassed, announcing that I was the Labour candidate, quickly withdrew and shut the door. "My God," she said, "I must put the chain on!" "A large Irish Catholic vote," I wrote in my diary, "which goes against Archer Shee, my Tory opponent, who is himself a Catholic, but opposed the Irish Treaty and is alleged to have taken part in Black and Tan atrocities. I feared some young Sinn Fein desperadoes might do him violence. I had met some of them, at O'Bolger's request, in the basement of his shop, and they had asked whether it would help me if they kidnapped him. I said I thought not, but that I was sure they could help me in other ways. They did. At one of Archer Shee's meetings a little old Irishwoman at the back of the hall asked if she could come to the front and ask a question. 'Certainly, Madam,' he replied. So she came forward and stood just below the platform and, looking up at him, asked: 'Do you recognise me?' 'Yes,' he said, 'I have certainly seen you before. Where have we met?' 'Ah,' she said, 'I was in the second row of the women and children when you ordered the troops to fire on the crowd in the streets of Dublin in 1917.' That broke up the meeting, and no doubt went the rounds, but I was told afterwards that that little old woman had never been out of Peckham in her life.

"On the eve of the poll the Tories were distributing a last-minute leaflet setting out my four previous defeats. Boys were taking supplies from the Tory Central Committee Room to push them through people's doors. But the boys didn't understand what it was all about, and I organised a party to intercept these supplies and persuade the boys to hand over the leaflets, which we then destroyed. This was pretty successful, and I took some part in it myself.

"It was a rather crude election. The Liberal candidate had no window cards. So I said, and our local speakers picked it up and repeated it, that no woman in Peckham thought him good-looking enough to put in her window. This started people laughing at the Liberals. And I tried, with some success, to get them laughing at the Tories too over the legend of Bilinski, who had been quoted in Archer Shee's election address as having made some discouraging observations in Moscow about the effect of the Russian Trade Agreement on employment in Britain. But I was officially informed by Paddy Coates, Secretary of the Anglo-Russian Parliamentary Committee, that no such person existed, and I made the most of this. Bilinski had several days start over Zinoviev in Peckham. Later, at all my meetings when the Zinoviev letter[1] was mentioned, and often before it was mentioned, I used to ask, 'Anyone seen Bilinski tonight?' or 'How's Archer Shee's friend Bilinski getting on?' And the laughs go round very quickly in a small area, densely populated with quick-witted Cockneys, and with many people attending a series of meetings and wanting the same jokes repeated, and passing them on, in their work places and in the pubs.

"Towards the end we have a sense of coming victory. A packed-out meeting at the Hippodrome on the last Sunday afternoon, October 26th, at which Laski makes a great impression, and a wonderful women's meeting, addressed by Ruth and me, in the Central Hall.

"Polling on October 29th and counting the same night in Wilson's Grammar School. It is soon clear that Emery, the Liberal, is well out of it. Shee and I pass and repass. When we are nearly through, he is 700 ahead and I have resigned myself to my fifth defeat. But there is a great heap of my votes on a slow-counting table. I come up, pass and go ahead, and finish 945 in front. Ruth and I mount the platform and prepare to take the cheers. Two of my young men from the L.S.E., who have canvassed and dug out like Trojans, and whom I have got into the count, are radiant and wildly excited. Then Shee, pale with anger, demands a recount. 'It is a matter of national importance to the Conservative Party,' he says. In this recount one vote of mine is found among his, and the final figures are:

---

[1] A letter supposed to have been written by Zinoviev, the Secretary of the Communist International, to the Secretary of the British Communist Party, urging British Communists to undertake subversive activities in the Army and elsewhere. Its authenticity was disputed. It was published in the middle of the election campaign.

DALTON · 13,361
ARCHER SHEE 12,414
EMERY 3,194
Labour majority over Conservative 947

"Labour gain!

"I move the vote of thanks, and tell the staff: 'You have had a long innings, a very long innings, and you have played the slow bowling very well.' Shee does not shake hands, or congratulate me, but is heard saying: 'I hear there are three Conservative gains in Salford.' Crowds waiting outside, singing, cheering, whirling rattles. Ruth and I make our way through them, after a short speech, and walk to Camberwell Green. Then fall into a taxi and drive home. It is 3 a.m. on October 30th. A strange sensation, this victory at last, while others are falling at the touch of the Zinoviev letter! The beginning of a new chapter in my life. . . ." I was 37 years old.

The results of the election were: 160 Tory net gains, 42 Labour net losses and 118 Liberal net losses. The Tories had a majority of over 200 and the Liberals were down to 40. Labour lost 47 seats and won five, four from the Tories and one from the Liberals. I was one of the four. A year before I had lost, swimming with the tide. Now I had won, swimming against the tide.

CHAPTER VIII

M.P. FOR PECKHAM

IN the first three years of my first Parliament I kept no
regular diary, and fewer notes of my doings and thoughts
—except for trips abroad, of which I speak later—than at
any time since the war, or since the end of 1927 when I took
to diarying again. I was fascinated and absorbed by my new
life. I spent much time in the Chamber and too much, as it
turned out, in my constituency. I determined, at the start, to
get to know all Labour M.P.s personally by the end of my first
session. I did not take any particular trouble to get to know
Tories or Liberals. Socially, at Westminster, I was a strong
Party man.

I became good friends with many Labour M.P.s whom I had
not known before, particularly among the miners, and with
Scott Lindsay, the very capable and cheerful Secretary of the
Parliamentary Labour Party. Vernon Hartshorn and I found
that we were well matched at chess—though not at a very high
level—and played many games together during all-night sittings.

In addition to my work in Parliament and in my constituency,
I was still teaching, part-time, at the School of Economics.
I was also making many political speeches in the country,
particularly at weekends, and doing a certain amount of
writing, both journalism and, in the later stages of this Parliament, a book on international affairs. So I was pretty fully
occupied.

I often wrote in the *New Leader*, the I.L.P. weekly, then
brilliantly edited by Brailsford, from whom I learned much
both as to style and substance. In January, 1925, I thus ended
an article entitled *First Impressions of Parliament; the Devil and
the Labour Members.*

"Parliament is a very comfortable place. The historic dignity
of its procedure and its precincts is very soothing. The sense of
unreality in debates, where speeches turn no votes, is enervat-
ing. The physical atmosphere of the House itself, through

156

which no fresh wind ever blows, seems designed to subdue the will and banish discontent. It is very easy to become a Lotus-Eater in a place where

> *No forked lightnings flit,*
> *And no thunders roll in it.*
> *Through the land a river flows,*
> *With a sleepy sound it goes;*
> *Such a drowsy noise, in sooth,*
> *Those who will not listen, hear not,*
> *But if one is wakeful, fear not—*
> *It shall lull him to repose.*

"Why kick against the pricks? Parliamentary tactics make a pleasant game from day to day. Asking Ministers a few questions, scoring a few points in debate, voting in a few divisions, attending a few committees—what more need one do? And 'the Devil, with sad and sober sense on his grey face, tells the rulers of the world that the misery which disfigures the life of great societies is beyond the reach of human remedy'. The Devil takes special pains to make himself agreeable to Labour members. He hopes, at any rate, to persuade some of them that he is not such a bad fellow as he is painted; and that the Labour Party, as he has always contended, when faced with responsibility and put in possession of all the facts, can be just as 'statesmanlike' as Tories and Liberals.

"It is well to face boldly, at the outset, the danger of this Parliamentary creeping paralysis. For, if enough of us face it together, we can certainly defeat it. We can keep alive, particularly in the comradeship of the back benches, our idealism, our Socialist faith and our fighting spirit. We can thus make it easier for the Front Bench to shake off the dust of office and to give a strong lead. We can make the House of Commons a sounding-board for words of hope that shall reach that greater audience outside, which stands waiting in the twilight. We can make this Parliament an interlude between the First Labour Government, which lived from day to day on the sufferance of its opponents, and the Second, which must live by a majority of its own. We shall not waste these oncoming Parliamentary years, if we spend them preparing the way for that majority, till the lobbies resound to its tread and the Chamber to its cheers."

I hope that sensations such as these will ever linger among Socialists in opposition, and among Socialists in office the sensation that democratic power is in their hands, and that they must use it powerfully while there is yet time.

My maiden speech in the House on February 16th, 1925, was on the Government's White Paper in favour of the "Safe-guarding of Industries" by tariffs. I said that this policy would not cure unemployment and would do more harm than good. On the other hand, I declared that "Free Trade is to me not a policy at all; it is a mere absence of policy"; and the controversy between Free Trade and Protection only "the mildewed straw of the last century". Arthur Ponsonby in the *New Leader* made this kindly comment on my speech: "There was no sense of strain. He spoke with ease and restraint, he was brief and to the point, he was clear, and adorned his argument with good Socialist doctrine. He gave the House the impression that he could do a great deal more if he wanted to." Others, whose judgment I valued, were also complimentary.

At a meeting of the Parliamentary Labour Party in my first session I spoke in favour of Imperial Preference. Snowden wanted us to vote against all the Government's proposals to charge lower duties on Empire than on foreign imports. I argued the other way, both on principle and also because, I said, such preferential reductions would help to reduce the cost of living—cheaper tobacco and cheaper wines and spirits from the Empire. We were in a minority, but it was decided to allow a free vote in the House. Some thirty of us, led by Jimmy Thomas, voted with the Tories in favour of preference; the rest, led by Snowden, voted with the Liberals against.

Snowden was not pleased with me over this. Nor with my attitude over two other questions which came up early in this Parliament. On both it was suspected that he had already committed himself privately while Chancellor of the Ex-chequer, and that the Tories were only doing what he would have tried to do. The first was Churchill's return to the gold standard at pre-war parity. I argued against this in the Finance Committee of the Parliamentary Party, urging that it was premature and would be deflationary, and that we should wait and see how things went in the next year or two before returning to gold at *any* parity. The second was Neville

Chamberlain's Bill for extending the contributory system of national insurance to cover widows' and orphans' pensions, now provided for the first time, and other improved benefits. I argued that the contributions, from employer and employed, should not be raised, but that the whole of this increased cost should fall on general taxation. I had prepared a memorandum, later published as an article in the *Labour Magazine* for July, 1925, showing that, if Churchill had not reduced the super-tax and standard rate of income tax in his recent Budget, he would have had enough revenue to provide widows' and orphans' pensions *at double the rates proposed by the Government* and the other improvements also, without any increase in contributions. These estimates of mine were quoted with approval by John Wheatley in a speech in the House. This helped my budding reputation as a "financial expert", though it irritated Snowden.

It was not very difficult in those days—it is harder now—to acquire a reputation in the House as a "financial expert". I got quite a long way by rising, in the middle of some pundit's speech, and saying: "The right honourable gentleman means Treasury *Bonds*, I think, not Treasury *Bills*." And the speaker confessed that he did.

I spoke mainly, in my first Parliament, on financial questions and took some part in Budget and Finance Bill debates. And in my first session I made an Empire-cum-Socialism speech, which pleased our Party. I said I would take the Tories for an Empire tour and see how much Socialism we could find. And then I catalogued it, Dominion by Dominion—and India and the Colonies as well—State Banks, State Railways, State Hydro-Electric Power, State-owned land, and so on. I think that one reason why our people liked my speeches was because I treated the Tories, and Liberals too, with a slightly contemptuous self-confidence.

I made another speech which angered the other side, when British troops were being sent to China to protect British-owned factories and offices in Hong-Kong and Shanghai. I asked why we should not recruit some "Pals' battalions" of shareholders instead—this was a term used in the voluntary recruiting drive in the war and was still familiar. I also asked why British capitalists preferred to invest their money in a troublesome place like China, rather than "under the Union Jack" in Australia or New Zealand. I supposed it was because Trade Unions were stronger and wages higher in the Anzac countries.

At the end of my first session, just before Christmas, 1925, I was, to my great surprise, elected to the Executive of the Parliamentary Labour Party. There was a vague desire for new blood, and Arthur Ponsonby had asked me whether he might propose me. Treating it as a joke, I agreed. I tied with my proposer for the last place. It was decided that Scott Lindsay should draw lots between us, and I won. Ponsonby told me afterwards that he had voted for me, but not for himself. I told him that, being pretty sure most other candidates *would* vote for themselves, I had voted both for myself and for him!

This success meant that I now had to sit on the Front Bench. And there, through subsequent sessions and Parliaments, I stuck. This cramped my style and limited my opportunities. I am sorry I didn't have a longer back-bench life. It would have been more fun.

But I reacted against respectability by getting myself suspended on April 15th, 1926. Neville Chamberlain had introduced an Economy Bill, penalising ex-Servicemen and a number of those entitled to benefits under National Insurance. It was a mean little Bill and, admirably led by Jimmy Thomas, we fought it obstructively. We kept the House up all night and divided whenever we could. Then, in the small hours, we started to go slow in the division lobbies. We dragged our feet and took our time. Then thirteen of us, having passed the clerks, who marked our names on the register as having voted, sat down in a circle on the floor, and refused to pass the tellers, who counted the number of those voting at the exit of the lobby. The division, therefore, could not be completed. The tellers continued standing at the door, and we continued sitting on the floor. This impasse lasted for three-quarters of an hour. Various members looked in on us through the glass door of the lobby. We exchanged pleasantries, and sang, to the tune of "John Brown's Body", "The Clerk will now proceed to read the Orders of the Day." Jimmy Thomas urged us, vainly, not to be such bloody fools. The Sergeant-at-Arms took a note of our names.

The next thing we knew was a rush of Tories coming through

WITH JOE COMPTON, M.P., 1927

the lobby behind us, and picking their way through our recumbent and obstructive forms. "What are you doing?" we asked. "Voting for your suspension," they replied. Mr. Speaker Whitley had been roused from sleep, since the House, being in Committee, was presided over by the Chairman or Deputy Chairman of Committees, but a suspension can only be moved with the Speaker in the Chair. The Chairman having reported our names to the Speaker, Mr. Chamberlain now moved that we all be suspended for six days from the service of the House. But now the impasse was repeated. A number of our friends, voting in the other lobby against our suspension, passed the clerks, but then sat down upon the floor, refusing to pass the tellers. The Speaker, however, after waiting another fifteen minutes, ruled that a reasonable time had now elapsed since the division was called, and summoned the tellers to the Table to announce the numbers of those who had actually passed through. The Division which we obstructed was called just after 5.30 a.m. The Division suspending us was concluded just after 7 a.m.

Thus did we draw attention, through the Press, to the injustices of the Economy Bill and to our own fighting spirit. The morning placards and the headlines blared: "Thirteen Socialists suspended. Amazing scenes."

My twelve associates in this demonstration included George Lansbury, John Wheatley, Jack Lawson and Joe Compton. I am the only one of the thirteen who is still alive and in the House of Commons.[1]

We all went down to East Ham, where there was a by-election on. It had been a Tory seat. But we asked the electors to give us Susan Lawrence and a Labour gain. And they did.

On our return to the House after our suspension we marched in in single file, led by George Lansbury, and were loudly cheered from the Labour benches.

Very soon after this, at midnight on May 3rd, 1926, came the General Strike. This, as Keynes put it, was one of "the consequences of Mr. Churchill" and his return to gold the

[1] A deliberate hold-up, not quite so long, and quite unknown to the Press, was, I am told, once perpetrated by a Noble Lord, then a member of the House of Commons, in opposition to some Liberal Bill. He retired into the lavatory in the lobby and there remained for half an hour. His Chief Whip told the tellers he was indisposed and so held them at their stations.

previous year at pre-war parity. The pound being thus "up-
valued", all our exports, sold at given prices in foreign currencies, brought us fewer pounds. Either, therefore, we must
put up our prices in foreign currencies, which meant that we
sold less and there was more unemployment in the export
trades, or we must reduce our costs, which meant wage cuts
and worsened conditions in the export trades. There would,
of course, have to be "some readjustments", Mr. Montagu
Norman had warned Mr. Churchill when advising the return
to pre-war parity. But neither of them seemed to think that
this would lead to any serious difficulty.

The first "readjustment" proposed was at the expense of
the miners. The coal-owners demanded a reduction in wages
and a lengthening of hours. The miners refused. "Not a penny
off the pay, not a minute on the day," cried Arthur Cook. So
the owners closed the pits and locked the men out. The Government refused to intervene unless the miners agreed that there
must be some reduction in wages. So a special Conference of
Trade Union Executives decided to bring their members out
on strike in support of the miners. All forms of transport,
printing (including all newspapers), iron and steel and allied
industries, gas and electricity for power purposes, and all building, other than housing and hospital work, were to stop.
Ernest Bevin declared that "even if every penny goes, and
every asset is swallowed up, history will write that it was a
magnificent generation that was prepared to do this rather
than see the miners driven down like slaves. I rely, in the name
of the General Council, on every man and woman to fight
for the soul of Labour and the salvation of the miners."

The strike lasted eight days. On May 12th it was announced
that "in order to resume negotiations, the General Council
decided to terminate the General Strike today". Sir Herbert
Samuel had made new proposals which seemed to the General
Council to offer a way out. But the miners fought on alone,
feeling themselves deserted, until November, by which time
a series of district agreements had been forced upon them,
reducing wages and reintroducing the eight-hour day.

It was, I think, inevitable that the experiment of the General
Strike should be tried. Political action seemed to have failed.
Trade Unionists felt that the first Labour Government had

not done much for them and had been put out of office by a dirty trick. Trade Union leaders who were not in Parliament were inclined to take a poor view of the politicians. And the standards of life of all workers would be in peril if the miners, the first to be attacked, went down. There was, therefore, a strong emotional swing from political to industrial action. After the General Strike there was a strong swing the other way.

But what was most amazing was the absence of bloodshed, or even serious violence and, indeed, the general good temper shown during the strike. Within the Labour Movement there was a wonderful spirit of comradeship and solidarity and, while the strike lasted, of exhilaration. Afterwards there was an emotional reaction.

A typical incident, unintelligible to most foreigners, was a football match at Plymouth between the strikers and the police. The strikers beat the police by three goals to one.

At Peckham our Agent and two other men were arrested for distributing a locally produced news bulletin. I went round to the Police Station, spoke to the Superintendent, whom I knew well, and got them released. Our Constituency Labour Party took the Peckham Winter Gardens, including a large boxing-ring, for a week. We used it as a Labour Club for Peckham strikers and their families, and provided simple meals and sing-songs and other amusements. We wanted to keep our people off the streets, thus reducing risks of trouble with the troops or the police, and to keep up their morale. I brought down Joe Batey, one of the Durham miners' M.P.s, and other speakers to address them.

Ruth and I both spent a good deal of time there. One night, when I was speaking, a man at the back called out that they wanted more ginger. I asked him: "Do you live in Peckham?" He didn't answer. I said: "You've come to the wrong shop. In this constituency the Member of Parliament has been suspended and the Agent has been arrested. Plenty of ginger here!"

King George V, as Harold Nicolson has now revealed, played an important part at this time in discouraging Tory Ministers from provocative acts and announcements. Mr. Churchill, taking a holiday from the Treasury, had become editor of the

British Gazette, issued daily on behalf of the Government. "The King", says Mr. Nicolson, "caused an immediate protest to be addressed to the War Office", following a provocative announcement in the *Gazette* about the possible use of troops. He also dissuaded the Cabinet from introducing, as they had decided to do, a Bill prohibiting the use of Trade Union funds for the benefit of the strikers. Nor did he share the Government's objection to Russian Trade Unions contributing to the British miners' relief fund. It will be recalled that the Prince of Wales, later King Edward VIII, also ruffled some Tory feathers by himself contributing to this fund.

The impact of the General Strike upon many younger people was profound. Thus my friend Hugh Gaitskell, at that time an Oxford undergraduate who had hitherto taken no particular interest in politics, immediately joined the Labour Party and drove a car for the T.U.C. In this struggle, so sharply and so clearly joined, between "the masters" and "the men", it was impossible for any generous spirit to be emotionally on the side of "the masters".

At the Labour Party Annual Conference at Margate in October, 1926, I was elected to the National Executive in the Constituency Party Section. It was the first time I had stood, and I had never made a speech at an Annual Conference. My election, I think, was partly a protest vote against the Old Gang. I was not re-elected in 1927, but I came back to the National Executive in 1928 and steadily held my seat for the next twenty-four years. Then, having had a very good innings, I was defeated in 1952 and immediately announced that I should not stand again.

Until 1936, when, during my year as Chairman and largely owing to my influence, the method of voting was changed, the whole National Executive, in all its Sections, was elected by the whole Conference. The elections in the Constituency Party Section were, therefore, largely determined before 1936 by the block votes of the big Trade Unions. After 1936 Trade Unions ceased to vote in the Constituency Party Section. The miners voted for me in 1926, and again in 1927 when I was beaten, and again each year until 1936. I shall always cherish the memory of this faithful support, and I hope I have been able to do something to repay it.

In December I was re-elected to the Parliamentary Executive, going up from twelfth to third place. The order of voting was Snowden, Graham, myself, Johnston, Thomas, Lees-Smith, Smillie, Trevelyan, Lansbury, Webb, Adamson and Henderson. MacDonald and Clynes, as Chairman and Deputy Chairman, and Tom Kennedy as the new Chief Whip, were ex-officio members. Henderson had previously sat on the Executive as Chief Whip, a post which he had resumed for the session after the 1924 election. On this occasion he had a surprisingly low vote, only three ahead of Wheatley, the highest unsuccessful candidate. (Next session, at the end of 1927, he moved up to second place, just behind Snowden.)

Each summer, during the 1924–9 Parliament, Ruth and I spent some weeks on the Continent. Partly for a holiday, partly to write undisturbed, partly on voyages of political observation. And though I let my diary lapse at home, I kept some sort of continuous record, even of trivialities, abroad. In 1923 we had been to Jugoslavia and Trieste and Fiume, and in 1924 to Sardinia and Sicily. In 1925 we went, via Provence and the Val d'Aosta, to Geneva to observe the Assembly of the League of Nations. In 1926, via Danzig, to Poland, where I found much that was well worth observing. In 1927 to Austria, chiefly in the Tyrol, where we climbed mountains and I finished my book *Toward the Peace of Nations*, which Ruth typed. She typed all my books, up to and including my Penguin, *Hitler's War*, published in 1940. In the summer of 1927 I carried her typewriter in a rucksack as high as Gurgl in the Tyrol. In 1928 we went via Bruges to Brussels for the Socialist International, where I was one of the British Labour Party delegation, and then to the Eastern Pyrenees, where we climbed and I finished a new and revised edition of my *Public Finance*.

In the next Parliament, in 1929 and again in 1930, I went back to Geneva for the League Assembly. But I was then a Minister and a member of the British delegation.

Of all these visits, my most vivid and abiding memories are of Poland. We spent six weeks there and covered much ground, both geographically and socially. We came through Danzig and Gdynia to Warsaw, went on to the Eastern Borderlands, stayed with one small and one large landowner—both had wonderful horses to ride, but no w.c.s, and the ruins from the war were not yet rebuilt—attended a peasant's wedding and drank their home-made spirit, with dire consequences, and rode through endless pine forests. Then to Vilna, full of Baroque churches by Italian architects, exotic so far north. Here I talked with Poles, including Socialists and Jews, and Lithuanians. Then back to Warsaw. Then via Cracow, very beautiful, to the Carpathians for a week, based on Zakopane. There we walked through magnificent forests (much better trees than in the Alps, since the heights are much lower), slept in mountain huts, climbed Swinica, the highest peak in Poland but quite easy, and followed up valleys past lovely little lakes deep in the woods—the best known is Morskie Oko, the Eye of the Sea. Then back to Cracow, where we were entertained by the University people, led by Kostanecki, the Rector, and his wife, whose son had been at the L.S.E; a distinguished and agreeable circle, rather like Oxford, high culture perhaps a little overdone, museums, libraries and lunch parties of Dons, and tombs of famous men in the Wawel. They took us to Koszcziusko's Mound and the State Salt Mines at Wieliczka, employing 800 men and dating back to the eleventh century. Here we saw wonderful chapels with a Byzantine suggestion, carved in salt by the workers in their spare time. In these they assemble for a service every day before starting work. Then to Lwow, moving again in University circles. There we met Twardowski, said to be the best philosopher in Poland, who studied ethics under Franz Brentano and knows the writings of Moore, Russell and Whitehead; *Principia Ethica* has been translated into Polish. Parnas, Professor of Chemistry, knew Cambridge well, and was a friend of E. J. Dent. I talked also with some Ukrainians. Then back to Warsaw for ten days. There we met many Socialist, Trade Union and peasant leaders—Daszynski, Zulawski, Rataj were the three who stood out—Polish Ministers, including Zaleski, the Foreign Minister, Polish Foreign Office officials, more Dons—Czyrzanowski, a little bearded economist, very like Cannan—some architects, musical and social Poles, Chopin's piano, the British Minister's wife—he was on leave—and the British Consul. I met some Ukrainian leaders, secretively in a suburb, who tried to make me drunk and asked whether, if they started an armed rising to free the Ukraine both from Polish and Russian oppression, a British Labour Government would send our Navy into the Black Sea to give them moral support; I said I would ask Mr. Ramsay MacDonald. Then we went for two days to a country house near Poznan, more riding, and back by train through Germany.

A pretty full six weeks! I came away aware for the first time of this most gifted and romantic nation, so brave, so gay, with so much good-looks and personal charm in both sexes. And such a history! "This Messiah among the Nations, this meteor of a country", as one of their own writers has said.

Polish cooking combined Latin art with Slav imagination. Sour cream and mushrooms—a wide range of edible fungi—constantly recurred. Mead and rye vodka were the best native drinks.

Politically there was neither Democracy nor Dictatorship, but a characteristically Polish half-way house. The strongest opponents of Pilsudski were the Right Wing Parties, against whom he had directed his coup. But the Jews and some of the Socialists still backed him. Social legislation was good on paper and said to be well enforced. The Ministers seemed, on the whole, young and able, but some reactionary militarists were influential and some minority problems, especially the Ukrainian, very prickly.

The story, told by their critics, that Poles always talked but never got things done, was disproved by the rapid building of the new port at Gdynia and by many other new developments.

It was this visit to Poland which finally determined me to try to rewrite the Foreign Policy of the Labour Party, with some change of emphasis. Many of the Party's established international "experts" were still stuck in old anti-French, pro-German postures. Pro-German and more than half Pacifist, an odd straddle! More sympathetic, some of them, to unwounded conscientious objectors than to wounded soldiers. They knew little in detail, or from direct study, of the League of Nations, or of the hopeful constructive work being done at Geneva, though we had some younger up-and-coming experts, such as Philip Noel-Baker and Will Arnold-Forster, to make good that gap in our knowledge.

As for Poland, she was picked up, like much else, in their

silly syllogism. "Everything that came out of the Allied victory
in the war, and the Treaty of Versailles, is bad. Poland came
out of all that. Therefore, Poland is bad." But few of these
"experts" had ever visited Poland or met typical Poles.

Lloyd George worked at Versailles against Poland and in
favour of Germany, on the issues in dispute between them,
notably on the question of the Silesian frontier. It would have
been far better to let Poland have East Prussia and the whole
of Upper Silesia at that time. This would have given her
greater economic and strategic strength and correspondingly
weakened Germany. Any consequent transfer of German
population would have been small compared with what took
place after the Second World War. The Poles would soon have
populated these new territories, and such accessions in the
west might have been made conditional on less ambitious
eastern frontiers, which would have meant less troublesome
minority problems.

Yet even Lloyd George could coin a memorable and sympathetic phrase when Polish troops, contrary to Allied wishes,
occupied Vilna. Poland, he said, "is staggering in the blinding
sunlight of her resurrection morning". She had lain in the
tomb, since the Crucifixion of the Third Partition, for more
than a hundred and twenty years.

I returned from Poland in September, 1926, believing that
the Poles had not been fairly judged, either by British public
opinion as a whole or by the British Labour Party. Compared
with the Germans, who bored on and on with their grievances,
the Poles were ineffective and amateur propagandists.[1]

I tried, therefore, in the years that followed, to correct some
false ideas.[2] But I could not know how close was to be my
future relationship with many Poles at critical hours in the life
of our two peoples; nor the fresh martyrdoms that awaited
Poland; nor that, in *our* fiercest test, the Air Battle of Britain,

---

[1] Lord D'Abernon in Vol. III of his *Diary* has a good saying. The German has
for the Pole "the contempt, ineradicable though unjustifiable, of the bass for the
tenor".

[2] Elsewhere I wrote: "I remember putting on paper in the Foreign Office in
1930 the argument, in opposition to the views held by others, that on grounds of
justice and in the light of all the facts there was no reason why we should back
German claims against Poland, and that, moreover, it could not be in British
interests to aggrandise at Poland's expense a Germany who had been, and might
soon again become, what Poland would never be, a grim menace to this country."
(*Hitler's War: Before and After*, p. 100.)

one German aircraft out of every seven brought down would be destroyed by Polish airmen flying in our skies. But all this belongs to a later chapter of my story.

I published my book *Towards the Peace of Nations* early in 1928. It was, on the whole, well received both inside and outside the Labour Party. Many of my political colleagues liked it, though I took a different line, and used a different tone, from that till then adopted by most of our speakers and writers on foreign affairs.

I defended the new map of Europe drawn at Versailles as being a great improvement on the pre-war map, more than halving the total of the "national minorities" west of the Russian frontiers. I combated the argument, at that time generally accepted in Labour circles, that the new frontiers should be "revised". I argued, on the contrary, that they should be left alone, but gradually rendered "invisible" by reducing tariffs and other trade restrictions and encouraging communications of all kinds, including the voluntary migration of members of "national minorities" who felt they would be happier with their own nationals on the other side of the new frontiers. While urging their fair treatment, I discouraged an excess of sympathy with the often highly organised complaints of the "national minorities", for, "if majorities are apt to be tyrannical, minorities are apt to be neurotic, to make mountains out of molehills, and to prefer the nourishment of a grievance to its remedy". There was also "the prejudice of conservatism" against the new map. "To many middle-aged people the Europe of 1914 was the real Europe, and the Europe of 1927 seems, by contrast, something artificial and unreal. They are disconcerted by the reappearance of Poland on the map, by the emergence of Czechoslovakia and Jugoslavia, uncouth and unfamiliar names, and by the shrinkage of the familiar outlines of Austria-Hungary. But those who experience such emotions are not even good conservatives. For the Europe of 1914 was only fifty years old, while an independent Poland had existed, before the partitions of the eighteenth century, for eight hundred years, and an independent Bohemia, before the Battle of the White Mountain in 1627, for more than seven hundred years."

I discussed at some length the League of Nations and its achievements and possibilities. I belaboured Sir Austen Chamberlain, our Foreign Secretary, with a mass of detailed accusations, and contended that the British Tory Government had "at every point obstructed the work and the growth of the League". I denounced them, most of all, for rejecting the Geneva Protocol of 1924. This instrument would have firmly linked, for all League members, Arbitration, Disarmament and Security. Any State which agreed to submit all its disputes with other States to arbitration (or other predetermined form of peaceful settlement) and which had carried out its obligations (under a Disarmament Convention to be hereafter drawn up) to reduce and limit its armaments, would be entitled to the full benefits of pooled security. This meant that, if such a State was threatened with aggression, defined as a refusal by another State to settle a dispute by peaceful means, all the other signatories of the Protocol would rally to its aid and would be prepared to "apply sanctions" to the aggressor, including, if need be, the sanction of combined military force. Arthur Henderson, then Home Secretary in the First Labour Government, with very shaky backing from some of his Cabinet colleagues, had been, with Herriot, the chief architect of the Protocol at Geneva. Had it gone through, it would have satisfied France and given a real inducement, such as never afterwards existed, to make an early success of the Disarmament negotiations. And it would have built a stronger League of Nations framework within which Germany could more safely have been accommodated later. There was keen and widespread support for the Protocol among members of the League. But Sir Austen Chamberlain could produce no better alternative than the Treaty of Locarno, a nine days' diplomatic wonder which led nowhere.

"Jealousy and vanity are the politician's chief temptations" —so I wrote in my diary just before Christmas, 1927, at the session's end, stirred to this opinion by observing MacDonald and Snowden, and by some good talks with Charles Trevelyan, best of political colleagues.

"But out at Le Trayas with Ruth, between the red rocks and the blue sea, I read the first volume of Sir Henry Wilson's life and diaries, and I find that soldiers are just as susceptible as politicians; also that H. W. kept a diary, even in the full rush of war. And this determines me for the future to do the same."

And so I did, after a fashion, but often very sketchily, and often with long gaps.

Before starting on 1928 I made some notes on 1927. "In the summer we were campaigning against the Government's Anti-Trade Union Bill, but making no headway. Very poor attendances at meetings. I spoke at one with five 'national speakers' on the platform and four people in the audience. Apathy and whipped-doggishness. Judging by by-elections, a Liberal revival is not quite a fantasy. I refused to become rattled, as some were, but was watchful for new signs. Uncle said 'for the first time since the last General Election I feel there is a check on'.

"Our Annual Conference at Blackpool in October was a good show, apart from my sideslip off the National Executive. But this was much less surprising than my sideslip *on* the year before. I was replaced this year by Mosley, following a well-timed attack by him on me in the *New Leader*.[1] The margin between us was narrow. In the Conference there seemed to be greater determination and unity. But in the autumn session I sensed great caution and anti-Leftism in the Parliamentary Party, chiming with the General Council's new inclination towards industrial peace and talks with employers. There is a distinct danger of courage evaporating.

"Programme Committee. Uncle has wanted a programme for next election for some time. He brought up a draft in the summer, the contents of which were not bad, but which was much too long and awfully dully written. This was turned down by the Parliamentary Executive, partly on contents, the Left objecting to certain omissions, and partly on style. The National Executive thought it best not to go on with this document, but to get a resolution from Blackpool authorising the preparation of a programme for the next election, assuming a Labour Government and a Parliament of normal length. This resolution was got at Blackpool, the programme to be submitted to the next Annual Conference or, if practicable, to a special conference if the election comes earlier. The new National Executive at its first meeting appointed a Programme Committee—J. R. M., Uncle, F. O. Roberts, Cramp, H. Morrison,

---

[1] On the use of the proceeds of a Capital Levy. He and I ran a lively correspondence in the *New Leader* on this. But his first shot was fired just before, and my first shot in reply just after, the vote at Blackpool.

C. T." (Charles Trevelyan), "George Lansbury, Ellen Wilkinson, Mosley. The last two were put on by Uncle in accordance with his regular practice of (1) encouraging the young and (2) 'crushing extremists' under a weight of official responsibility. On the whole, distinctly a good Committee.

"But it has had some severe rows already. C. T., G. L., E. W. and O. M." (Oswald Mosley) "sent in a joint signed document and gave the unwise appearance of being a Left Wing Cave. Then O. M., who often shows a surprising lack of judgment, rang up Middleton and asked for an advance copy of certain official drafts, because he 'wanted to talk them over with some other members before the next meeting of the full Committee'. G. L. very disgusted with him over this.

"Then a great row over drink! E. W. moved that 'there should be no reference to the drink question in the Programme'. I had urged her to do this. This was carried by 7 to 2, only Uncle and J. R. M. voting against. On this Uncle offered his resignation from the Committee, silly old ass, and the National Executive, at the end of a meeting when many had left, only asked him to take it back by 7 votes to 6! He told me this on one of our walks home from the House"—he had a flat in Artillery Mansions and I in Carlisle Place, near Victoria—"at the end of the session. I urged him to stay on, and said that we must recognise that the Party was very divided on drink policy, and that many of our members were much embarrassed about it. I thought the furthest we could go was to set up a Royal Commission on it, if we came in, as the Labour Government had promised to do in its election manifesto of 1924. He was not against this, but said that the Programme Committee hadn't even left him this loophole. But I suspect that he hadn't raised this at the Committee, only his damned old Local Option.

"His electoral sense on drink is very much at fault. He thinks of 'Temperance people' as an important electoral asset, which they aren't—particularly as compared with the great army of moderate drinkers—and also of a 'Temperance vote' which could be won by us from the Liberals—which it couldn't be, whatever we said about drink. He also declared that there was more drinking in the House among Labour M.P.s than ever before, which may be regrettably true, but wouldn't be altered

even if we adopted Local Option. C. T. and I had agreed, in a
conversation early in 1927, that Uncle would be the best successor to J. R. M. (whose health was then so bad that the
problem of succession seemed as if it might be imminent).
C. T. said truly that he is the type who has often made an
excellent Labour Premier in the Dominions. But his bad temper on Committees and his habit of 'dancing on everyone' is
an awful pity. I think C. T. is now a little shaken in his view.
But who else would be better?

"Snowden and the Surtax. This is a tiresome tale. At the
beginning of 1925 J. R. M. personally appointed a number of
small Committees to work out various branches of policy.
Most of these seem to have died out, but one showed great
vitality. This was a Committee on Finance, consisting originally of Willy Graham and Sydney Arnold. They were appointed without Snowden's knowledge and it is intelligible
that, on hearing of the existence and activities of this Committee for the first time considerably later, he should have been
piqued. The relations of J. R. M. and P. S. during the Labour
Government, as before it, had been very bad. Graham had the
thankless job of go-between. They were not often on private
speaking terms, and P. S. was on the point of resignation over
the London Agreement on the Dawes Plan. J. R. M. had
negotiated the finance of this himself, without a word to P. S.
(who after all was Chancellor of the Exchequer) until it was
all settled. P. S., who thought the agreement much too kind
to France and much too hard on Germany, in addition to
feeling that he had been personally slighted, had gone as far
as sending for the *Manchester Guardian* correspondent, to give
him a statement of his reasons for resignation. Then he was
dissuaded. His wife keeps on stoking up his hatred of J. R. M.
and it is rumoured that, if L. G. holds the balance in the next
Parliament, he will support a Labour Government on condition that J. R. M. is sacked, and replaced by P. S. as P.M.
This rumour was mentioned at one of our informal 'At Homes'
of the Parliamentary Executive last November. P. S. said
nothing. And then, after an interval of other talk, remarked
that he very seldom saw L. G. in Surrey"—they were near
neighbours—"and that the last time was some months ago
when he had been up to see a private cinema show at L. G.'s.

But no direct denial! It was very clear, during this talk, that P. S. was all for the closest co-operation with the Liberals. 'I want a Parliament of achievement,' he said, and praised the quality of the Liberals in the last Parliament, and scouted the possibility of our winning more than 250 seats next time, and thought we should lose some in London. He and J. H. T., who, however, saw the practical difficulties more clearly, evidently favoured a Labour-Liberal Coalition Government. But I think no one else did. Tom Johnston said to me afterwards that many of our people's hair would stand on end if they could have heard that discussion.

"But back to the Surtax! Graham and Arnold co-opted Lees-Smith, Pethick Lawrence, Gillett and myself, making a committee of six, which had many meetings in Graham's room upstairs during 1926 and 1927. The earlier meetings were during the sittings of the Colwyn Committee on National Debt and Taxation, on which Lees-Smith sat. We evolved the idea of the Surtax as an alternative to the Capital Levy. I was alone on the Committee in wanting to retain C. L., the others thinking that 'the time has passed'. I could have played the part of Casabianca, both honestly and probably with some political profit on the Left. But I decided against this and in favour of co-operating to find an alternative. The Surtax, in the end, was the chief feature of the Minority Report of the Colwyn Committee signed by Lees-Smith, Barbara Wootton and two others. The Report came out just before the Budget of 1927. The question was whether the Party should back the Surtax officially. Our committee of six made a short memorandum, proposing that the next Labour Government should raise at least £100 million a year of new revenue, £85 million from a new Surtax[1] averaging about 2s. in the £ on unearned income, but graduated and exempting the first £500 a year, plus £15 millions from higher death duties and land values. Further, that about a quarter of this should go to increase the Sinking Fund, and the rest to taking taxes off food and increasing social expenditure. At this stage P. S. was called in. It was an awkward job explaining to him what our committee was! Graham funked this, but Arnold did it, shrilly and

[1] Additional to the Supertax—now called the Surtax—on all incomes, earned or unearned, over £2,000 a year.

brusquely. P. S., however, swallowed our plan whole, raising no criticism but saying, with a sour smile, that he was surprised at our moderation and thought such a programme could be realised 'in the course of two or three Budgets'. But I had thought of it as tying him or his successor down to do it in his *first* Budget!

"P. S. also took the chair for Lees-Smith, when the latter explained the Surtax, in relation to the Colwyn Report, to the Parliamentary Party. He showed no sign of disapproval. I think that, at this stage, he was so delighted to have got rid of C. L. that he was not greatly interested in the details of the substitute. So we went ahead. The dropping of C. L. wasn't seriously objected to by anyone, rather to my surprise. Later, however, disputes developed both as to the use of the proceeds of the Surtax and as to its yield."

These are not worth recalling now. But at one point Snowden became very isolated and seemed likely to fall out of active leadership, if not actually to resign from the Party. After the Surtax had been approved by the Blackpool Conference, which he did not attend, he wrote to a correspondent a letter which got into the Press, saying that he had had no part in drawing up the scheme and that, "of course", if the estimated yield was wrong, "the whole scheme fell to the ground". He also wrote to the *Manchester Guardian* attacking the Geneva Protocol, immediately after J. R. M. had written supporting it. But he had second thoughts about his general position, and the bright hope of losing him soon faded.

At the year's end I noted "Our leaders! What a crochety lot they are! J. R. M., Uncle and P. S. all, in their way, very difficult. C. T. and I agreed that it was the very devil. You have to focus them so carefully, and pick your words and approaches so gingerly, that time and energy both evaporate before you can get to the point. How good it is to be able to be quite straight and direct, as C. T. and I, for instance, can be with one another." As the years have passed since then, I have tried to retain that ease of the straight and direct approach—and some of my friends say I have succeeded.

"February 6th, 1928. Eve of Session dinner of Parliamentary Executive. Rather a cold affair. J. R. M. says that he has had a most pressing invitation to look in at the Londonderrys' official

(Tory) reception. Would our Party object more than the Tories if he went? Would any of us like to go with him? A silence. Then Uncle says to Adamson, the only miner present, 'Well, Willy, wouldn't you like to go and see the inside of a coal-owner's hovel?' Then more silence. J. R. M. looks vexed.

"I walk round with Uncle to our own Eve of Session reception. He thanks me for sending him my *Peace of Nations*. He is in the middle of reading it. I say I want him to go to the Foreign Office in the next Labour Government, and so do many others, including the best of the Geneva Secretariat. This is the first time I have put this to him. He tells me again of his difficulties with J. R. M. He says that it seems that, unless one feeds him with admiration and adulation, one can't hope ever to get very near him.

"March 12th. Endless talk at Parliamentary Executive on Zinoviev letter." We had demanded a Parliamentary debate on it, nearly four years after the event, but we had had a long and rather futile enquiry into it going on inside the Party. "J. R. M. has a confidential letter from one Dombrowski, from a Paris address, offering to put at our disposal some real information as to the authorship of the document. The English of the letter is so bad that we can't make out whether the suggestion is that the document is forged or authentic. But, in view of next Monday's debate, we decide to leave no channel unexplored and send off Tom Shaw to Paris by the next train to interview D. Quite like a film story!

"J. R. M. says that at the F.O. there were always two schools of thought on Russia, one, led by Eyre Crowe, which attached no importance to attempts to improve Anglo-Russian relations and regarded the Russians as dirt—this school triumphed as soon as Austen Chamberlain came in—the other hoping for and believing in the possibility of improved relations, and anxious to take up, firmly and in detail, particular breaches of the Trade Agreement", which prohibited interference in each other's internal affairs. "This second school represented J. R. M.'s own view. But Crowe was too easily convinced of the authenticity of the letter, because (1) the Secret Service Agent who gave it to the F.O. had received it from a man who 'had never been known to make a mistake' and (2) a police spy had reported a meeting of the C. P.

ARTHUR HENDERSON, 1926

Executive at Great King Street, where it had been stated, only a few days before, that an important letter from Zinoviev was on its way. So convinced was Crowe, that he had not troubled to ring up J. R. M., then campaigning in his constituency, to give him this information! The whole stage had been set, by previous events, for the bursting of the bombshell. The steady anti-Russian propaganda of the Tories, the mishandled Campbell Case, the Russian Treaty with its guaranteed loan. And the irrational effect of the mere publication of the Z. letter was bound to be tremendous, whatever J. R. M. or anyone else had said or done.

"March 15th. Executive discuss Shaw's mission to Paris. He says that Dombrowski, whose real name is Riczewski, is a tuberculous degenerate. He and a companion, better educated and with a stronger personality, are admittedly professional forgers. They claim to have forged the Z. letter themselves and sold it to a person whose photograph they have kept but whose name they don't know, who alleged that he was acting for the British Secret Service. They sold forged documents to many other governments, including Spain and Portugal. The agents of the governments said what particular document they wanted forged and it was done. These two are Russians. They worked for the White Russians who have now chucked them. They were denounced three years ago by the Soviet Ambassador in Paris, found guilty of forgery in the course of a private examination by the French police, and one of them is now officially 'en fuite'. In fact, the police know that he has simply changed his name from R. to D. and is still in Paris. This pair offered Shaw 'an exact copy of the forged Z. letter, including the signatures, and a dossier showing how the business was handled by them'. The price of this would be £20. Shaw had already paid them several hundred francs! At a meeting this morning of J. R. M., J. H. T. and Maxton—the speakers in Monday's debate—with Shaw and Ponsonby, it was agreed that Shaw ought to go back to Paris and pay £20 for this dossier. But J. H. T. has since had second thoughts. What if these rascals are double-crossing us, and the Government here know what is happening, and we are challenged, during the debate, to deny that we have just sent an ex-Cabinet Minister to Paris to pay £20 to bribe two White Russian spies? He moves that we postpone further action till after Monday's debate. I second, supported by C. T., Tom Johnston and Webb. Snowden, Lansbury, Shaw and one other against. Carried by 5 to 4. Uncle in the Chair. J. R. M. away. J. H. T.'s instinct is certainly right. And, apart from all else, how convenient for the Tories to be able to sidetrack the whole debate from the leak to the *Daily Mail*, back to the authenticity of the letter!

"March 16th–18th. Five meetings, two in the Frome Division, one at Neath and two in the Aberdare Division. A specially warm greeting at Neath. But it is a horrible business coming down to speak in poverty-stricken mining areas like Mountain Ash. One feels that one has no real message with an immediate meaning, and that it's almost indecent to try to make them laugh!

"March 19th. Z. debate rather a fizzle. But Baldwin, in the course of his speech, said that he understood we were going to produce an affidavit by the real forgers of the Z. letter. At this point Uncle nudged me on the bench and winked. Weren't we wise to stop Tom Shaw before he had committed us too far!

"March 23rd. After a public meeting at St. Pancras, go round to C. T.'s 'to celebrate the Thirtieth Year of the Hunt, 1898–1928'.[1] A crowd well spaced across the years, including Geoffrey Young, whom I last saw eleven years ago in a garden at Gorizia, the week before he lost his leg on the Bainsizza plateau. Tonight, in his beautiful voice, he recites a new Hunt Poem. And then much singing.

"April 19th. Rajchman, Pole from Geneva, fears that a British Labour Government would be heavily on the German side in controversies with Poland. He wants J. R. M. to visit Warsaw. Claims that *he* warned J. R. M. against the beautiful Polish lady, who was sent by the British Intelligence to spy on him during the war. I had said that this lady, of whom J. R. M. often talks, typified modern Poland to him.

"May 1st. The spring is wonderful this year. Everyone in a good mood. J. R. M., for once, looks me between the eyes and seems interested in what I say. P. S. too is full of smiles. Probably we are all less tired, and that is all there is to it.

[1] This was the Lake Hunt, founded by the Trevelyans and the Youngs. I went to it several times, both before and after the First War. Each day four of our party were hares, the rest hounds. We hunted within a defined area in the Lake District.

"May 9th. Meet to decide our attitude to Government's Currency and Bank Notes Bill", transferring control from Treasury to Bank of England. "We get P. S. to agree to a motion of rejection, pending 'an investigation into the constitution, powers and policy of the Bank of England'. This will put everything in order which any of our people may want to say about the Bank.

"May 14th. Currency Bill Second Reading. Snowden does quite well, except that he doesn't understand that 'the fiduciary issue' means the issue *not covered by gold*! But our great essay in adult education is showing some progress. I make a short and rather bored speech late in the evening. Today at our E.C. P. S. was in doubt whether to divide on our amendment! Fortunately I was able to push him into a division.

"June 5th. Wind up on Second Reading of Finance Bill. Not very interesting. I hate speaking in the House at present. Everything is so dull, including our own people.

"July 20th. To Liphook to spend the night with the Webbs and walk next morning. They are getting old gently but surely, she the faster of the two and the more self-consciously. We talk, rather flatly, about people and, rather old-fashionedly, about unemployment and poor law. We agree, whatever else we may think about him, that Mosley is 'very uninstructed'. Webb says J. R. M.'s snobbery is terrible, but he is the only leader, not least because of his hold in the country among the simpler people who incline our way. Graham Wallas was wrong when he said that one of the secrets of the working of the British Constitution was that Numbers 10 and 11 Downing Street intercommunicated, so that the two leading members of the Government were always in touch. When J. R. M. was at No. 10 he hardly ever saw Clynes, who was at No. 11, except in the House and at Cabinets, and Mrs. Clynes was never once asked inside No. 10." Someone else told me later that J. R. M. had had the intercommunicating door locked and had taken away the key. "When J. R. M. and" his daughter "Ishbel had the Duchess of York to tea, no wives of Cabinet Ministers were invited, though Mrs. Trevelyan went, thinking that it must have been a mistake that she had received no invitation. No Cabinet colleagues ever spent a weekend at Chequers, though the Londonderrys did at least once. The lack of touch was so bad that, after a while, it was agreed that Clynes, Thomas, Snowden, Henderson and Webb should lunch once a week at No. 10. But Ishbel and the Dutch housekeeper were always there too, so that no intimate political conversation was ever possible.

"The Webbs are not enthusiastic about C. T. They once went round the world with him. He was aggressive and used to shout people down in argument. Webb said he had never really grown up, though he had mellowed a bit with age. None the less, he had often been rather assertive in Cabinet on foreign policy and other matters on which he had no special knowledge. I said that I admired his vigour and directness and the way he kept clear of personal quarrels within the Party. Webb said that, perhaps, this was calculated and that, if there was a heavy mortality among the leaders, he thought the Party might have to fall back on him. I said I didn't think he thought of this, or was ambitious for it.

"Mrs. Webb spoke well of Cole's work and influence at Oxford. He, too, she thought, had much improved. She quoted, half in malice and half in approval, his tribute to 'the Webbs who have the courage of their obsolescence'.

"July 24th. We are all re-elected on the Parliamentary Executive, though Webb only saves his seat by one vote. There was a feeling that he oughtn't to stand again, as he was retiring at the end of the Parliament. Uncle at the top instead of Snowden. A splendid change this! I am seventh. Mosley only misses the wooden spoon by one vote, twenty-third out of twenty-four candidates for twelve places.

"September 30th. To Annual Labour Party Conference at Birmingham, our last before the General Election. The Conference carries the election programme, and critics and opponents cut a very poor figure." This programme, entitled *Labour and the Nation*, was based on a first draft by Tawney, not improved, either in style or substance, by other hands.

"Uncle makes a good statement on family allowances. Barring a Trade Union veto,"—the Trade Unions were all being consulted on it—"it will be in the election manifesto. He says that a large majority of the Joint Committee" of the National Executive and the General Council of the T.U.C. "is in favour of the principle, and that he himself is in favour of it."

But we were counting our chickens too soon! Resistance to

family allowances in the Party, and particularly among some of the older Trade Union leaders, was obstinate and formidable. The latter feared that these allowances might lead to reduced wages—might deprive them of a useful argument in wage negotiations in terms of the cost of living of a man with a wife and several children, and might lessen the attractiveness of Trade Union membership. And Snowden hated the idea like hell. We didn't, in the end, get the Party fully committed to it till half-way through the next war, in conditions which I will describe later. But I was steadily and keenly in favour of it—on a non-contributory basis—and gave it a high priority among plans for redistributing income. And I am proud that I was the Labour Chancellor of the Exchequer who found the money for it in 1946, as from the earliest date when my friend Jim Griffiths could get his paying-out machine ready to start. I hope we shall carry it much further in the future.

At the Birmingham Conference I spoke in favour of that part of the programme which included the nationalisation of the Bank of England. I discounted vague fears of bankers' "sabotage", with which a determined Labour Government would be unable to deal. The banks, I said, didn't want a panic, which would cause a run on their reserves. "Bank chairmen don't stay on deck in heavy seas. In August 1914 it was only the strong hand of the State and the organised community that led the faint and tottering figures of the bank chairmen through the storm." I got a great ovation. Some said they liked the way I said it even better than what I said! I was re-elected to the National Executive, after a year's absence, just displacing my friend Jack Hayes, the ex-policeman and Labour Whip, by a short head. Mosley also was re-elected. I said to him, when I knew that he and I had two of the five places in the Constituency Party Section: "How reassuring to find that this little world is large enough to hold us both!" He replied: "Yes, rather a surprise, isn't it?"

"New National Executive appointed a Committee to draft the election manifesto, consisting of J. R. M., Uncle, Morrison, Susan Lawrence, myself, Cramp, Dennison and Mosley. This will be a job!

"December 4th. Uncle in an expansive mood tonight over coffee with Will Arnold-Forster and myself. We spoke of the

Geneva Protocol of 1924. He said there were no clear principles laid down by the Cabinet before he and Parmoor went to the League Assembly. They just had to do their best. The Commission on the Protocol finished its job at 1 a.m. Uncle was awakened, soon after he had gone to bed, by a visit from an Admiral. He was very sleepy. The talk went somewhat like this:

ADMIRAL. I am Admiral X.

UNCLE. Are you?

A. The Admiralty are very much alarmed at the reports in the Press about what you and your colleagues have been doing here.

U. Are they?

A. I have brought with me a memorandum suggesting various changes in the draft of the Protocol.

U. You are too late. We finished our work at 1 o'clock this morning.

A. But you could have the Commission called together again.

U. You don't know much about international conferences if you think that a Commission like this can be recalled after its work is finished. You are too late, I tell you. You should have come here earlier if you had anything important to say to me.

[Exit Admiral.]

"December 5th. Parliamentary Executive confronts the problem of what a Labour Government should put in its first King's Speech, and do in its first session. Snowden, Webb, Shaw and Graham to draft a plan, with special reference to unemployment. Snowden thinks the repeal of the Betting Tax would be very popular! I say afterwards to C. T. that it will be a poor starveling of a policy that this Big Four of the Right will produce. He and I and G. L. and T. J." (Tom Johnston) "must act together to stiffen it.

"February 13th, 1929. First Parliamentary Executive meeting to consider the draft programme for the first session of a Labour Government. Uncle, G. L. and T. J. all absent, ill. C. T. and I the only two stalwarts present. Rather tiresome this chancy business, with people being sick! C. T. and I had fed together beforehand and agreed to praise the draft in general, but to ask for something stiffer on the mines. J. R. M. goes round the circle and comes to me fourth. I say I am not satisfied at

Nationalisation of the Mines not being in. C. T. backs me up. And then old Adamson, the only miner on the E.C., says that he no doubt takes even more interest in this question than either of us and that he quite approves of the programme as it stands. Full of suspicion and resentment that we should even mention mines. If this sort of carry-on were known outside, what a row there'd be!

"February 14th. Further meeting of Parliamentary Executive. Uncle, still ill, had seen J. R. M. and persuaded him that it was necessary to have consultations before the election with the miners and the T.U.C. This now agreed, and solves many difficulties." So I thought at the time. The consultations led to a reasonably satisfactory programme being drawn up, including raising the school age, earlier retirement pensions, big development schemes and mines nationalisation, if we had a majority for it. But the Second Labour Government, taking office less than four months later, ran away from this programme from the first day.

"March 13th. The National Executive's Election Manifesto Committee met in J. R. M.'s room. A thin meeting. Only Uncle, H. Morrison (who is not in the House), Mosley and myself, in addition to J. R. M. In attendance Greenwood, Will Henderson, Middleton and Tawney. The latter had been brought along by Uncle, who wanted him to draft the Manifesto, as he had already drafted *Labour and the Nation*. Tawney, wanting to know what to put in the draft, pressed J. R. M. for figures for increased unemployment benefit, larger pensions at an earlier age, etc. J. R .M. very sticky. Doesn't want to be 'flashy' or 'attractive'. 'That', said Tawney, 'is your Puritan upbringing.' Tawney is cheerful and irreverent. But my underlying sense is one of intense annoyance. We are letting L. G. and Mond-Turner and the rest simply march past us. We are led by timid, nerveless old men."

These were the days of *We Can Conquer Unemployment* and *Can Lloyd George do it?*, with Keynes and Hubert Henderson expounding on behalf of the Liberals a lucid positive Employment Policy. Most of our elderly leaders weren't *against* such a policy. But they missed most of the points and put it all so dully. Colin Clark was alive to all these hopeful possibilities, but few others in our Party were.

"At the Parliamentary Executive this afternoon J. R. M. asks that Snowden and Thomas should join the Election Manifesto Committee. This is agreed to. Then he says that he was 'amazed' to see Tawney at this morning's meeting, and 'disturbed' at some of the suggestions made. P. S. and J. H. T. both sniffing and asking 'Who is Tawney?' " My recollection is that, after putting in a draft, Tawney got fed up with some of them and chucked it!

"April 10th. Election Manifesto Committee. Snowden boggling at maintenance allowances, increased pensions, etc. But fair progress made.

"Living Wage Committee, joint between National Executive and T.U.C., met this afternoon on Family Allowances. (I had been a witness before them, but was not a member.) The majority by 8 to 3 had decided in favour of the principle, M. Bondfield, Citrine and Elvin dissenting. But the Unions, who had been circularised, had returned halting and uncertain replies, so that now nothing can be done. This great redistribution must come in the Second Wave! How many years hence? Some of our people are positively terrified of anything that would either win votes or do good!"

The Election Manifesto of 1929, in retrospect, looks unexciting. It was, of course, mainly a boil-down of *Labour and the Nation*. There was no specific nationalisation in it, except of the coal mines, and then only if we had a majority. There was no mention of the Bank of England. There was to be "reorganisation of railways and transport". But there was a long list of useful measures, including a number dealing with "national development" which, if we had really pushed them through during the next two years, as well as taking other action required by events we could not then foresee, would have bettered history.

In July, 1928, I decided, and publicly announced, that I would not stand again for Peckham at the next General Election. I had spent too much time in the constituency and had unwisely allowed myself to become too much involved in the running of the Party organisation. Soon after my election I had been pressed by my leading supporters to become Chairman of the Constituency Labour Party. I had agreed to this, thinking it would be not much more than a nominal title. Then, when personal differences and animosities developed in the Party, both sides begged me to come and take the Chair at meetings of the General Management Committee. This, they said, would bring both sides together. I again agreed, but the experiment was not successful. The differences within the Party became worse. They were wholly conflicts of personalities and not of politics. But, after having vainly tried to compose them, at much cost in time and nervous energy, and having made various practical suggestions, which were not adopted, I decided, after a further vain effort had been made by Labour Party Headquarters to improve the situation, to bring my official relationship with the constituency to an end.

Ruth had been elected to the London County Council for Peckham in March 1925. This was the first time we had won the County Council seats for Labour. She polled 6,398 and her Labour running mate 5,695. Then followed a Tory with 2,988 and a Progressive with 2,833. It was a magnificent victory. She had been re-elected in 1928, with a substantially increased vote. She did not stand again in 1931.

But she has served in all for eighteen years on the Council, including twelve years, in two separate innings, as an Alderman. She enjoyed most being Chairman of the Parks Committee, again in two separate innings. She retired in 1952, but she was responsible for the destruction of many sooty Victorian shrubberies, for the development of the Green Belt outside London and for the layout of new parks inside the County. She was also responsible for the redecorations and reopening of Kenwood House, after it had been transferred to the L.C.C. by the Iveagh Trustees.

CHAPTER IX

ABOUT PEOPLE

YOUNGER people sometimes tell me that 1929–31 now seems a very obscure period. What *were* MacDonald and Snowden worth? Why did people follow them? And what about some of the other leading figures in the Labour Party at that time?

I hope my narrative will help to answer these questions. But something may, I think, usefully be added here. MacDonald and Snowden both built up their position in the Labour Party, and primarily in the I.L.P., by public speaking all over the country, often to quite small audiences. General socialist propaganda, with more of eloquence and warmth than positive detail. They also wrote, MacDonald more than Snowden, a number of small books and many articles in socialist periodicals. But neither books nor articles were much read outside the still narrow, though ever-widening, circle of the converted. When they got to Parliament their national reputations grew, and when, in 1923, they became Ministers for the first time— MacDonald Prime Minister and Foreign Secretary and Snowden Chancellor of the Exchequer, neither having had any previous experience of office—their national and international reputations swelled still further with a loud blast of sudden fame. But, with both of them, it all began with public meetings. Nowadays there are other possible beginnings. Wireless, television, weekly columns in widely read newspapers, offer alternative approaches to notoriety.

But what manner of men were they? To supplement my own answers, which emerge gradually in the course of this book, I here draw on some most revealing descriptions by Raymond Postgate, from his admirable *Life of George Lansbury*, his father-in-law.

"If it is difficult to explain to a later generation the importance of Keir Hardie," he says, "it is doubly difficult to explain that of Ramsay MacDonald. It is difficult indeed to portray the man at all. He was to attain the highest office in the State, to head the first two Socialist Governments, to inspire extreme devotion and extreme contempt, to turn on his own party and drive it to the worst disaster it had known. A man (one would say) obviously of strongly defiant and possibly violent character, whether he be hated or admired. Yet this, most of all, he was not. His most contemptuous opponent, Winston Churchill, called him 'the boneless wonder'; he was not so much a boneless as a hollow man. The outside can easily be described: reasonably tall, slim, well-proportioned, with a noble head and handsome profile, a big and flowing moustache; early greying dark hair, with a big quiff at the front. The voice exceptionally fine and deep, resonant with a great variety of tone and sufficient of a Scots accent to give it charm. The manner all that could be required of courtesy and dignity. But the contents of the splendidly delivered speeches were very small—they amounted in earlier years to no more than generalities about the Socialist future and to involved warnings against rash actions; in later years they amounted to nothing at all; and some of his speeches then were incomprehensible in the literal sense of the word. . . . He had a political theory, or at least a political metaphor. Society to him was an organism; it could be described in biological terms, and its future could be predicted as assuredly as Darwin could trace the evolution of species. In his *Socialism and Society*, published in 1905, he elaborated this thesis. Society was moving at its own pace towards Socialism. It should be assisted on its way, of course; but the prodding which MacDonald was prepared to give it was of the gentlest kind." In the House of Commons, "what served him was his knowledge of Parliamentary technique and his admirable Parliamentary manner".[1]

"That queer, vain simulacrum of a statesman," said H. G. Wells; "The greatest snob on earth," said Winston Churchill. "*Ah!* my friends," I so often heard him say, and once to a deputation of clergy, "You are doing our work in your way and we are doing your work in our way." A lady friend of mine told me she had the most profound distrust of J. R. M. She always felt like that about people who might equally well be actors or clergymen.

[1] *Life of George Lansbury* (Longmans), pp. 98-9.

He hated the Webbs and the School of Economics because they would not let him teach economics there. But neither would they let J. A. Hobson. They preferred Cannan and Foxwell.

I have written of MacDonald elsewhere as follows:

"Like all who have travelled great distances, he has had his lucky days. At three of the most critical moments of his career he has been the victim of mistaken identity. The first was in 1900, when, as a comparatively unknown young man, he was elected the first Secretary of the Labour Party. (Mr. Will Thorne, M.P., who was present, relates that 'James R. Mac-Donald was chosen as Secretary. But many of the hundred and twenty delegates were under the impression that they were voting for James MacDonald, Secretary of the London Trades Council, who had played an important part in the preliminary stages'.) The second was in 1922 when, by a narrow majority over Mr. Clynes, he was elected Leader of the Party in Parliament, and thus became Leader of His Majesty's Opposition and prospective Prime Minister. On this occasion he owed his success to the votes of a number of Clydesiders, newly arrived at Westminster, who desired to give their confidence to a robust Socialist of the Left. The third was on August 24th, 1931, when he seems to have been mistaken by the King for a Party Leader, whom a majority of his followers would still follow."[1]

Between MacDonald and Snowden there was no love lost. Snowden said, in my hearing, in 1929: "I wish I were Prime Minister only for a month. I'd show him how to do it." "Both", says Postgate, "knew real poverty when young (Mac-Donald as the illegitimate son of a Scots girl of straitened resources; Snowden as one of the children of a Yorkshire weaver); both early came into the ranks of the lower middle class. Snowden was a Civil Servant until a bicycle accident crippled him for life; those who watched him hobbling about the House of Commons on his sticks could not but wonder whether the accident which had twisted his body had not also twisted his mind."[2]

His "proclaimed Socialism was merely a form of words. All industries (he believed) should be nationally owned and controlled, but how this could be done he had never thought out."

[1] *Practical Socialism for Britain*, p. 24.   [2] *Life of George Lansbury*, p. 100.

When, for political reasons, nationalisation was off the map, "his mind became politically a void. There were still the sharp nose, the arrogant manner, the tight mouth and vindictive tongue, the obstinacy and the angry blue eyes." When at the Hague Conference in 1929 he "beat down and outwitted the French" and snatched from them some of the German reparations discussed there, "this fairy gold (for it was never to be received) and the deafening applause in the Press went to his head. He believed himself to be a great statesman; he had never listened much to others; and now he did not listen at all.

"But Nature abhors a vacuum, even in politicians' heads; and Snowden's lost Socialism was replaced by a primitive Liberalism. Two things became sacred to him, Free Trade and the Gold Standard," neither of which had anything to do with Socialism. "The Budget must at all costs be balanced; the gigantic waste of the 'dole' must somehow be ended."[1]

And finally, of Postgate's admirable characterisations, Henderson. He "was a silent, unimaginative man, loud-voiced, stiff, red-faced, with deep pouches under his eyes; an ironfounder by trade, a Nonconformist lay preacher from an early age; patiently hard-working, but rather rough and short-tempered in politics; a rigid teetotaller; with few individual characteristics beyond a trick of shooting out his white cuffs at subordinates whom he rebuked". But "this dull-looking man was an almost solid block of integrity. . . . He might be influenced when his mind was not clear; he had deferred too long to Lloyd George" in the War Cabinet, "and he was in the future to defer too long to MacDonald. But when he saw his duty clear, he would do it; he might not even trouble to explain. Moreover, his loyalty was not to Lloyd George's Cabinet but to the Labour Movement which he represented in it."[2]

This was a good description of Henderson in 1916, at the age of 53. Later he mellowed much, and he always went on learning.[3] But he never quite escaped, in public, from pomposity. And always, till his last years, when he was shrunken through

---

[1] *Life of George Lansbury*, pp. 253-4.   [2] *Ibid.*, pp. 171-2.
[3] Someone who saw him in the Chair at the Disarmament Conference at Geneva said: "Il est comme tant d'Anglais; il a l'air bête, mais il ne fait pas de bêtises; alors on doit penser qu'il n'est pas bête." Quoted by Freya Stark, *Beyond Euphrates*, p. 330.

illness, he gave a sense of weight. Garvin said of him: "He is not exactly a rusher, but he is a moving weight." And one of the League Secretariat at Geneva said: "He is slow to start, but, when he does, he is like an elephant going through jungle." Molly Hamilton writes of him that: "Certain words invariably came from his mouth with capital letters. They were words of collectivity. Rarely did he speak in the first person singular; but when he said 'Party', 'Party Conference' or 'Socialist Movement', something big loomed up. 'This Great Movement' —does any phrase bring him back more vividly? He conveyed the sense, most actual to his mind, and constant in it, of a mighty confraternity, whose solid centre would swing on, no matter what snarlings or scufflings might be happening on the wings."[1]

In 1918, Webb and Henderson, Postgate says, "had produced and imposed on the Labour Party a Socialist programme, detailed and practical, called *Labour and the New Social Order*", and "Henderson had reorganised the Party, giving it a modern structure to go with a modern programme, and in particular setting up local Labour Parties with individual members. In the end those parties were to make the I.L.P. superfluous."[2]

Next in the line were Clynes and Thomas. Clynes combined, as did none of the others, a natural dignity and courtesy, sincerity, loyalty to colleagues, and a command, in speech, of good and simple English. A Tory Cabinet Minister told a friend of mine that, in his view, no member of any Party in the 1918 Parliament spoke purer and better English than Clynes. He had started work in a cotton mill when he was twelve, and was wholly self-educated. He was very small of stature, having had too little to eat, and too little fresh air and exercise, while a child.

In March, 1922, he came to speak for me in the Cambridge by-election. He was Leader of the Opposition then, Mac-Donald and Snowden being still out of the House. He told a large audience in Cambridge Guildhall that, of all the younger men in the Labour Party, I was the one he most wanted to see in Parliament. And I remember, when there were some Tory undergraduate interruptions, his quiet comment, which drew a great cheer from our Trade Unionist supporters: "I am well

---

[1] *Arthur Henderson*, p. 266.　　[2] *Ibid.*, p. 180.

aware that there is a great mass of educated ignorance in this place."

At the first meeting of the Parliamentary Labour Party after the General Election of 1922, he was defeated by MacDonald for the leadership. It was by four votes only, with a total Party strength of 142. The I.L.P. turned up in full force and voted for MacDonald—except Snowden, who voted for Clynes. They had fixed this at a meeting of their own beforehand. Several Trade Unionists, who would have voted for Clynes, had not arrived when the vote was taken. Before the vote MacDonald got in a short speech complaining that the officers of the Party had made no proper arrangements for accommodation for the increased number of Labour M.P.s, and demanding greater energy in the conduct of our affairs. This probably turned a vote or two. Clynes took his defeat with perfect poise and with complete composure. That very night he moved a vote of confidence, at a public meeting, in the new leader. Nor, to the best of my knowledge, did he ever afterwards intrigue against him. He was, more than any of the other leaders except Henderson, a team man.

Immediately after the 1935 election, when the leadership of the Party was again in question, I went to consult him at his house at Putney. He said then that he thought I should be leader, and offered to support me. He himself was too old, he said, and I agreed. But I was not willing to stand. I was, in fact, canvassing for another candidate, as I shall relate later.

Though politics is, of necessity, a highly competitive profession, not least in the Labour Party, we have a strong sense of social security near the top. To do a man out of his job, at that eminence, is against good followership. In the thirty years since 1922, there has been no case of a man once chosen to be leader of the Labour Party being deposed by a vote at a Party meeting, though MacDonald, as we put it, "expelled himself" in 1931, and Lansbury resigned in 1935, and there was a strange move, which came to nothing, at the time of the 1945 election. But that too must wait its turn in my story.

MacDonald would have been far less loyal to Clynes as leader than Clynes was to MacDonald. And this might have led to much trouble in the Party. But I am sure that, taking all into account, that Party Meeting's vote in 1922 was wrong.

Jimmy Thomas was what Arnold Bennett called "a card". He had complete self-confidence and he enjoyed life. He ate and drank, and gambled and negotiated, and liked telling and hearing funny stories of a rather obvious kind. The Duke of Windsor in his *King's Story* tells how Thomas used to entertain King George V in this way, and Harold Nicolson confirms that soon after his operation in 1929 "the King received Mr. J. H. Thomas who was always apt to regale His Majesty with ribald jokes. The King laughed so hilariously at some of Mr. Thomas's stories that he had a further relapse."[1]

He showed an increasing propensity, which Low illustrated, to put on evening dress, and he made quite amusing, rather cheeky, after-dinner speeches. He astonished elderly hereditary noblemen by calling them by their Christian names the first time he met them. In conversation he overworked what police witnesses call "the B words" and he reversed, with great consistency, in both directions, all correct practice regarding the initial H. In my first session of Parliament, I observed that, having only just arrived, I was still very innocent. Whereat he pushed his spectacles down his nose, and replied. "You bain't so bloody hinnocent! Hi think you're bloody hartful."

He gambled on anything—cards, horses, the Stock Exchange. He would even bet on which of two flies going up a window-pane would reach the top first. It was reported that his luck varied from time to time, but that he generally won at cards.

He was a wonderful negotiator. He did as much as any Trade Union leader of his time to improve the working conditions of his members, the National Union of Railwaymen. He was very persuasive, very resourceful, quick as a flash when he saw an opening.

He was a Monmouthshire Welshman, and I once heard him say that he had been back to Newport and looked at an office door-knob, which he had had to polish as a boy. "But", he added, "I felt no bitterness." Once, when all his diplomatic gifts seemed to have failed, and a strike on the railways had been declared, he sat in his office at Unity House, his head in his hands and the tears streaming down his cheeks. "Me poor bloody 'eart's broke," he sobbed. "We're beat." Then he was told the Press were waiting to see him. In an instant he

[1] *King George V*, p. 432.

recovered, went into an outer room with a confident step and a serious look—he *could* look very serious when he chose. "Boys, we're winnin'," he told the Pressmen, " 'cos our cause is just." And, after a short stoppage, he got a pretty good settlement.

As a Parliamentarian, he was very ready in debate, but did not prepare his speeches. I remember him more than once organising an all-night sitting, when we were in Opposition, and leading it throughout the night most amusingly and effectively, without a single note.

He often declared that he was not a Socialist, and I have heard him add, "and I don't read any of those bloody books". MacDonald liked him much the best of all his colleagues. Thomas could always break into his room unannounced, which none of the rest were allowed to do. He didn't embarrass MacDonald by talking shop or trying to push him towards the Left. And, as Brailsford once said to me, he never embarrassed MacDonald by talking about some book MacDonald had not read.

It was Arthur Balfour, I think, who first said that "in politics there is no friendship at the top". And J. A. Spender has even suggested that friendship is easier between members of opposing parties than between members of the same party, because then there is no direct personal competition between them. But this, in my opinion, in the conditions of modern politics, is true of very few. Balfour's saying was pretty true of this particular group of Labour leaders. MacDonald and Thomas were friends, and so, though not so intimately, were Clynes and Henderson. But that was all the personal cement there was. I recorded in my diary during the 1929–31 Government these words, spoken to me by a high Civil Servant of great experience. "I have never been so conscious of personal difficulties and frictions in any Cabinet I have known, as in this one. Baldwin used to have terrible trouble with Winston and Jix, but it was only occasional, and one knew when it was coming. In this Cabinet one has to be on the look-out all the time. The rivalries and suspicions are always just below the surface, ready to burst out at any moment." The Labour Government of 1945–51 was much more of a band of brothers, though even there one or two jarred each other and there was increasing tension near the end.

I now turn from these eminent and well-established men to my own experience as a young politician. When, after the war, I had become active in the wider Labour Movement, and had become first a Parliamentary Candidate and next a Labour M.P., I had expected to be received by many with suspicion and reserve, which it would take some time and effort to break down. Particularly did I expect this from Trade Unionists, who might look twice at one with my social and educational background.

It was not so at all. I was surprised, and rather shocked, to find that most of them took me at more than my own valuation. To be well received at Cambridge, when I became Parliamentary Candidate there, was not so surprising. I had had roots and a past record there. But, as I moved about the country, speaking at Labour meetings, attending Conferences and so forth, I found warm welcomes everywhere. That I was my father's son; that I had become a Socialist in 1907, converted by Keir Hardie; that I was earning my living teaching economics at the L.S.E.; that I was particularly associated with the advocacy of the Capital Levy; that I seemed to be something of a financial expert, rather a rare and valuable bird, they thought; that I was regarded as a better-than-average public speaker, who tried always to combine the three elements, clear exposition, purple passages and humour; that I treated both Tories and Liberals with an easy and open contempt; that I could drink beer in any pub or Workman's Club in any company; that I was, most genuinely, pleased by a variety of companionship; all these things helped me.

But it was still surprising to me how little consciousness of class difference there was within the Labour Movement. Henderson's famous phrase, "workers by hand and brain", written now into the Labour Party's Constitution, did express a real unity. We all wanted the same thing. So what did it matter where we came from?

At a village in Kent I was once billed to speak as "Hugh Dalton, M.A., D.Sc.". Two villagers were looking at the bill. One asked the other: "What's D.Sc.?" The other answered: "Doctor of Socialism, I suppose."

So, too, when I became a Labour M.P. There were sections, of course, within the Parliamentary Labour Party. A Trade Union group, a separate Miners' Group, an I.L.P. Group (to which I belonged, but with no sort of an exclusive loyalty), a Temperance Group (to which I did not belong), and others. It was necessary, in forming Labour Governments, or even Party Committees, to keep a proper balance between sections and, in particular, to ensure a reasonable representation of Trade Unionists. If this were not done, there might be a sudden, and quite justifiable, outburst of resentment. But, if it *was* done, we were very near to being, and feeling ourselves to be, a party without internal class differences. "This", as a Yorkshire miner, now dead, said to me, when I first entered Parliament, "is a great communal home."

One of the most attractive privileges of active politics is what almost amounts to a recognised right of entry to other people's homes. An M.P., or even a prospective candidate, can knock at any door or address anyone in street or field, and very seldom be rebuffed. This wide social span can give an understanding that could come no other way. "Begin with the policemen, the parsons and the publicans," an old hand once advised me. "But don't end there."

I have a very grateful and affectionate memory of older men in the Labour Party who helped me and encouraged me when I was young.

And of four above all the rest: Arthur Henderson, Charles Trevelyan, Josiah Wedgwood, Johnny Clynes, in that order. Two Trade Unionists and two sons of famous families. These last two both entered Parliament as Liberals, but moved forward to Socialism. And I am grateful too to Sidney Webb, but in a different fashion. Of my relationship with Arthur Henderson, I need say no more here. It comes out clearly in the course of my tale. But though none of them were as close to him, or for so long, as I was, he took trouble also with a number of other Socialist Intellectuals as they are sometimes called. With Cole, Laski and Tawney, in particular, he kept in touch. "I think", he said to me once, "that I am the only one who knows how to handle these chaps. I get them to come and see me and have a talk. And then I ask them to write me a memorandum. That pleases them and keeps them quiet for a time. And I often learn quite a lot from what they write." Certainly he was the only one of Labour's Big Five at that time who could even begin to "handle these chaps", or thought it worth while to try. But Henderson had a special feeling for Universities, and for University recruits into the Labour Party. "I want", he once said to me, "to see a great alliance between Labour and Learning."

Nor do I need to say much here of my relationship with Charles Trevelyan. That too comes out in the story. I met him first, I remember, when I was an undergraduate, at breakfast with Lowes Dickinson. And I remember that he held forth, at length and with emphasis. And then I used to meet him at the Lake Hunt at Whitsun, and often at his house in Westminster, in Great College Street, and occasionally at his home at Wallington in Northumberland. He was not a man of letters, like his brother George the historian, or his brother Bob the poet. But he had great character and determination and great physical fitness. Bertie Lees-Smith once said to me that he played politics like a rather rough game of football, a lot of heavy charging and hearty tackling but not much finesse. He was, indeed, good in the open air, very keen on his Northumbrian estate and a very good shot. He used, I am told, to scandalise the neighbours by shooting birds on warm days, stripped to the waist. And, as Socialist Lord Lieutenant of Northumberland, he scandalised some Tories by painting a Hammer and Sickle on his entrance gates—or was it painted by some other Tories?

Josiah Wedgwood has written his own story in several attractive books.[1]

I have heard it said by some who were there that he was the bravest man on Gallipoli; let us believe at least, in that immortal band of heroes, as brave as any other.

---

[1] *Essays and Adventures of a Labour M.P.*, *Memoirs of a Fighting Life* and *A Testament to Democracy*. This last book he published in 1942, less than a year before he died. I was then President of the Board of Trade, and he sent me a copy with this letter.

My dear Hughie,
   I think it possible that you may like this book. At least it will be *good* for you, and your lady may have an idle hour to pass awaiting your return at night. The Chapter on Bureaucracy is for your Secretary; the one on Reconstruction for yourself.

Ever yours,
Jos.

Only a short time before his death, at the age of 71, he was still firewatching and, as his niece Miss C. V. Wedgwood says in her excellent short life of him, he made his own epitaph when he wrote, autographing a book for a friend: "To a firewatcher, from an incendiary." (*Last of the Radicals*, p. 244.)

As I saw him in politics, he was a Socialist individualist, a vigorous combative man, with a tremendous chin, great gaiety and charm, a passion for freedom and a faith in the taxation of land values as a cure for nearly all our ills.

When I came to Parliament in 1924, he took me to sit beside him on the third bench back, above and just next to the Gangway on the Opposition side. And there he coached me on procedure, and told me stories about people, and when to make my maiden speech. On the first day, some industrial Tory, moving the Address in reply to the Gracious Speech, lapsed, contrary to Parliamentary tradition, into controversial personalities. And Jos remarked: "What I say is, if a man *must* be a Tory, at least let him be a gentleman." I have always treasured that one!

He never refused when I asked him to come and speak for me, and once, at Cardiff, embarrassed me a little by declaring: "Hugh Dalton and I both belong to the master class" (the "a" in both these last two words pronounced as in "gas"). "We were taught at school that it was better to be dead than a slave. But they never taught that to you."

He spoke to me most frankly about his own hopes and political ambitions which were never fulfilled.

I tried to repay some of my debt to him by working out, as I have already mentioned, a compromise between land nationalisation and the taxation of land values. The central point was that the proceeds of a tax on privately owned land values should be used to buy land for public authorities. He was very pleased with this plan and we got it adopted by the Party. But nothing more was done about it.

His son, Josiah, took over the family business, served for a time on the Court of the Bank of England, before nationalisation, and on the very ineffective Monopolies Commission set up by the Labour Government of 1945. He worked under me as a Research Student at the London School of Economics and, on his own initiative, followed up some of the lines suggested in my book *The Inequality of Incomes*. His own book, *The Economics of Inheritance*, to which I wrote a preface, is still worth reading. If his health had been stronger, he would, I think, have come to Parliament and made his mark there.

Johnny Clynes was a gentle and modest person. He never

obtruded his counsel or his company upon me. But I knew that they were always there, in the background, to be had for the asking. And, when I *did* ask for them, I was always glad.

Sidney Webb I think of in a different way from those four others. With gratitude, indeed, for he helped and influenced me greatly. But my relationship with him, and with Beatrice, had no warmth, not much human interest surrounding the business on hand, little inclination to wander into by-ways and amusing irrelevancies. I felt, as did so many others, that I was regarded only as a means to the Webbs' ends, never as an end in myself. And this I found repellent, both to my Cambridge ethics and my sense of humour.

Yet let us not undervalue the Webbs. Bertrand Russell says truly that they "did a great work in giving intellectual backbone to British Socialism. The Webbs and the Benthamites shared a certain dryness and a certain coldness and a belief that the waste-paper basket is the place for the emotions. But one should not demand of anybody all the things that add value to a human being. To have some of them is as much as should be demanded. The Webbs pass this test, and indubitably the British Labour Party would have been much more wild and woolly if they had never existed."[1]

Age comes upon politicians, even more than upon men living less active and exciting lives, unawares. At the end of a five-year Parliament, all the members are five years older. This is a solemn platitude and, for most, a disability they are unwilling to admit.

Older people, particularly in politics, should cultivate a sense of the succession. They should be looking ahead, and looking out for younger people to replace them.

To be spoken to by older people in a tone of friendship, and with frankness, and on a footing of equality, to be confided in, to be consulted—all this may lift the morale of the young. It certainly did mine. And it may help the old too.

Personal relationships across a wide age-gap must, in the nature of things, be more difficult to sustain than between contemporaries. I have experienced this from both sides of the gap. Of how it feels from the older side I shall write later. Here

[1] *The Listener*, July 31st, 1952, p. 178.

I have recorded something of how it felt from the younger side, while I was still under forty. And that is still very young for a politician in ageing Britain!

The vilest of all emotions, the sin against the Holy Ghost in my scale of values, is when the Old grow jealous of the Young. Each of us, in the endless procession of the ages, has his appointed place. Let no one try to cause a selfish block in that procession. Let the Young, and the Old too, move on.

As between different political parties, the distinction between Right and Left is generally obvious. Democratic Socialists are to the Left of Communists, Conservatives or Liberals. Within a political party, having a common policy to which all its members (more or less) subscribe, the distinction is less easy. But most people, in a Party of the Left such as the Labour Party, like to be thought to be on the Left of the Party. Jimmy Thomas, as we have seen, was an exception.[1] People, reputed to be on the Right, sometimes speak of "the so-called Left", hinting that this is bogus and that they are the real thing. New arrivals nearly all make their entry from the Left. The I.L.P. leaders did, including MacDonald and Snowden. So did the Clydesiders. So did Mosley. So did I, when I was first elected both to the Parliamentary and the National Executives. So have some later arrivals, after 1931. But much that looks and sounds Left is in manner, not matter; in an appearance of "dynamism" and high blood-pressure and an impatient sense of urgency. It is a common trick of debate, or internal party propaganda, to label others "Right" and oneself and one's friends "Left".

The older leaders of a Party are generally thought "to be more to the Right", partly because they *are* older and less resilient than they used to be, partly because "experience" and "a sense of responsibility" often cramp their style, even when out of office. The simple meaning of Right and Left is that the Left are bolder, keener on big changes soon, and the Right more cautious, with a keener sense of all the difficulties. Judged by this standard, much of the talk of Right and Left is meaningless. And, when it isn't, the relative position of individuals is

[1] In Tarascon Railway Station, near dawn, Ruth and I once heard a railway porter singing: "Je suis du Midi, du pays de l'aïoli." She said: "You would never hear a railway porter sing 'Je suis du Nord.' " But Jimmy Thomas did.

often wrongly estimated. Henderson, for instance, was well to the Left of MacDonald on many issues, as my diary shows. The Left is sometimes only a mystique, a snobbism. I was asked once whether I was Right Wing or Left Wing, and I replied: "I fly on both my wings, but my heart is on my Left." And a Lancashire M.P., not long since, paid me a tribute which I treasure, moving a vote of thanks to me after a public speech. "The Right Wing thinks he's Left, and the Left Wing thinks he's Right, but I know he's flying on both his wings, straight towards Socialism."

CHAPTER X

M.P. FOR BISHOP AUCKLAND

IN July, 1928, as I have said already, I had decided not to
stand again for Peckham and to let it be known that I was
available to fight some other constituency. Uncle had
strongly advised me against this course, but I had insisted. I
told him I had taken my political life in my hand before, and
was quite prepared to do it again. He thought it doubtful
whether, with a General Election bound to come in less than a
year, and with nearly all good seats fixed up, I could hope for
anything else as good as Peckham. I said I was fed up with
Peckham and would risk it.

"July 26th. Much interest and some concern among my
friends over the Peckham announcement. Most assume it must
be C. P. I rather tire of explaining that it isn't. Lunch at the
House to Uncle to celebrate the twenty-fifth anniversary of his
return for Barnard Castle, the first Labour victory in a three-
cornered fight."

Very soon after this I had a tentative approach from Bishop
Auckland. Ben Spoor, the sitting member, had announced that,
for health reasons, he couldn't stand again. He had never
recovered from the effects of malaria on the Salonika front in
the war. Uncle, having failed to persuade me to stick to Peckham, now, characteristically, did his best to help me to get
Bishop Auckland, which, since the redistribution of 1918, included part of what had been the Barnard Castle division
when he won it in 1903. He had given the Durham miners, who
had approached him as Secretary of the Party, a favourable
report on me, and had written personally about me to Peter
Lee. I was nominated—by the Bishop Auckland I.L.P.—along
with about a dozen others, for the prospective candidature.
They took a preliminary vote, without summoning any of us,
to reduce the number to three. The three chosen were myself,
Anderson Fenn, husband of the Labour Party Woman Organiser for the North-east, and Dr. V. H. Rutherford, ex-Liberal

M.P. for Sunderland, now turned Labour. Among those
eliminated at this stage were Will Lawther, later M.P. for
Barnard Castle and now President of the National Union of
Mineworkers, and Will Davis, a local schoolmaster, who will
reappear in my story. He became, and still is, my closest personal
friend in my constituency.

At the beginning of September, when Ruth and I were in
the Eastern Pyrenees, walking and working on a new edition
of my *Public Finance*, I got a telegram from the Rev. William
Hodgson, Vicar of Escomb and Secretary of the Bishop Auckland Divisional Labour Party, inviting me to attend a Selection Conference. They did their selecting very thoroughly.
I went up two weekends running, stayed at the vicarage at
Escomb and there met a number of the leading members of the
Party. I addressed a private meeting of workers during the first
weekend, and two public meetings, one indoor and one outdoor, during the second, when Ruth came with me. The Vicar
gave me to understand that *he* was supporting me. But the other
two candidates were coming up during the next two weekends
to stay at the vicarage and to be put through *their* paces.

On October 7th I wrote in my diary: "Wire from Hodgson
and Worden" (Chairman of the I.L.P. branch) "that I have
got Bishop Auckland! This should be a seat for life, barring
grave accidents. Voting at Selection Conference: Dalton 108,
Fenn 17, Rutherford 4. Then a unanimous vote for me. Clouds
pass away. My position, with a safe seat and a place on both
Executives in this critical year, is a very strong one, come what
may."

But I also wrote: "To represent these fine people will be one
long heartache, until we can make tremendous changes. We
must do that soon." Most of those whom I had met at the
vicarage, and seen at public meetings, were unemployed miners.
Pits had been closing, and mass unemployment and poverty
had settled down on what had been, only a few years earlier,
a busy mining area.

Pits were being flooded and abandoned, because the private
coal-owners would not co-operate in the comparatively simple
job of pumping out the water. So one pit after another, going
eastwards, was drowned out, and the livelihood of the little
mining villages, with no alternative employment, was drowned

out too. And seventy million tons of the best coking coal in Britain were submerged beneath the waters of an underground lake, these capitalists' chief contribution to the amenities of my constituency!

So now, in 1928, human values had depreciated almost to nothing. White-faced women who starved themselves to feed their children; children certified by doctors as "suffering from malnutrition"—that meant having been half-starved long enough for it to become obvious—being fed at school; men sitting silent in Workmen's Clubs, too poor to buy either a drink or a smoke; every second shop in Newgate Street, the main street in Bishop Auckland, shuttered up and the shopkeeper ruined, because the people had no money to spend; old clothes and old boots being collected and distributed by charitable persons; others organising the departure of boys and girls, as soon as they left school, to be bell-hops in London hotels or kitchen-maids in rich private houses.

And no new industries would come to the district. There was too much Trade Unionism and Labour politics here, we were told. And the North Eastern Railway Company were talking of closing the railway shops at Shildon, our largest remaining source of employment. That would have been the end, but I took this up with Sir Ralph Wedgwood, the Chairman of the Company, not unsuccessfully. That he was Jos Wedgwood's brother, and that the latter was a friend of mine, helped.

Bishop Auckland and the surrounding area, and my personal contacts in the months and years that followed, taught me the meaning of a "distressed area". As will appear later, much of my political effort—before, during and after the Second World War—was devoted to this question. And we succeeded in "making the tremendous changes", which led to full employment and new life and new health in my constituency, and in others like it. I am very proud of my share in this resurrection. Had I stayed at Peckham, I should have missed that direct experience of achievement.

And others might not have achieved as much as I did, for three times, in later years, I was particularly well placed to help. First in 1936, when I was Chairman of the Labour Party's National Executive, and Chairman of its Distressed Areas Commission. Then in 1942–5, when I was President of

the Board of Trade in the Coalition Government, and devised
and introduced, after much resistance, the Distribution of
Industry Bill and began to steer new industries into the
"Development Areas", a new and more hopeful title which I
had invented. Finally, in 1945–7 when, as Chancellor of the
Exchequer in the Labour Government, I prodded the slow
coaches and found the money for all this new work "with a
song in my heart", as I declared in Parliament, a phrase the
Tories often quoted out of context.

From the moment of my selection in October, 1928, I was
received into a great community—that of the Labour Movement
in County Durham. I have belonged to that community for
twenty-four years now. I have been well content to be faithful.
Before I came to Bishop Auckland I had flirted with many
constituencies. I had even broken with Peckham, deliberately,
after victory, through boredom, not because I feared defeat.

But with Bishop Auckland I settled down for the rest of my
political life, and I have never wished to change again. When
I lost the seat in 1931, I accepted, without a flicker of doubt,
the call to win it back. I stayed out of Parliament, refusing
by-election offers, but spending much time in Bishop Auckland,
till 1935. Since then I have been returned in four Parliamentary
elections, in 1935, 1945, 1950 and 1951. The area of the constituency was increased, following redistribution in 1950, from
50 to 200 square miles, gaining more in natural beauty in the
Teesdale than in Labour strength. But our strength is still
sufficient.

When Clem Attlee became Prime Minister in 1945, he took
five members of his Cabinet, and his Chief Whip as well, from
County Durham. But in the Churchill War Government I
was the only Minister of Cabinet rank representing a constituency in an old Distressed Area. It was lucky there was one!

The greatest power in this great Durham community are the
Durham miners—stormtroops in peace and war, in industry,
in politics, in the armed forces and on the football field. They
have had a succession of leaders, many of whom have been my
personal friends. I count conspicuous among these Peter Lee,
W. P. Richardson, Jack Swan, Will Lawther and, today, Sam
Watson. And, among the many good men and true who have

come from the Durham pits to Parliament, I have known no
two finer characters than Jack Lawson and Willy Whiteley.

The Durham miners' gala, on the last Saturday in July, is
the most moving event of its kind which I have ever seen, when
more than a quarter of a million people converge, marching
with their colliery bands and banners, upon the old city of
Durham, in perfect order and with the minimum of traffic
control. Out of this tremendous demonstration of democratic
Socialist comradeship and industrial power, I get my biggest
political kick of the year. I never miss it.

Of the miners, as indeed of many other elements in the County
of Durham, once one wins their confidence, one can lose it only
by one's own fault. An opponent of mine at a Parliamentary
election once spoke angrily of my supporters' "stupid, pug-
nacious loyalty to that b—— Dalton!"

Bishop Auckland, even before the redistribution of 1950, and
still more after, has ceased to be a mining constituency, in the
sense that a majority—or even a substantial minority—of the
electors are miners and their womenfolk. But the proportion is
higher among the old people. And the memory of the miners'
struggles, the tradition of their solidarity and their present
strength, still permeate the whole county.

I am very fortunate to have come to Durham.

On December 20th, 1928, the House separated for Christmas.
All seemed straight sailing. But two days later Ben Spoor died
suddenly. This caused a by-election at Bishop Auckland and a
most unusual situation.

If I contested this by-election myself, I should have to resign
from Peckham, and this would cause a second by-election
there. Moreover, John Beckett, now M.P. for Gateshead, had
been adopted as my successor at Peckham. He was a friend of
mine at this time, and had great energy and some ability. His
later association with Mosley surprised and disappointed me.
If he stood at Peckham now, this would cause a third by-
election, at Gateshead. But, if I didn't stand, what would
Bishop Auckland say? There were, at the most, only ten months
left before the General Election, and the by-election couldn't
happen for another month and a half. Uncle was out of London.
It was Christmas Eve. Frank Wise rang up to say he would be

willing—indeed, I gathered, was really very anxious—to fight it for me, and to have a month or two in the House, and then go back to Leicester, where he is prospective candidate, at the General. I wonder!

I spent Christmas at Windsor. Back on Boxing Day, in time for tea. Still no Uncle on the telephone! Ruth and I had planned to spend ten days at Langdon Beck, in Upper Teesdale, and then do a round of meetings in my new constituency.

I wrote in my diary: "December 27th. Attend Spoor's funeral. Local Party at B.A. want Ruth to stand. They say they don't want any other warming-pan. They want to get people into the habit of voting Dalton.

"To Langdon Beck late that night. She has arrived and Uncle has told her on the telephone in London late last night that she ought to stand. She is willing—though she says she has been more interested in an Edgar Wallace thriller than in the prospect of being an M.P.!

"December 19th. I go down to B.A. and meet the General Committee, some seventy in number, and they unanimously decide that R. shall be asked to stand. No other name is mentioned. I say she is willing.

"Then we stay on for a week at Langdon Beck Hotel; a jolly spot, even under snow, though this grows monotonous after a few days. We walk down to High Force, and across to Weardale, and up to Cauldron Snout, and back along the Tees in the dusk, picking up a young guide at Widdybank Farm for the last few laps. We shall, I think, come back to Langdon Beck."

We did, and I quite often. Since 1950 all the Upper Teesdale is in the Bishop Auckland Division. I much enjoy visiting this part of my constituency. And, while I was Minister of Local Government and Planning in 1951, I designated the Pennine Way, the first long-distance route in Britain, which runs right through it, touching both those two fine waterfalls, High Force and Cauldron Snout.

"Thus strangely and dramatically ends 1928," I wrote. "And in 1929 anything may happen, as a result of the General Election. May it be an *annus mirabilis*, and a turning-point in British, yes and in world, history!"

"January 7th–12th, 1929. Twenty-one meetings in six days, at all of which R. and I both speak. And she speaks jolly well and they like her. She is less tired at the end than I had feared. The poverty and hopelessness are shocking! But they are wonderful people."

The special correspondent of *The Times*, reporting the by-election on January 22nd, wrote:

"A terrible story was told me here. Scores of the miners' cottages present to the world the usual clean curtained windows and carefully scrubbed doorsteps, but if you get a peep inside there is no furniture. Lodgings for visiting political workers have been looked for in the hope of giving a helping hand to some poor family with a furnished bedroom to spare. It is almost impossible to get such a room because the furniture has gone."

"January 13th–25th. In London. Meanwhile in B.A. Gibbin (our North Eastern Regional Organiser) is in charge, slow and fussy, but safe and experienced, booking halls and speakers and getting on with the clerical work.

"School term begins and Parliament meets. As usual after a holiday, all in good spirits. The General Election seems very near now, and hopes run high. We are inclined almost to take for granted a Labour Government in a few months' time.

"Very interesting talk with C. T. and A. P. (Arthur Ponsonby) at 14, Great College Street. Partly suggested by Haldane's posthumous revelations of his influence on J. R. M. Vitally important that this next time J. R. M. should have a sound Labour man as Principal Private Secretary.

"Shall J. R. M. make his Cabinet unaided, or rather unofficially aided by a few intriguers and lickspittles, or shall he have something in the nature of an official advisory committee? We are all for the latter. Preferably a committee of five— Clynes, Uncle, Snowden, Thomas and C. T., we think. We are to raise this with Uncle and G. L." Actually this *was* the committee, except that C. T., to my regret, wasn't on.

"January 25th. To B.A. And then till February 7th an election campaign, rather exhausting physically, but with the curious new quality of victory sure, and only the size of the majority uncertain. Far too many meetings are arranged, and too many national speakers. But the constituency has been very starved of meetings for years, and a lot of this ought to do for the General Election without much repetition.

"One of our most valuable and likeable visitors is Harry Stoddart" (for many years, and still, Labour Agent at Jarrow). "He has large, brown, faithful eyes out of which he looks at R. Wonderfully good at getting on with all types.

"The Tories seem only half-awake. The Liberals rather more formidable. Curry is one of the specious kind, quotations and misquotations: 'much more advanced than the Labour Party', etc. Rather an irritating little bounder.

"Eve of poll meeting at the King's Hall, Bishop Auckland, addressed by Snowden, C. T., F. O. Roberts, Peter Lee and other Durham miners' leaders, and local speakers, the candidate's husband, and the candidate herself. Very impressive, particularly F. O.'s leading of community singing on his fiddle. R. arrives very late, having been put by the Rev. William Hodgson, without an escort, into a very decayed taxi, which finally broke down at Eldon. So she had had to walk, pick up buses, etc., in order to get round to a long list of meetings. When she arrived, she had a great reception and spoke very well for five minutes. Then F. O. started, 'For She's a Jolly Good Fellow!' and immediately afterwards, to wind up, 'Abide With Me' sung with great fervour by the audience. This combination is very English. Whitehead in *Process and Reality*, it will be remembered, says that the first two lines of this hymn are the key to philosophy.

"February 8th. Declaration.

RUTH DALTON (Lab.)	14,797
CURRY (Lib.)	7,725
THOMPSON (Con.)	3,357

Labour majority over Liberal	7,072
Labour majority over Liberal and Conservative	3,715
Conservative saved his deposit by	123

"This is better than Spoor ever did. His best majority over the two combined was only a few hundreds in 1923. And his best in a straight fight was 2,900 last time.

"R. is wonderfully adequate to the end, but almost fainting with fatigue when we get to London. Journalists are waiting at our flat. I have to drive them off with airy nothings.

"February 9th. R. in bed, but slowly recovering from fatigue, and buried under letters and telegrams of congratulation. It takes her some days—poor little object!—to begin to see herself as a conqueror, and as the momentary centre of all eyes. But it comes gradually. I am very proud of her.

"February 12th. R. takes her seat, walking up between me and Tom Kennedy, our Chief Whip. Everyone very congratulatory and friendly on our side; the others rather interested and watchful. She does it jolly well, of course.

"February 19th. Dine with Snowdens at the House to meet Bernstorff of the German Embassy. My relations with P. S. are good at the moment.

"J. R. M. talking ghastly nonsense in the Lobby about the difficulty of a British Foreign Secretary having to consult the Dominions about everything, the consequent impossibility of carrying out a Party policy and the desirability of 'taking the F.O. out of Party politics, like the Speakership'. That such ideas should even cross the brain of this tired man is disastrous. Rumours of J. H. T. for the F.O. link up with this line of helplessness. C. T. and I discuss and he says, for the first time, that he thinks Uncle should be at the F.O. I had never told him that this was my view, since I thought that both he and A. P. might be thinking of themselves for this job. But I am delighted with C. T.'s opinion, and urge him to tell Uncle, and to raise again the question of the Advisory Committee for J. R. M. in making a Labour Government. He goes off to see Uncle (still ill) that afternoon.

"February 20th. R. asks her first Parliamentary Question (very confidently).

"March 13th. R. makes her maiden speech in the House on the Lord Mayor's Fund. A great success. Our people very delighted with it. 'Composed and compact,' says *The Times*. Listening to Eustace Percy's account of how no one was hungry, or ill clad, or depressed any more, any nervousness she may have felt turned to indignation. And she went for him with a vigour unusual in maiden speeches. Many congratulations afterwards."

A few days later J. R. M. invited her to tea. He said he hoped that, though, of course, she would be releasing Bishop Auckland to me at the General Election, she was sufficiently interested in Parliament to be willing to stand somewhere else. She said she found the L.C.C. much more interesting than the House. "There we *do* things," she said. "Here it seems to be all talk." She said she had never wanted to be an M.P. and was only here now to help me out of a difficulty. Not very tactful!

On April 10th Uncle went off with J. R. M., Clynes, Snowden and Thomas to discuss at lunch somewhere the next Labour Government. Uncle told me, some days later, that the talk was rather inconclusive. J. R. M. said he hoped they would all put themselves in his hands, "or rather in your own hands". He seemed to regard the other four as an informal committee to discuss and advise on appointments, without any formal departure from the constitutional practice by which the Prime Minister alone selects ministers. At this stage J. H. T. had said: "That's all very well for Philip. His job's decided already." And P. S. said, rather sourly, "Is it?" J. R. M. had hinted that he couldn't combine the two jobs, P.M. and F.O., again, so someone else would have to take the F.O. No names mentioned for this. J. R. M. would lead the House, and perhaps preside over the Unemployment Committee. Clynes would have to take a Department this time.

And so the weeks drift past as the election draws nearer. All the life goes out of Parliament. Ruth speaks, very successfully, at the Albert Hall for five minutes on April 27th, along with other by-election victors, and J. R. M. makes a disappointing programme speech. She is very popular with the comrades in the House. We both go up to Durham for the May Day weekend, and launch our campaign in advance. The Election manifesto is completed. Not a thrilling document, but improved as we go on discussing it.

Parliament was dissolved on May 10th. I spoke on the 9th in North Dorset for Colin Clark, and was howled down at Blandford by Liberals, who had hoped to win the seat back in a straight fight with the Tories and were furious at Colin's intervention. On the 10th I spoke for Sanders in North Battersea, and was howled at by followers of Saklatvala, the retiring Communist M.P., whom Sanders knocked out this time; on the 11th for George Dallas at Wellingborough on the way north.

My estimate, seat by seat, was:

287 Tories
268 Labour
55 Liberals
5 Independents[1]

It was expected to be a dull election.

I got to Bishop Auckland on May 13th, Ruth following a few days later after addressing meetings for candidates on the way.

I recorded: "May 13th–30th. This election is the easiest thing I have ever had. It seems hardly fair to take the money! Aaron Park, our agent, is almost too calm, and everything is a bit late and casual. But it all comes out well enough in the end. I speak, in addition to meetings in the constituency, in Darlington, Stockton, Barnard Castle, Durham and at Wheatley Hill in the Seaham Division. Darlington is a terrific fight against the wealth and influence of the Londonderrys. But in our constituency the recent by-election has spoiled the pitch for all parties.

"May 30th. Polling Day. . . . After the close of the poll, we go to the King's Hall to hear the results. There is a good rush of Labour gains. . . . Holding Darlington and winning Stockton are specially applauded.

"May 31st. To our own count in very leisurely fashion after noon. It is finished by 2.30.

DALTON	17,838
CURRY (Lib.)	9,635
THOMPSON (Con.)	4,503

Labour majority over Liberal 8,203
Labour majority over Liberal and Conservative 3,700

"There is an increase in the absolute majority since February, but a slight decrease relatively. I am disappointed not to have 10,000. We were very weak in the town of Bishop Auckland. Still! Nothing much to grumble at!"

After speeches of thanks to supporters, we make our way to Darlington to catch the 5.15 for London. We have won 18

[1] As it turned out, I gave the Tories 27 too many and us 21 too few. But I got the Liberals within 3. They went up from 43 to 58, after a tremendous propaganda, paid for out of the Lloyd George Fund, for their Employment Programme.

seats out of 19 in Durham, including all the County Divisions. Only the Hartlepools stay Tory.

There was a great crowd at Darlington Station, nearly all our people, waiting for J. R. M. It was a train-load of Labour victors, green and white everywhere—Keir Hardie's old colours —waving from the windows of the train, waving from the crowd. And then, amid all our waving and cheering, just as the train was moving out, Harold Macmillan, who had been beaten at Stockton, came to a window, and waving his Tory colours—red and gold I think they were—all alone, and with tears streaming down his cheeks, called for "three cheers for Baldwin!" "In politics there are ebbs and flows," I said to him afterwards.

"I have a few words with J. R. M., but only a few, on the train. The last time he and I travelled back on the same train after an election was from Cardiff in 1923, on the eve of the First Labour Government. Since then both he and I have moved from South Wales to the North-east. Now at each stop, York, Doncaster, Grantham, great crowds gather on the platforms, cheering and calling for a speech, and we buy new editions of the evening papers, and our gains go mounting up. It is certain now that we shall be the largest Party, but fall a little short of a clear majority. Certain too that the Liberal revival is a myth, and that my estimate of the Liberal total will be very near the truth, though I had under-estimated Labour gains and Tory losses. . . .

"At King's Cross at 11 p.m. a vast crowd, cheering like mad outside the station. We go home to bed."

Some quotations from my diary follow:

"June 1st. I read in my *Daily Herald* that at J. R. M.'s house last night there was 'quite a family party. His son Malcolm was there and Sir Oswald and Lady Cynthia Mosley.' So *they* had lost no time!

"June 2nd. See Sydney Arnold in the afternoon. J. R. M. is talking with Clynes, Henderson, Snowden and Thomas. Nothing more is known, but Jowitt has told Arnold that a bunch of twenty Liberals will back us, regardless of L. G.

"See Uncle Arthur in the evening. F.O. not yet settled—nor anything else!

"June 3rd. See Lees-Smith at the School, and discuss our

future arrangements here if we go into the Government. Baldwin is resigning without meeting the House. The crisis of Labour Government making is right on us!

"June 4th. See Greenwood in the morning. The Press is beginning to be full of fancy Cabinets. Even the staid *Times* takes a turn. I am suggested for the War Office. Not very attractive, nor even very likely. Laski says he saw J. R. M. on Sunday and Uncle yesterday. One must discount all he says, but, according to his own account, he told them both who ought, and who ought not, to be in each job!

"He says J. R. M. asked him whether I should make a good Minister of Agriculture, and that he replied 'Yes', but that I should be better still in certain other offices. The battle of Uncle *v.* Thomas for the F.O. is still raging. Snowden is said to be indifferent to everything else, provided he is Chancellor, and Clynes is a broken reed. Laski says Mosley stayed with J. R. M. till 1 a.m. the night J. R. M. got back from the north, was in again next day, and took J. R. M. out to lunch the day after! Also that X", now a Labour Peer, "was on the doorstep and couldn't be moved for several hours yesterday.

"I end the day feeling very tired. I have wired Charles Trevelyan, who was to have been at Durham tomorrow for an Honorary Degree, to come back without fail. He is coming. Baldwin has been down to Windsor today to resign. J. R. M. goes down tomorrow.

"June 5th. Breakfast with C. T. at 8. *What* a good fellow he is! Straight, sensible, honest talk. Horrified at idea of Thomas at F.O. Will do what he can to back Uncle. Will see J. R. M., if he can, about it. Thinks Lees-Smith, Tom Johnston and I should all be in the Cabinet. For himself, wants to go on with Education. I suggest Admiralty, but he says he wouldn't take that, except on clear terms that the Navy is to be cut down ruthlessly. Fears he may be offered India, owing to his family tradition, but wouldn't take that, for he is conscious of knowing nothing about it, and has never been there. I say that, if I had a clear field of choice and he was somewhere else, I would prefer Education to most other things. He says I am quite right, though, for various reasons, the job won't be quite so easy this time.

"National Executive at 10.30. Routine business and reports

arising out of election. J. R. M. at Windsor. C. T. sees Uncle in a corner, and reports that Thomas is still going baldheaded for F.O., but that consultation among the Big Five is still proceeding.

"2.30. Joint meeting of National and Parliamentary Executives. J. R. M. comes in at 3, looking very tired. Says King has commissioned him to form a Government; that His Majesty was very friendly; that old Ministers will hand over seals on Friday and new ones be sworn in on Saturday; that our supply of capable people far exceeds demand; that he is having a terrible time trying to fit people in; appeals for team spirit and loyalty; those who have to take less important posts than they expected may be assured that, if they acquit themselves well, 'the ladder is open, right to the top'; that he is very much exhausted and is going to take a holiday next week; that he has already given orders to certain Departments, with Baldwin's consent, for memoranda to be prepared which will enable a quick start to be made. Ends rather more brightly by referring to our great victory and great opportunities.

"A lot of hanging about in passages afterwards. I bring Tom Johnston back to tea. J. R. M. saw him just after the meeting, and offered him Under-Secretary for Scotland, under Willie Adamson, who is to be made a peer! But the thing not quite settled, because W. A. has a son, which J. R. M. didn't know, and now says may make the King unwilling to agree to the Peerage. T. J. should be in the Cabinet. This is a poor offer. He is inclined to accept it, if Adamson goes to the Lords, but, if not, he's doubtful." (He *did* accept it, though Adamson *didn't* go to the Lords.) "8.40 p.m. Telephone message from C. T.'s maidservant. He's done the best he possibly could at H.Q. He's just rushed straight out again."

"June 6th. *Times* says Uncle *may* go to F.O. *Herald* says Thomas *will* deal with unemployment. I conclude that Uncle has won. To Transport House about 11. Meet Phil Noel-Baker coming downstairs. Uncle is Foreign Secretary, he says, and has asked him to be his Parliamentary Private Secretary. Perfect! I see Uncle, to whom I first sent in a personal letter, provisionally congratulating him and saying that, so far as I am concerned, if not in the Cabinet, the only two jobs which really attract me are Financial Secretary to the Treasury or

Under-Secretary at the Foreign Office—the latter especially under him. He is all smiles, not unnaturally. 'I stuck to it,' he says, 'though it was rather painful at times.' Snowden said, 'I'm sorry, but I can't help you in this.' Having got what he wanted, he did not care much about anyone else. But indirectly Snowden had put Uncle in, for, when it had been proposed that Thomas should be at F.O., and Uncle Lord Privy Seal to deal with unemployment, Uncle had said that he would only consider accepting if the job carried Deputy-Leadership of the House, and Snowden had objected that Deputy-Leadership belonged to the Chancellor of the Exchequer. So Uncle refused, and wouldn't budge, and yesterday Thomas had said, when they met after the Joint Executives, 'Well, Arthur, you'd better take the F.O.' And, after a pause, J. R. M. said, 'Well, Henderson, will you take it?' And Uncle said, 'Yes, if *you* want me to'—and at this point in his narrative he gave me a heavy wink. And then Uncle said: 'Well, Jim, you'd better take Lord Privy Seal and deal with unemployment.' And J. H. T. said: 'All right, if you'll all back me and if Philip will find the money.'

"Uncle said that Tom Shaw was to be offered the War Office, and Greenwood to be Minister of Health, Wheatley being left out altogether, which Uncle thought was a great mistake. A lot remained to be filled in. Last night neither Lees-Smith, nor I, nor Mosley had been fixed. But I gathered that all our names were on some list that meant something, though not necessarily, nor even probably, the Cabinet. Of the two jobs outside the Cabinet mentioned by me, Pethick Lawrence was to go to the Treasury. Uncle would very much like to have me at the F.O. and would say so, if he got a chance, but J. R. M. might want to allocate Under-Secretaries without consultation. Last time, when Uncle was Home Secretary, he had actually asked Frank Hodges to be his Under-Secretary, 'and then Rhys Davies walked in!' He suggested to me, as another possibility, Under-Secretary at the Home Office. Clynes would be a good head and the work would be important and varied. Uncle had pressed, as a matter of principle, for one woman to be in the Cabinet. There had been opposition, though J. R. M. was in favour. But Uncle had insisted, though not pressing any one name, and had got his way.

"3 p.m. See C. T. at his house. He thinks he may have had something to do with keeping Thomas out of F.O. He appealed very solemnly to J. R. M. on this; negatively, not mentioning Uncle. He pressed my claims on J. R. M., but was clearly vexed by the lack of response. Usher is to be one of J. R. M.'s Private Secretaries at No. 10. This is good in principle, since Usher is a member of the Party and has been a Labour candidate for Parliament. C. T. will now go round and see Uncle right away, congratulate him and urge him to ask for me at the F.O.

"4.10 p.m. C. T. rings up that Uncle, of his own accord, said that he wanted me and would ask for me, but J. R. M. might want to make the allocations himself. This, said I, in view of J. R. M.'s general attitude towards me, and his special interest in the F.O., may be unsatisfactory! He may want one of his own henchmen to keep him informed about Uncle's doings. But C. T. has done all he could, and has been a great friend. He said at the end today, 'I know what a rotten business this is. I've been through it all myself. But *vita longa*. You can, if the worst comes to the worst, afford to wait a year or two.'

"June 7th. 10.30 a.m. Ring from Uncle, surprised that I have heard nothing. A little later a ring from Scott (his Private Secretary) saying that I am to call at No. 10 at 2.45.

"This I do, and find Usher, looking very pale and rattled, only a day and a half old as P.M.'s Private Secretary. After a quarter of an hour's wait I go into the Cabinet Room, where J. R. M. is alone. He is friendly in manner, though, I thought, a little apprehensive. He begins by explaining that 'there are three or four of you with about equal claims', for whom he has had to try to find roughly equal positions. (I assume he means Lees-Smith, Tom Johnston, Mosley and myself.) So we are none of us to be in the Cabinet. Some people have taken a different view about some of us, but he can't help it. 'You will all have to win your spurs, like we had to do.' Henderson has asked for *me* at the F.O. At this I endeavour to become very agreeable. This, I say (quite truly) is the Department, the subject-matter of which most appeals to me. In other Departments I have intellectual interests or social sympathies, but here a passion. I should be proud of the chance to do something for Peace and to carry forward *his* work. He says he can offer me the Under-

Secretaryship at the Foreign Office, subject to it being one of about twenty appointments which have to be fitted in together. But it is practically certain that this one won't have to be changed. I express sympathy with him in this business of fitting people in. 'Yes,' he says, 'it has been terrible. I have had people in here weeping and even fainting.' (I wonder *who*?) I said, 'May it be counted to me for righteousness that I have kept off your doorstep!'

"Going out I meet Uncle, and Jowitt, who has just joined the Labour Party and is to be our Attorney-General. We are photographed together on the doorstep of No. 10.

"Uncle and I go up to Hampstead by car with Will and Little Arthur. The Henderson family are to do a talkie film. General air of satisfaction! Uncle says that, when he said he wanted me, and that he had got Phil as P.P.S., J. R. M. said, as though a march had been stolen on him, 'Quite a strong team!', to which Uncle replied, 'Yes, that's what I'm after.' "

So far my diary took the story then. But many years later, when Uncle was dead, his son Will told me that the day after his father had been appointed Foreign Secretary, i.e. some time on June 6th, probably in the evening, he said to J. R. M. "I have appointed Hugh Dalton to be my Under-Secretary." "What!" said J. R. M. in astonishment. "You have appointed him?" "Yes," said Uncle, "it is laid down in the Statute that a Parliamentary Under-Secretary of State is appointed by the Secretary of State, not by the Prime Minister." And that was good law, though neither of them put it to me in those terms at the time.

As regards our backers for the Cabinet, Henderson told me afterwards that he and Clynes had been in my favour; the other three against. With Lees-Smith, Tom Johnston and Mosley, the line-up had been different, but none had a clear majority of the Big Five.

CHAPTER XI

FOREIGN OFFICE

ON June 10th, 1929, at 2.30 p.m., Uncle and I take over the Foreign Office. Just we two. No Ministers of State or Duplicate Parliamentary Under-Secretaries of State then!

"2.30–5. Fascinating $2\frac{1}{2}$ hours in Secretary of State's room. Walford Selby, who was Sir Austen Chamberlain's Principal Private Secretary, is in attendance. Uncle is in great form. We see first Sir Ronald Lindsay, Permanent Under-Secretary of State. He then introduces the three Principal Assistant Secretaries; then a crowd of about twenty next seniors; then three legal advisers.

"To this gathering Uncle makes a speech, in his own style, more familiar to me than, as yet, to them. This, he says, is the fourth Department of State, with which he has been associated. Contrary to an opinion 'which is widely held in our Movement', he believes that we can count on the loyal co-operation of the Civil Service 'in spite of the Bolshevik character of the new administration'. (A loud guffaw by the Secretary of State, a slight guffaw by the Parliamentary Under-Secretary, silence elsewhere.) He recalls with great pleasure his work at Geneva in 1924. Although the Protocol, which he was instrumental in drawing up, came to nothing, we must now make a fresh start. He believes that much can be done in the direction of arbitration and disarmament, and that he can rely on their support.

"Then a long talk à trois with Lindsay. Uncle says there can be too much continuity in foreign policy. I observe that there was no continuity over the Geneva Protocol. 'Our point of view', says Uncle, 'is diametrically opposed to that of the late Government on the Optional Clause.' Also on the recognition of Soviet Russia, to which we are definitely committed."

After discussing private secretaries and other preliminaries, "Lindsay brings up two 'urgent matters'. First, the Lateran Treaty. He suggests that Uncle should send telegrams of congratulation to Mussolini and the Pope. 'What?' says Uncle. 'Congratulate Mussolini? I doubt if he would appreciate a message from me. Do you know that a few months ago I denounced him at an International Socialist Conference in Vienna as the murderer of my old friend Matteotti? And the Pope? But I am a Wesleyan, and the Prime Minister is a Presbyterian.'

"Then Trotsky, who wants to come to England for medical treatment. Lindsay wants to refuse him a visa. 'From our point of view there is no advantage in letting him in; from the point of view of the Home Office there are obvious objections.' 'That is a new way', says Uncle, 'of approaching the matter, to ask whether there is any advantage to us in letting him in. Is there not still a right of asylum?' In any case, he adds, this is a matter which should go to the Cabinet, and it can easily wait a week or so.

"Uncle then mentions the Press Service. This, he says, must be directly under him and me, and his P.P.S. will be helpful here. 'We find', says Lindsay, 'that a P.P.S. is no use for work like this. He is a very inexperienced person.' 'That will not be so this time,' says Uncle. 'My P.P.S. is a man of very great knowledge and experience. I daresay you know him, Philip Noel-Baker.' I could hear Lindsay's jaw drop. 'I didn't know he was in Parliament,' he said.

"Uncle said to me afterwards: 'Stupid of that chap to try to rush me like that the first day. He should have had the gumption not to bring me those papers just as we were going.' " And I remember his saying to me, after we had been some time at the F.O. together: "The first forty-eight hours decide whether a new Minister is going to run his Office, or whether his Office is going to run him." Both then and later I was a great admirer, and a conscious imitator, of his technique.

He decided to keep on, for the present, Walford Selby and the other two Private Secretaries who had been with Sir Austen Chamberlain. Actually he kept Selby till the end of his term, and was most loyally served. I, on the other hand, said I would like to make a change. I asked Lindsay to find me, as my Private Secretary, "somebody fresh and bright and young". He recommended Gladwyn Jebb, now known to tens of millions in the United States on the television screen. For me this was a

most happy recommendation. Our first interview went like
this:

I. You were at Oxford?

He. Yes.

I. What relation are you to the great Jebb of Cambridge?

He. None.

I. Are you a Roman Catholic?

He. No. Are you?

I. No. But you'll do!

The first small job I gave him was to make me a chart showing
who in responsible positions in the Foreign Office *were* Roman
Catholics. There was so much talk outside of Catholic domina-
tion here that I wanted the facts. The chart showed that only
one Head of a Department—the Near Eastern Department it
was then called—was a Roman Catholic, and that no other
held any key position in the Office. This did not, of course,
cover our Diplomatic Missions abroad, where the number was
larger.

I found Gladwyn Jebb not only an admirable Private
Secretary and a most delightful social companion, but also an
outstanding personality and an intellectual power in his own
right. He worked most perfectly with me while I was at the
Foreign Office, and we had a second innings together during
the war, when I was Minister of Economic Warfare. Of that
chapter I hope to write later. Here I simply put it on record
that, in my judgment, no man of his generation in the Foreign
Service, or of the older generation whom I knew, has a more
exceptional combination of high qualities—a handsome presence, brains, initiative, ingenuity, charm (when he cares to
use it), humour, courage, energy, physical and mental endurance, and unswerving loyalty to those from time to time
set in political authority over him.

On June 17th and 19th I accompanied Uncle at his first
reception of the Diplomatic Corps. This, and the fact that no
official was present, though Selby announced them at the door,
caused, I heard, some comment in diplomatic circles. My tailor
had made me a morning coat just in time for this ceremony. I
have very seldom worn it since, but still possess it, though I
have somewhat outgrown it! The Portuguese, the Albanian
and one of the South Americans spoke in French, and I translated.

"Of the Ambassadors," I wrote in my diary, "the Spaniard, Merry del Val, was much the best. He spoke of Spain's love of peace, and said that she prized especially good relations with Great Britain and France; he deliberately, he said, placed them in that order. He offered at any time to conclude an all-in arbitration treaty with us. Fleuriau, the Frenchman, was a little thin wisp of a man. Sthamer, the German, was a fat, crumpled old thing. He said to Uncle, with typical Teutonic tact, 'You must find this office very strange. I don't suppose you have travelled abroad much.' And Uncle replied, 'I've attended international Socialist conferences in most of the capitals of Europe.' The Brazilian, dark and elegant, spoke only of trade. The Italian was away on leave.

"The Ministers, on the 19th, were hustled past, almost at the double. Only three minutes each were allowed. Uncle said: 'I shan't ask them to sit down, or I shall never get them out.' Looking, before the march-past began, at the long typewritten list of their countries, he said, 'Many of these wretched little places must be only about half the size of Yorkshire' and, when it was all over, he yawned and stretched himself and said: 'So this is what self-determination leads us to—all these snuffling little countries.' "

In those days Ministers were many and Ambassadors few. Now they are all Ambassadors and the title is worth nothing. I heard soon after that in diplomatic circles it was being put around by the Germans that Uncle was a fair-minded man without prejudices, but that his Under-Secretary was pro-French, "and even pro-Polish".

The first three objectives Uncle gave me to work on were the signing of the Optional Clause, the renewal of relations with Russia, and the evacuation of the Rhineland. We accomplished all these within the first few months, but none of them without hard fighting.

At the end of June Uncle asked me what I would think of his inviting Lord (Robert) Cecil to join our League of Nations delegation to Geneva, and generally to advise on League of Nations questions, and what I thought the Party would think of such an arrangement. I said that I would think very well of it. Though Cecil was not a member of the Labour Party, he had great knowledge and great prestige in League circles, he had resigned from the Tory Government on the Naval Disarmament Treaty and, I understood, shared all our views and supported all our immediate aims in international policy. The Party, I thought, if we were carrying out our own policy, would accept this arrangement in his particular case, but it would, of course, be much more satisfactory if Cecil would actually join the Labour Party.

This last point was put to him by Uncle, but he hesitated to commit himself to all our domestic policy.

"July 3rd. Cecil to see me. He will be a great new strength. He will have a room here and will import Will Arnold-Forster as his Private Secretary"—one of our best experts on League affairs, served in the Admiralty (blockade section) in the war, son of a Tory Secretary of State for War, not widely known to be a Socialist, all most edifying! "We are rapidly building up a superiority of gunfire over the officials. Lindsay looked in while Cecil, Phil and I were together. He retreated hastily. Cecil said to me 'Now you are found out!'"

But the officials said they could not find a room for Cecil. Ten days passed. Then:

"July 13th. Selby again mentioned difficulty of finding a room for Cecil. I said I was being driven to the conclusion that Cecil's co-operation was unwelcome to the Office. Uncle said gruffly: 'Of course, I could see that from the beginning. No room in this great building? Let us go and look.' So he and I and Selby went, and he walked straight across the passage, through what is called the Locarno Room into what is still called the Cabinet Room, where Cecil's father, the great Lord Salisbury, held his Cabinets. Uncle asks: 'Who uses this great room?' Selby says: 'It is sometimes wanted for Conferences.' 'How often?' asks Uncle. 'Twice in the last year,' says Selby. 'Well,' says Uncle, 'when it is wanted, Cecil can be asked to clear out.' Meanwhile he is to have a desk by the window, under his father's portrait. And Will A.-F. will have a desk at the far corner.

"July 17th. Cecil came to see me today. He is installed in the Cabinet Room. He said he felt like the line in the child's alphabet, 'N is a Nobleman in a large room.' He had proposed W. A.-F. as his Private Secretary and the Office had jumped at it, not wanting to provide a Secretary from their own staff. I told Cecil that Uncle was rather too immersed in detail. He said, 'Yes, the Office will try to drown him in detail, so that he shan't have time to do any mischief.' "

Meanwhile, "June 25th. New Parliament assembles. The Government benches are a glorious spectacle! G. L. said it almost made him cry. Row upon row of Labour victors. Much younger in the bulk than I had imagined. I felt really proud of our Party. Young middle-age predominates. But C. T. says that raising the school age is not to be in the King's Speech." He named a list of influential Ministers who were against it! And, of course, nothing on retiring pensions. And nothing positive about development schemes to increase employment. "This bloody Cabinet", I recorded, "is far behind our Parliamentary Executive and its 'secret programme' of last session."

On the Foreign Office front we were soon heavily engaged with Parliamentary Questions and controversial debates. On P.Q.s neither Uncle nor I were satisfied with many of the drafts submitted by the Office. Going through these and correcting them took a lot of time. He said to me one day, with a slight note of surprise in his voice, "I don't believe some of these chaps have ever read any of our Annual Conference Resolutions." I said it didn't look like it and suggested that it might be useful to circulate copies of *Labour and the Nation* in the Office. He told me to do this, with a suitable covering Minute.

I, therefore, ordered two dozen copies from Transport House, to be charged to the Foreign Office Vote, and sent them round with a Minute from which these are extracts.

"The recent heavy crop of Parliamentary Questions has occasionally resulted in a last-minute rush, which the Secretary of State and I have found very inconvenient. Some answers, raising important points of policy, have had to be passed after very scanty consideration. It is desirable to take all possible steps to prevent this in future, and to work out an orderly and punctual timetable for the handling of Parliamentary Questions in the Office." Then followed details designed to this end. "Time will be saved if replies are drafted so as to harmonise, as closely as possible, with the declared policy of the Labour

Party on foreign affairs. For general guidance on this point
a copy of *Labour and the Nation* is attached. The passages dealing with foreign affairs will be found on pages 45–49. Should
it be necessary to give a reply in apparent or partial contra-
diction with any statement contained in this pamphlet, the
answer should be worded in conciliatory terms and should, if
possible, contain some assurance that the Secretary of State
will consider the matter further if circumstances change.

"In general, so far as Labour (and, to a lesser extent,
Liberal) Questions are concerned, replies should be friendly
and helpful in tone, and all abrupt statements, which might
be interpreted as snubs, should be avoided."

The story, and the substance, of this Minute got into the
Press. It caused great pleasure in the Labour Party, and
improved the quality of our draft Parliamentary Answers. But
about a year later, when we were fighting the General Act of
Arbitration through the Cabinet and Uncle had asked me to
prepare the Cabinet Paper, the Office draft began with a
quotation, with acknowledgments, from *Labour and the Nation*.
But Uncle cut out this reference. "I find now", he said, "that
it always puts Them against a thing, if I tell Them it's in
Labour and the Nation."

Our first big Parliamentary fight was over Egypt and Lord
Lloyd's resignation. There was nothing in *Labour and the
Nation* about Egypt. This was a bonus! But within our first
fortnight the Office proposed to Uncle the heads of a possible
Egyptian Treaty, and suggested that this was a good moment
to try for it. They also began to prepare his mind for the re-
moval of Lord Lloyd, our High Commissioner, who was, from
their point of view, an "outsider", not a professional diplomat
but a Tory politician, who had been a thorn in their side under
the late Government, and well to the Right of Sir Austen
Chamberlain.

Uncle decided to have a try for an Egyptian Treaty and,
having studied the papers, decided that Lloyd must go. If he
had been to the Right of Austen, he would be far too much to the
Right of us to be any use as our tool. Uncle wrote Lloyd a letter,
then saw him and was offered and accepted his resignation.
Sir Percy Loraine, a professional diplomat, succeeded him.

"July 24th. A great day!" I recorded in my diary. Then

four heads. (1) and (2) recorded progress with Russia and the Optional Clause, of which more later.

"(3) We stage a private notice question, on which Uncle tells the House that Lloyd has resigned and his resignation has been accepted. Winston and some Tory backbenchers howling with fury. Uncle is quite splendid in standing up to them. He squares his shoulders and answers a shower of angry supplementaries with slow deliberation. His letter to Lloyd was couched in such terms as would have 'led most people to anticipate that their resignation was expected'. He will make a statement, if desired, on Friday. The laying of papers is a matter which needs careful consideration in the public interest. Roars of cheers from our delighted supporters!

"(4) J. R. M.'s statement on Anglo-American Naval negotiations. Well phrased and good content. More fury from Winston and others. More cheers from our benches.

"Our morale in the House today is the highest since the first day of the session. A buzz of triumph everywhere. 'If only we could have a day like this once a month, we should be quite content,' said one. The Tories begin to realise that they are out of office, and that we are taking and enforcing decisions. Winston shouted across the floor to me, 'You can't bully us!' I and others had been shouting 'Order!' at Tories who tried to put supplementary questions when the Speaker was on his feet.

"July 25th. Uncle preparing his speech for tomorrow on Egypt on basis of an Office draft, from 6 to 10.30 p.m. He and I and Phil dine in a private room at Phil's club. Old man very slow but sure. By the end not much of the original draft was left.

"July 26th. Lloyd debate on the Adjournment. An overwhelming Parliamentary triumph for the Government. Uncle direct, frank and self-assured. Discloses all the clashes between Lloyd and Austen, whom, as he reports, the Cabinet several times overruled in Lloyd's favour.[1] Winston in a terrible state.

[1] He cited five cases. First, in the early summer of 1926, whether or not H.M.G. should oppose the resumption of office by Zaghlul, leader of the Wafd. "My predecessor was strongly in favour of non-intervention." Lord Lloyd disagreed. "After a lengthy telegraphic dispute, Lord Lloyd's view was accepted by the Cabinet." Second, in the winter of 1926–7, "Lord Lloyd wished to insist rigidly on the retention of a large proportion of British officials in the Egyptian service generally and on the State railways, and in some departments on an actual increase in their

Rose without a Tory cheer. Attacked the F.O. Got the worst of it in exchanges with Uncle. Even began to lose the House. J. R. M. attacked him very effectively. Samuel supported us. Baldwin quite half-hearted. Austen very wisely kept right out of it! Tremendous elation in our Party. A strong finish to this first bit of the session. 'If *only* the other Departments can do as well as the Foreign Office,' several say to me rather wistfully. Ruth in the Speaker's Gallery, the sole supporter of the Government amid a cloud of Lloydite ladies, including Lady Lloyd herself. Uncle tells me later that, immediately after this debate, there was a Cabinet at which he was greeted by his colleagues, as he entered, with cries of: 'See the conquering hero comes!' Only J. R. M. at the head of the table sat silent. 'He has never thanked me for anything I have done these six and twenty years,' says Uncle to me.

"July 29th. Echoes go reverberating round the political sky, still thundery with Lloyd's going. The King is said to be very disturbed. He does not feel that he has been kept fully informed of what is being done at the F.O. and he thinks Lloyd has been badly treated. The Army have been running to the Palace. So have Lloyd's friends. Stamfordham is coming to the F.O. tomorrow. J. R. M. has written Uncle a fussy letter about Mahmud—the Egyptian Prime Minister with whom we were negotiating—'a drowning man' he thinks—and about the

number. (Hon. Members, 'Hear, hear') I think some of those 'Hear, Hears' had better be deferred. My predecessor held that such a reversal of policy was unjustifiable in itself, and calculated to defeat its own object by generating ill-feeling. A very lengthy exchange of telegrams and despatches resulted in Lord Lloyd being overruled." (Hon. Members, 'Cheer now!') Third, in the summer of 1927, "Lord Lloyd considered that the Egyptian Army was a grave threat to our position in Egypt. My predecessor" did not agree. "A protracted exchange of very long telegrams took place, and continued for some weeks. Finally the issue went to the Cabinet, who decided mainly in favour of Lord Lloyd. Battleships were despatched to Egyptian waters." Fourth, in the spring of 1928, "Lord Lloyd held that, unless the Assemblies Bill was withdrawn, it would be necessary to dismiss Nahas Pasha's Government and dissolve Parliament. My predecessor informed Lord Lloyd that H.M.G. did not desire to tear up the Egyptian Constitution. Nahas Pasha postponed the Bill. Lord Lloyd still wished to proceed to extreme measures, but was overruled." Fifth, in the early spring of 1929, the Egyptian Government proposed some new taxes on British subjects in Egypt. "Under the capitulations, these taxes could not be imposed without our consent. They were moderate and reasonable in themselves. But Lord Lloyd strongly opposed any concession whatever in respect of most of them. After a telegraphic argument he was overruled. . . . In addition to these five cases, numerous minor differences of opinion revealed themselves and . . . during the early part of this year things became so bad that the conduct of business became difficult, since on few, if any, points was Lord Lloyd able to accept the views of my predecessor, and *vice versa*."

Sudan, hesitating about our proposed terms. Uncle says that, if he is to be pulled about much more, he will suggest that J. R. M. should become Foreign Secretary himself, and be done with it. 'On Egypt the P.M. has a diehard streak, you know,' Selby said to me. Uncle told me, and the officials, that the Palace and the P.M. seem to be echoing one another, and that it's difficult to fight such a combination. To me alone he said that he knows he's unpopular at the Palace, but that doesn't worry him. J. R. M., no doubt, is disowning him behind his back."

He was quite right, as Mr. Nicolson's narrative shows. "'The Prime Minister,' Lord Stamfordham wrote to the King on July 31st, 1929, 'has written to Mr. Henderson criticising the handling by the F.O. of the negotiations with Mahmud, which he did not consider had been skilful. . . . The impression given by the P.M. was that he had been beaten by the F.O. and that the alternative would be the resignation of Mr. Henderson, although he did not say this in so many words. . . . From all the P.M. told me, and from all I have heard, I am convinced that he is not happy at what has been done."[1]

I continued in my Diary:

"July 30th. It is clear that not only Lloyd and Winston, but Admirals and Generals are in the habit of running to the Palace behind the backs of Ministers. It is sardonic that the F.O. officials should be the objects of attack and abuse now, and that on Egypt they should be to the Left of J. R. M.!

"July 31st. J. R. M. rather easier over Egypt, in view of Sir J. Maffey's excellent letter on the Sudan." Maffey was Governor-General of the Sudan and Commander-in-Chief of all troops there, and warmly backed our draft treaty, including the proposal which had so much upset J. R. M. and, as Mr. Nicolson relates, been so strongly disapproved by the King, of the return, subject to conditions, of one "token" Egyptian battalion to the Sudan.

I never really met Lloyd until we became colleagues in the Churchill Government in 1940. We then got on well together, taking wholly the same view about the war. An amusing incident happened in the early days of the new government. Our

[1] *King George V*, pp. 443-4.

security measures against spies, assassins and other saboteurs were then at their height. Gladwyn Jebb gave Lloyd, who was now Colonial Secretary, a lift in his car from some club, where they had both been lunching, to No. 10 Downing Street. A policeman, who knew Jebb but not Lloyd, stopped the car at the bottom of Downing Street and demanded Lloyd's identity card. Lloyd carried no card, but indignantly asserted his identity. The policeman, only half-convinced, asked Jebb: "Do you vouch for this man?" "Yes," said Jebb. So Lloyd was let through.

J. R. M. used to talk as though Uncle's *Heads of a Treaty* with Egypt had been drawn up, and made public, without proper consultation or Cabinet approval. This was not so.[1]

Uncle first saw Mahmud, who was on a visit to this country, uninvited by us, on June 27th. Mahmud had taken the initiative by sending him two days earlier a memorandum on the broad lines, as he saw them, of a possible Anglo-Egyptian settlement. Uncle reported this memorandum and conversation to the Cabinet. He had told Mahmud that any proposal made by the latter would have to be considered by the Cabinet as a whole. A Cabinet Committee was appointed, which held several meetings, and reported their findings to the Cabinet, as a result of which "the proposals took the shape found in the White Paper, with all the notes with which the proposals are accompanied".

Main features of the Heads of Proposals were the withdrawal of British troops from Cairo and Alexandria to the Canal Zone, as soon as the Egyptians had provided the necessary accommodation and amenities there; the end of the occupation and an Anglo-Egyptian Alliance instead; British support for Egypt's application to join the League of Nations; the abolition of the capitulations; and "while reserving liberty to conclude new conventions in future modifying the conventions of 1899, the High Contracting Parties agree that the status of the Sudan shall be that resulting from the said conventions".

"A proposal for the return to the Sudan of an Egyptian battalion, simultaneously with the withdrawal of the British

---

[1] What follows is taken from the Foreign Secretary's speech in the House of Commons on December 23rd, 1929.

Lord Lloyd, on December 11th, had said in the House of Lords: "I could not but concur" with the Government "that I was not a suitable agent for the execution of their present policy in Egypt."

forces from Cairo," would be "examined sympathetically, if, as H.M.G. earnestly trust, the treaty is worked in the same friendly spirit in which the proposals were negotiated."

The Proposals were not offered to Mahmud exclusively. They were offered to Egypt and, in particular, the White Paper stated, to "the newly elected Egyptian Parliament". It was made clear to Mahmud by Uncle that this Parliament must be, as he told the House of Commons, "freely elected" and also, what he did not say publicly, that the existing electoral law, providing for universal suffrage and direct election, should not be changed. There had been talk in Mahmud's entourage of the advantages, from their point of view, of indirect election and a restricted suffrage.

I, however, spoke on August 13th, at Welwyn at an I.L.P. Summer School. (The I.L.P. said they had invited all Ministers to address this school, but only Ben Turner, the Yorkshire textile workers' leader who was now Secretary for Mines, and I had accepted.) I said that Mr. Henderson "had made it a condition that Parliamentary Government in Egypt, which had been destroyed in the days of Lord Lloyd, should be restored. There was moreover to be no change in the existing electoral law." This led to some commotion in the Foreign Office, and to a rather chilly correspondence between Lindsay and myself. Mahmud first threatened to resign, but thought better of it. The Wafd were delighted. Uncle was quite unmoved by all this. What I had said was true. And no Treaty without the Wafd's signature was worth a damn.

Mahmud went home and the Wafd won the election. We had an Egyptian second innings with them in 1930. But there was no treaty. All else was cleared, but we stuck over the Sudan. This has now just been cleared, twenty-three years later.

"As regards Soviet Russia, we find, rather to our surprise, that there is no question of fresh 'recognition'. That carries on from 1924, when the First Labour Government gave it. The problem is how to resume diplomatic relations, which the Tory Government broke off in 1927. Some of our pro-Russians say that nothing short of an immediate exchange of Ambassadors will soothe Soviet pride, suspicion and inferiority complex. But Uncle won't have this. He proposes to invite Moscow to

send a special representative to discuss all questions in dispute.
If they refuse, he will have no hesitation in telling Parliament
so.

"Russia is still, in the whole field of foreign affairs, the subject
on which we are under most pressure from our own Party for
quick action. We are lobbied by Labour M.P.s and there is a
swarm of would-be intermediaries, politicians, Labour journalists—some turned violently anti-Russian later—and business
men, buzzing round our head. Frank Wise buzzed loudest. He
knew all the answers, and was always offering himself as a
go-between. Sometimes he went with our cautious blessing,
sometimes without it. We doubted his discretion and he had,
as he freely admitted, a personal axe to grind, as an employee
of Centrosoyus.

"July 15th. After delays, note to the Russians went this
morning. We are willing to establish normal diplomatic relations, and invite them to send a special representative to discuss
with Foreign Secretary all outstanding questions. Meanwhile
at question time in the House today J. R. M., in reply to a
supplementary, commits himself to a statement that a Russian
Ambassador can't come until Parliament has ratified the Government's decision to invite him. At this season of the year, with
the summer recess coming, this may mean nothing done till
October. Damn this slow caution!"

This answer caused a storm in the Party, and Uncle, I
gather, made a row about it next day at the Cabinet.

"July 17th. Suddenly summoned tonight to P.M.'s room. He
wants me there for F.O., while he receives a deputation of our
M.P.s on Russia. In front of them he is like a vain fractious
child, complaining of complaints, threatening to resign, etc.
Frank Wise jaws at immense length, but doesn't really make
his point. Involved quibbling between him and J. R. M. Then
a division bell rings. Then I catch J. R. M. who doesn't want
to go back to his room and go on with the discussion. I corner
him and explain that the points are two: (1) we shall lose four
months this way; (2) the Liberals would have backed us the
other way. He expresses great astonishment at (2), but in the
end drafts a motion of prospective authorisation of resumed
relations, to be put down tomorrow for an early day. I show
this to Uncle at his flat at midnight. He smiles sardonically.

This morning, he says, J. R. M. persuaded all of them, except himself, at the Cabinet that everything was all right."

But, "July 18th. Russia has fallen down again! Uncle, the morning after, takes the view that he can't now go back on J. R. M.'s supplementary answer, wrong though it was. We should have all the Press against us and the danger of 1924 all over again. 'Russia has brought us down once. We can't afford to let it happen twice.' Russia, after all, is not the only pebble on the beach. Uncle has made this view prevail with J. R. M. He is right, I feel, on second thoughts. But it's a weary business making fruitless efforts to recover ground which need never have been lost.

"July 24th. The Russians, contrary to my fears and to the general expectation, have accepted our invitation and are sending Dovgalevski, their Ambassador in Paris, to talk to us. This is convenient, because it allows of coming and going, rather than of steady sitting in London which might become tiresome.

"July 25th. Long jaw on Russia. I finally persuade them to send a simple invitation to D. to come on Monday. He couldn't come today because Tyrrell", our Ambassador in Paris, "wasn't authorised to give him a visa!

"July 29th. D. arrives. An hour and a half alone with Uncle. Apparently a good start." He was recalled to Paris two days later.

"August 7th. Uncle at The Hague. J. R. M. sends me a very reasonable version of our requirements on Russian propaganda and debts. This he wants conveyed discreetly to some of our Russophils." This I do.

"August 17th. The King has protested against the reception of a Soviet Ambassador in this country.[1] Lindsay has told Stamfordham that he is very much embarrassed by this, and does not propose to reply in writing to Stamfordham's letter." Lindsay had said to me, when there were difficulties with the Palace over Egypt and Lloyd, "It isn't the work that gets you down. It's the bumble-bees."

Uncle's talks with D. dragged on, but in the end things came out well. The decisive talk took place at the White Hart Hotel at Lewes, the day before Uncle gave an account of his steward-

---

[1] Compare Nicolson, *King George V*, p. 441 n.

ship as Foreign Secretary to our Annual Party Conference at Brighton on October 2nd. This speech, I recorded, was "the outstanding event of the Conference. A plain survey of all that has been done—Iraq, Palestine, Egypt, evacuation of the Rhineland, Geneva, Russia. At the end an ovation such as I had never heard before at a Party Conference. Not carried away by rhetoric or sobstuff, but conscious of honest, big achievement all along the line. Applause, quiet at first, but rising steadily to a crescendo, till everyone is on their feet; applause for straightforward policy and straightforward character. He had been sick for several days and had been dealing also with all the small details of the Conference, just as if he was still simply the Secretary of the Party and nothing else.

"There were few changes on the National Executive. I was re-elected with a higher vote, both relatively and absolutely, than ever before. Trevelyan and Hayes didn't stand again. Mosley did, but was defeated. Morgan Jones and George Dallas came on in his place and Trevelyan's. My vote was, no doubt, partly due to solid satisfaction at the work of the F.O."

There were many aspirants to be Ambassador in Moscow, including a number of Labour M.P.s. To one of these Uncle only said stolidly, having listened to a long speech of self-praise, "Well, I'll tell the Cabinet that you've applied for the position." He had made up his mind in favour of appointing a professional diplomat who could speak Russian. Finally the choice fell on Sir Esmond Ovey. He began well, but ran into difficulties later. No one, in my view, did better as our Ambassador in Moscow in the succeeding years than Sir Archibald Clark Kerr, later Lord Inverchapel, who was there during the latter part of the war. He was, in my judgment, by far the best British diplomat in his age group, until, at his final post in Washington, he got tired and lost interest. I shall speak more of him later.

On November 5th we had a debate in the House on resuming relations with Russia. We had Liberal support and a good majority. "Uncle makes another strong, solid speech, much approved by our people. He says that 'H.M.G. could not recommend Parliament to pledge the credit of the British taxpayer to any loan raised by the Soviet Government'. For this I am responsible. I pressed it on him, partly because, if we didn't make our position clear now, we might be embarrassed in the House later; partly, and even more, because, in my view, this was our cardinal error in 1924. There is just no case for such a guaranteed loan. Uncle spoke to J. R. M. about it, and both agreed it should be refused in advance. Tory leaders very half-hearted in opposition to our motion. L. G. backed us all the way and wished 'God speed to the Foreign Secretary'. Phil made a perfect maiden speech, well proportioned, well phrased—sometimes an echo of Pigou in his youth—well argued, with a touch of emotion at the end. I wound up for the first time for the Government in an important debate. The House was very full. I got an excellent reception from our people. They back us up very well in this House—a great contrast to the last Parliament, when they used to sit like gravestones behind the Front Bench. The Tories were flushed and noisy. In this last half-hour I made a provocative fighting speech, a counter-offensive. Our people were delighted with it, though some Tories who had intended to vote with us wouldn't after my speech—three did, however—and some Liberals, I heard, hesitated and were annoyed, though I didn't attack *them*. But I was warmly congratulated by Snowden.

"Uncle had some difficulty with the King about the Soviet Ambassador. The King said he couldn't shake hands with one of the gang who had murdered his dear cousin the Tsar. Uncle had had this difficult conversation at Sandringham last weekend." He said to me, "I didn't argue or interrupt. I just let him run on. And then I said: 'Well, your Majesty, that's the Cabinet decision, to exchange Ambassadors, but perhaps the Prince of Wales could receive him for you?' " And that is what was arranged.

And who was the new Soviet Ambassador to be? I heard that they had it in mind to send Kamenev, whom L. G. expelled for propaganda and for selling jewels to subsidise the old *Daily Herald*! Later, on November 13th, we heard that Sokolnikov had been substituted. It is possible that I had something to do with this. I told Wise that Kamenev would be hopeless, and asked why they couldn't send us a man like Sokolnikov. All I knew about *him* was that he talked about economic questions and had just made a very sensible speech at some

international gathering, saying that there was no reason why
Communist and Capitalist States should not peacefully "co-
exist". Wise expressed agreement and bustled off, and the
change was made.

Sokolnikov spoke French—he had been at the Sorbonne—
but no English. Physically he was a small man. He often
looked like a hunted animal. He had to refer every new detail
back to Moscow. It was difficult to see him alone. Some other
member of his staff seemed always to be within earshot. Ruth
and I asked him and his wife to lunch in our flat to meet three
or four Labour M.P.s. On the morning of that day a voice
rang up from the Soviet Embassy and said: "Madame Sokolnikov has a chill, but Mr. Bogomolov will come with the
Ambassador." Bogomolov was the Counsellor, a larger and
more jovial man than his chief. I had not invited him, but I let
him come. Once or twice during lunch he stopped in the
middle of a conversation to listen to what Sokolnikov was saying at the other end of the table.

And once, at the Soviet Embassy, when I went away with
Sokolnikov into a corner, we had hardly begun our conversation when Bogomolov left a group with whom he was talking
on the other side of a large room, and came across and joined
us.

The exchange of Ambassadors was clearly right. But it led
to no immediate improvement in Anglo-Soviet relations,
though it paved the way for possible co-operation against
Hitler some years later when Litvinov was Foreign Commissar
and Maisky was Ambassador in London. But the British
Government of that day failed to make the most of these
possibilities.

In our time not much good seemed to come out of the
resumption of relations—only tedious and inconclusive talks
about propaganda and debts. The Tories put an immense
number of Parliamentary Questions on these subjects and on
alleged religious persecution and slave labour in Russia, and
raised a series of debates on these matters in the House. These
questions and debates worried Uncle a good deal. I tried to
persuade him to take all this Tory stuff more lightly, and to
brush it off as obvious party politics. But I did not, as a rule,
succeed. An Anglo-Soviet Trade Agreement was signed in

April 1930 and about a year later, when Tom Johnston became Lord Privy Seal, responsible for reducing unemployment,
he showed much more initiative than his predecessors in encouraging exports to Russia. But that was about all.

We all believed, mistakenly, I am afraid, as history turned
out, that an early and complete evacuation of the Rhineland
by the Armies of Occupation would do much to create an
atmosphere of peace and goodwill in Europe. In fact, it
ministered to German arrogance and accelerated the growth
of the Nazis. But Snowden, though pro-German and anti-
French, was the most dangerous obstacle to early evacuation.
He wanted to reopen the Reparations Question, boggle over
the Young Plan, abuse the French and Italians and claw back
some millions a year from each of them. All this he tried to do
at the Hague Conference that summer, in 1929.

Uncle finally succeeded in carrying out his promise that "our
British Tommies shall eat their Christmas Dinners at home",
and in getting the agreement of both the French and the
Belgians to evacuate five years ahead of the timetable laid down
in the Versailles Treaty.

But only after a long fight against Snowden, who, snapping
insults at foreigners, particularly the French, "won rapturous
applause", I recorded, "from all the worst jingo elements in
England. Like a man with £1,000 a year turning the world
upside down for £2 10s. 0d., as Brailsford said. Swollen-
headed and fanatical, he begins even to talk of *his* duty to
restore England to 'her rightful place in international affairs',
and of our 'prestige' and even our 'supremacy'. Poor, pale,
historical shadow of a pacifist!

"August 17th. M. Norman and Lamont" (American banker)
"saw P.M. and told him that effects, in sphere of international
finance, of breakdown at the Hague would be grave. P.M.,
therefore, sent telegram *in clear* to Treasury telling Snowden to
ease up, and instructing Treasury to send this *in code* to The
Hague. The telegram reached the Treasury on Saturday
afternoon. Everyone had gone, except a second-division clerk
who, wishing to show initiative, telephoned the telegram in
plain English to The Hague. The telephone conversation, of
course, was overheard and soon everyone in The Hague knew

about it. P. S. wired back to P.M. that we were all in the soup and that P.M. must now send another telegram for publication, backing him up. P.M. caved in and did!"

A settlement was finally reached[1] on August 27th, the day before I left for Geneva for the League of Nations Assembly.

"August 28th. Snowden's face was hissed at a Paris cinema last night. The Prefect of Police has forbidden its further exhibition.

"August 31st. Uncle and his party, including Phil, arrive at midday. Uncle very tired, but very happy. He has got a great Press at last on the political side of The Hague. The tale of The Hague comes out by driblets. Still more at dinner with Phil. Uncle had to ask Mrs. S. to leave the room, because at a delegation meeting she persisted in interrupting on P. S.'s behalf. She came later and looked in on them still sitting, and asked crossly: 'How much longer am I to be kept out of my room?' P. S. sat passively in his hotel, seeing no foreigners unless they sought him out, glum and obstinate.

"To the Germans, when they came to beg him to compromise with the French, so as to save their financial situation and permit of evacuation, he said, 'You are asking me to condone a felony. I cannot do it.' Mrs. S. wrote to one of the League Secretariat: 'Some people here have no realisation of the principles that are at stake. They ask us to compromise, as though it were only a question of a small sum of money. Philip Baker, in particular, has played an unworthy part. He is always proposing new compromises.'" Political wives aren't always emollients! Yet Snowden, as a reward for his performance, got the Freedom of the City of London. But he never got the additional money he had screwed out of the French and Italians. The financial crisis swallowed all that.

Signing the Optional Clause of the Statute of the Permanent Court of International Justice meant accepting the jurisdiction of the Court in "justicable" disputes between our Government and other Governments. It meant, in short, compulsory arbitration in legal disputes. This had been in our programme and was, we held, the first step towards an orderly system of

[1] On Henderson's personal contribution to this see Mrs. Hamilton, *Arthur Henderson*, pp. 315–18.

predetermined procedures for settling all disputes between nations. "Law, not war," we said.

It was a simple, good idea and plainly right. We knew the Tories were against it. But we also ran into unexpectedly strong Departmental resistances. Signature by the Government of the U.K., it was argued, would be unwise, unless qualified by a number of reservations of which no fewer than nine were recommended. Uncle thereupon summoned me and the principal officials concerned to his room. He sat in his chair, with a stubborn look, and declared that the Government were in favour of signing the clause with the least possible delay. He did not wish to "hear a lot of legal arguments" about reservations. He, in his speeches during the election, had not spoken about reservations, but about *signing the clause*. If there were any real difficulties which they could put up, he was willing to consider them. But he expected that, when they put up difficulties, they would also suggest ways of overcoming them. All this produced rather a shattering effect, and after the meeting Uncle said to me, "Don't these chaps know what our policy is?" and, of one of our legal advisers, "Did you notice X? He didn't say a word, but he looked as though he was going to burst." He then told me and Phil to form a Committee with the principal officials and work out the details.

We had some sticky meetings, but we gradually won our way through. Uncle and I, Cecil and Phil and Will Arnold-Forster all worked together, on various planes and by various methods, to overcome obstruction and hesitation. We were supported by Sir Eric Drummond (later Lord Perth), who was then Secretary-General of the League of Nations. As an ex-Foreign Office official of high repute he could not be lightly brushed aside by our objectors. I showed him, on July 1st, the list of reservations proposed by the Office. "He is horrified. It would create a disastrous impression at Geneva. Better not sign the clause at all. Either we trust impartial judgment or not. Some people in the F.O. will, of course, be frightened out of their lives by the idea of arbitration." But some of the Office proposals, he says, are "simply cheating". This was my first experience, as a Minister, of what later became very familiar to me—the Whitehall obstacle race—of trying to push or pull some piece of policy over, or through, a long series of obstacles. These included, in this case, first, some of our own officials in the Foreign Office; second, some other Departments, particularly the Service Departments; third, some members of the Cabinet; fourth, some of the Dominion Governments.

Of the Dominions, Canada had for some time been anxious to sign, and was inclined to do so on her own, if no agreement with the rest of the Commonwealth could be reached.[1] And on August 21st, "I instigate Will" (Arnold-Forster) "to make contacts with the Irish and stimulate them to declare that the Irish Free State will sign the O.C. *anyhow*. (A certain X goes to Ireland today on this errand.) That would burst some people's idea of an Empire united only to do nothing. Cecil says we shall, if we admit the right of veto of one Dominion, have a worse Constitution than the U.S. Senate. More like the Polish Liberum Veto. Parmoor tells me that he may even resign if we give way over O.C. There is something rather dignified in his attitude. 'I am an old man, with very little time left now, but I was hopeful that we could do something quickly on behalf of Peace. If not, I can be of no further use to the Government.' I say to him that it is good to find him so strong, when others are so weak."

In the end, on August 27th, the day before leaving for Geneva, agreement was reached at a meeting with Dominion representatives that we should all sign at Geneva, and discuss reservations further, among ourselves, during the Assembly. J. R. M., in the chair, did very well. "He is always at his best", I wrote, "when just back from Lossiemouth and without too much time to waste." Phil had persuaded him that a "British Monroe doctrine" reservation[2] refusing arbitration in respect of "certain" unnamed "regions of the world" where we had special interests, pressed on us by some of our advisers, really would not do. At Geneva, "we succeeded at last in signing the O.C. I was in doubt, till the end, whether we should really ever do it. But Uncle did it on September 19th after lunch, in the Glass Room with a crowd of photographers and journalists and spectators looking on. And New Zealand and South Africa

[1] See Cmd. 3452 of 1929, p. 13.
[2] Copied from Sir Austen Chamberlain's graceless acceptance of the Kellogg Pact (Cmd. 3109 of 1928, p. 25).

and India did it with him. And so did France and Czechoslovakia and Peru. Ireland did it a few days earlier, without
any reservations, all by herself, good luck to her! Australia and
Canada did it the day after—they had been waiting for instructions—in the same formula as the rest of the Empire, bar
Ireland. This, following discussions with Dominions here, was
our London formula with only a few minor amendments—no
reservations that look reactionary or that weaken the principle
of acceptance.

"Our announcement that we were going to sign made a land-
slide. Scialoja went and signed for Italy, early in the morning,
before anyone was up, a day or two before us." And a large
number of others just after us.

"Jan. 27th, 1930. O.C. ratification approved by the House
without a division, after defeat of a Tory amendment proposing
to add a further reservation on belligerent rights. This is the
crown of $7\frac{1}{2}$ months' labour, against opposition from many
quarters. Uncle makes a solid speech in moving his resolution.
Samuel and Mander support us from the Liberal benches, the
former declaring that this is a contest between two centuries,
1930 and 1830. Jowitt winds up very well for us. Phil speaks
admirably. Angell and Seymour Cocks make their maiden
speeches. On the other side Austen is very moderate and
Mitchell Thomson very laboured. The debate goes off very
well; we have a tremendous preponderance in argument."

We had put out a White Paper, in composing which I had
some hand, defending our policy and meeting the chief objections. It is, I think, still worth reading.[1]

This seemed to many of us an historic milestone along the road
to a well-organised Peace. Since then that particular road has
become almost lost in the jungle. But we have found our way
several times to the Court, on a dispute with Norway, for
example, on fishing-grounds, when the decision went against
us and, most recently, in 1952 on our dispute with Persia over
the properties of the Anglo-Iranian Oil Company. Here the
Court first issued an interim injunction which the Persians
ignored and then declared by a majority that they themselves
had no jurisdiction, the British judge, Sir Arnold McNair, my

---

[1] Cmd. 3452 of 1929. *Memorandum on the Signature of H.M.G. in the U.K. of the
Optional Clause of the Statute of the Permanent Court of International Justice.*

old friend of Cambridge days, voting with the majority. And it is an ironical reflection that Persia was one of the "regions", in respect of which some of our Foreign Office advisers of 1929 would have declared a British Monroe doctrine, reserving the right to refuse arbitration and use armed force instead. Had the folly of that approach been fully understood by all those in responsible positions, even as late as 1951, when a British Labour Government had to deal with Dr. Moussadek?

It was decided to send an exceptionally strong delegation to the Assembly of the League in the summer of 1929. The Tories had sent one woman in their last team, the Duchess of Atholl. Of her, because she was instructed to object to every new proposal involving increased expenditure, Albert Thomas, with his large projects for the I.L.O. and for international public works, had said: "You call her the Duchess of Atoll. I call her the Duchess of Not-atoll."

Uncle, always on the lookout for going one better than the Tories, said that we must send *two* women. And this was agreed in principle, before the names were picked. The delegation, as finally fixed, was as follows: Prime Minister, Uncle, Willy Graham, Lord Cecil, myself, Woman No. 1, Sir Cecil Hurst (our Chief Legal Adviser, who later became a Judge of the Permanent Court of International Justice), Phil and Woman No. 2. The two female parts were given to Mrs. Swanwick, an old I.L.P. pacifist buddy of J. R. M., and to Molly Hamilton, a much more notable person. Molly (Mrs. M. A.) Hamilton had just been elected, after a number of unsuccessful fights, as M.P. for Blackburn in this new Parliament. She was, in my judgment, the ablest of the women Labour M.P.s in that House. And she was a great success at Geneva, both socially and in the grind of Committee work. She was P.P.S. to Attlee, both when he was Chancellor of the Duchy of Lancaster and Postmaster-General. Right at the end, as I shall relate, after the break-up of the Government, she was elected by the Parliamentary Labour Party to their Executive and to a seat on the Front Opposition Bench. With all the rest of us, she lost her seat in 1931. That finished her Parliamentary career. Had things gone otherwise, she would have been an admirable Minister in a Labour Government. She wrote many books—mostly novels and political biographies. Of these, *Arthur Henderson; a Biography*, published by Heinemann in 1938, is, as befits its subject, much the most solid and enduring. It is, indeed, an indispensable book for the understanding of the growth and character of the British Labour Party. I commend it, even on a very short reading list, to all younger people in our Party.

She was at one time an admirer of MacDonald, but gradually she came to see how little, that was firm and praiseworthy, lay behind those striking good looks and that beautiful voice and that facility for phrase-making. And, as she came to know Uncle, and saw him in action, she became, as I was, a convinced Hendersonian. This appears not only from her life of Henderson, but from another of her books, *Remembering My Good Friends*, published by Cape in 1944.

For writing her life of Uncle, I lent her some of my diaries and, especially in her chapters on the period 1929–32, she draws on them for incidents which I also narrate, sometimes a little more fully, in this book.

Since she saw, at closer range than most, much that was happening then, I quote her, though with a slight blush, on my relationship with my Chief at the Foreign Office.

"In the selection of his collaborators, he showed shrewd judgment. Having selected his men, he knew how to give them scope. Entirely without jealousy or any touch of the 'inferiority complex', he knew where he was strong and where he was weak and, knowing, did not care if others knew likewise. To his Under-Secretary, Hugh Dalton, he committed an unusually large share of responsibility over the detailed working of the office, and in the handling of papers. The combination of the long-headed Trade Unionist and the product of Eton, King's and the London School of Economics worked admirably. It rested on entire mutual confidence and entire agreement both as to large aims and immediate methods. On Committee and in debate, Dalton has athletic mental quality, and an unusual quickness of uptake; a powerful speaker, with a capacity for eloquence when eloquence is in place, he has a trained mind, a genial approach, and an easy command of Latin languages. A slight Latin bias was of no disadvantage at a period when a firm line had to be taken with France, yet no international achievement was possible without a full and sympathetic comprehension of the

French position—not always present in the pacifist section of the Party. Both at Westminster and at Geneva Dalton's friendliness and frankness of manner helped; and if his breeziness irritated opponents, it was a constant encouragement to supporters, suggesting, as it did, and rightly, that in the Foreign Office big things were being tackled with good heart and high corporate enjoyment."[1]

"What was good in Geneva," she wrote in her later book, "was the marvellous country into which one could get out. Some of us used to escape on Saturday night; sleep at some country hotel, generally in Savoy; on Sunday walk all day; and end with a really slap-up meal. Hugh Dalton was the main architect of these expeditions. He and Ruth are both good walkers, as I am; and on these outings I laid the foundation of a friendship that grew closer through the thirties. . . . For Geneva walks you had to have two qualifications—you must be able to walk, and you must be able to forget your Committees and your pet subjects. The combination was, unhappily, not as common as it might have been. Neither A nor B nor C[2] quite fulfilled the second condition, though the first two would have got full marks on the first. Generally Zilliacus used to drive us out in

---

[1] *Arthur Henderson*, pp. 288–9 and the footnote on p. 50.

And Ellen Wilkinson in her *Peeps at Politicians*, reprinted from the *Evening Standard* in 1930, wrote that, "in spite of the large head and the tall body and the booming voice, there is a lot of boyishness left in Hugh Dalton. As the son of a Canon of Windsor he thinks it is enormous fun to treat the entire Tory party with the air of a super-dowager glaring through high-powered lorgnettes. As a teacher of economics in the London School he loves to answer questions from obstreperous Tories, as though he were instructing his dullest and newest student in the first page of a primer. Nothing delights him more as an old Etonian than to face a group of his ex-schoolfellows on the warpath at Question Time, as though he were the headmaster come down in wrath to deal with a Rag." It wasn't quite untrue, and I find in my Diary for May 14th, 1930, "Twenty-two F.O. P.Q.s. The House is soon a bear-garden. Tories yelling with passion, and good response from our side. Some think I was 'provocative', others that I adopted a 'superior tone'. I had instigated some supplementaries from our side and, when young Herbert Gibson rose to put one, immediately after Austen had put one, the Tories started to shout 'Answer! Answer!' I said, 'If honourable members opposite will show a little courtesy, I am quite prepared to answer the right honourable gentleman. But I am not prepared to have my honourable friend behind me shouted down.' Then the row started, and grew, and continued throughout my ration. And perhaps I *might* have gone out to meet trouble a little less than half-way! The *Star* placards, as I walked over to the F.O. a little later, had 'Uproar in the Commons'. But it was really Red Ellen who made me do it. For precisely today she had a Bo-peep sketch of me, uncannily full of insight, in the *Evening Standard*, and I had to live up to it!"

[2] I have suppressed the names of three distinguished men, who can, however, be identified by referring to the book.

his fast and powerful car; Elliot Felkin of the Economic Section
seldom did much walking, but he would plan a quite super-
lative meal for us, when we got down from the mountains to
Sallenches, or Nantua, or wherever it might be."[1]

I spent three and a half strenuous but very instructive weeks
at Geneva in 1929. In addition to work in the Assembly, I
deputised for Uncle, both at the start and the finish, on the
Council. "Delegates remain for the most part depressingly
drab-suited," wrote Wilson Harris, "even in so torrid a September as had to be endured in Geneva in 1929, and the
severely orthodox were seen to shake their heads in pained
disapproval when Mr. Dalton so far outraged the decencies as
to make his first appearance as British representative at the
Council table in attractively comfortable grey flannels."[2] I also
persuaded Uncle, one day when he and I had been playing
tennis with others on the court in Drummond's garden, to take
a Press Conference immediately afterwards in white flannel
trousers and tennis shoes and an open shirt, I accompanying
him similarly clothed. This made a most favourable impression
on the Press, except for one small and self-conscious country
whose representatives thought they were being slighted. Once
or twice, to work off the effects of heavy official dinners,
Gladwyn Jebb and I played tennis before breakfast against
Benes and Fierlinger, then Czechoslovak Minister at Berne.

The British delegation kept the Assembly and all its Committees very busy. "In those weeks," I wrote afterwards, "one
had the sensation that the moral leadership of the world had
returned to this country, as when Mr. MacDonald and Mr.
Henderson had first gone to Geneva in 1924. The League
seemed to have come to life again, and to have gained a new
significance."[3] And Wilson Harris at the time declared that
"what chiefly struck the observer this year was the Assembly's
sustained vitality" and "it was the considered opinion of most
foreign observers that the activity of the British delegation was
the factor which, beyond all others, imparted to the Assembly
that new stimulus of which everyone was conscious".[4]

[1] *Remembering My Good Friends*, pp. 186–9.
[2] *Geneva 1929. An account of the Tenth Assembly of the League of Nations* (League of
Nations Union), p. 6.
[3] "British Foreign Policy, 1929–1931" (*Political Quarterly*, Oct.–Dec. 1931), p. 495.
[4] *Loc. cit.*, pp. 101–2.

In addition to signing the Optional Clause, we moved to amend the League Covenant, so as to cut out dead wood and bring it into line with the Pact of Peace (or Kellogg Pact). This terrified all the lawyers, but, after debate, a drafting committee was set up. We urged a "tariff truce" for two years, within which time negotiations for tariff reductions should take place. We arranged for an international conference of coal-producing countries on hours, wages and conditions in coal-mining to be held by the I.L.O. next June. We sought to reopen one or two questions which had been provisionally settled, we thought unsatisfactorily, by the Preparatory Commission for the Disarmament Conference. And we proposed a Committee of Enquiry into recruitment, promotion, pensions, etc., in the League Secretariat and the I.L.O. This proposal, contained in Uncle's opening speech in the Assembly, was entrusted to me. "Caused a great commotion," I wrote in my Diary. "Paolucci (Italian Under-Secretary) thought it was aimed at him. Drummond thought he should have been consulted first. The Small Powers were excited at the prospect of a larger share of the bigger jobs. The Italian Press thought it was an attempt at British hegemony at Geneva. Osuski (Czech) and Reveillaud (French) of the Supervisory Committee thought it was a vote of censure on them. But the staffs of both organisations were delighted. My speech in Committee in support of Uncle's proposal upset a lot more people. Drummond said his position had been rendered very difficult. He felt, he said in Uncle's room, in the presence of Uncle, Cecil and myself, that a great stir had been caused. 'Well,' said Uncle, at his best, 'this place has been stagnating for some time. It will probably do it good to be stirred up a bit.' The Smaller Powers, Drummond thought, had got above themselves and lost all sense of realities. They thought that England was leading them, and that they could defy the Great Powers, who were the real backbone of the League. His secretary, I heard, had been rushing round saying how awful it was that I had said that all the chief posts should go to Small Powers. What I had actually said was that the Small Powers had a genuine grievance, so long as all the chief posts were reserved, as at present, for nationals of Great Powers"—Secretary-General British, Deputy S.G. French, three Under-Secretaries, Italian, Japanese and

German. "In the end a huge Committee of Thirteen was appointed to enquire and report." The obvious remedy was to have more chief posts than Great Powers.

We worked hard at our personal relations. Ryrie, of Australia, was a real character. I always called him "General", his temporary rank in the war. He liked this. At some social function I asked him how many people he thought were present. He took a quick look round. "About a hundred and thirty," he said. "That's quick," I said. "Yes," he replied, "I'm used to counting sheep." He intervened in a long and solemn discussion as to the number of members who should sit on a certain Committee, and told us—it had to be translated afterwards into French—"I've always found a small Committee's the best, whether you're running a cricket match, or a horse race, or a dance. It's the same in politics. When I was a candidate once in Australia, they formed a very large committee in one place to support my candidature. And they sent me in a very big bill for drinks. But on the polling day I only got one vote there, and that was the scrutineer I took out with me. So I'm always in favour of a small committee." And Sir James Parr, of New Zealand, said: "Of course, I'm not a socialist, but I don't think Henderson's the sort of man to let the Empire down."

I thought our delegation had done well. "Next year," I wrote, "if we come again, we shall all, I hope, do better still."

MacDonald visited America at the beginning of October, 1929. He made a number of public speeches in New York and Washington and, on his way home, in Canadian cities, and he spent several days with President Hoover in a log cabin on the Rapidan River. His object was to create an atmosphere of friendship and understanding, to improve Anglo-American relations and to prepare the way for the Naval Conference of 1930. His visit was a very great success. The relations of the two countries had fallen into a bad state, following the failure of the Naval Conference of 1927, which had led to Lord Cecil's resignation from the Baldwin Government. There was even talk in some not wholly irresponsible quarters of the possibility of war, arising from competitive naval building, between us. The Americans demanded "parity" on which they put their own interpretation, and we had seemed reluctant to concede it.

MacDonald swept all this away. His speeches, largely impromptu, full of generous generalities and homely images, perfectly suited his audiences. To the Senate in Washington he said, "Parity? Take it, without reserve, heaped up, and flowing over. That was the only condition under which competitive armaments could be stopped." He invoked the Pact of Peace—the Kellogg Pact outlawing war—"a great event that I believe will stand up like a monument in history". He spoke of "taking risks for peace" and of British "national honour" being engaged by our signatures of the Peace Pact and the Optional Clause. In the "joint statement of President and Premier" issued from the meeting-place on the Rapidan River it was declared that "distrusts and suspicions arising from doubts and fears which may have been justified before the Peace Pact must now cease to influence national policy. We approach old historical problems from a new angle and in a new atmosphere. On the assumption that war between us is banished and that conflicts between our military or naval forces cannot take place, these problems have changed their meaning and character, and their solution, in ways satisfactory to both countries, has become possible. In view of the security afforded by the Peace Pact, we have been able to end, we trust for ever, all competitive naval building between ourselves with the risk of war and the waste of public money involved, by agreeing to a parity of fleets, category by category." I wrote in my diary:

"November 1st. Welcome J. R. M. home at Euston. He looks very fit and happy. He has made for himself an eternal niche in the temple of history. Our American Department at the F.O. contains some pessimists. But the immediate prospects seem good."

J. R. M. had told the King on June 5th, the day he went down to Windsor to kiss hands, when the battle between Uncle and Thomas for the F.O. was still undecided, that, "whoever was appointed to that post", he himself "would retain in his own hands the conduct of Anglo-American relations, to which he attached supreme importance".[1] And his conduct of them was admirable and by far his most effective contribution to our foreign policy.

---

[1] Nicolson. *King George V*, p. 435. "The King suggested that Mr. J. H. Thomas, owing to his close intimacy with Mr. MacDonald, might prove an excellent Foreign Secretary."

On November 4th Uncle told me that J. R. M. had proposed
to him that Lindsay should go to Washington as Ambassador,
in succession to Sir Esmé Howard, who was retiring,[1] and that
Sir Robert Vansittart, then Principal Private Secretary to the
Prime Minister, should succeed him as Permanent Under-
Secretary at the Foreign Office. This last would be a somewhat
dramatic appointment, involving the passing over of a large
number of older members of the Foreign Service who had
pretty good claims. Uncle had agreed to both proposals.
J. R. M. had asked him: "Do you think you could manage
without Lindsay?" He had replied, he told me with a smile,
"I shall have to try."

Both he and I soon found Vansittart a most welcome change.
He had a much quicker and less conventional mind, was a
much readier talker and a much more amusing companion.
He had, moreover, great personal charm and distinction. He
was a master of English prose—he wrote some plays and poems
in his spare time—and tried to improve the style of the Office.[2]
He shared my wish to give young men their chance before they
grew too old and was, therefore, not popular with the older
diplomats, whom he retired, almost without exception, at the
earliest age permitted by the regulations. He had a very ex-
tensive knowledge of foreign affairs, gained in a succession of
diplomatic posts abroad as well as in the Foreign Office, and
from much private travel and wide reading. "Quite a cultivated
chap, for a Civil Servant," I think it was Lord Hankey said.
He was one of the first to sense the German danger at the
beginning of the thirties, and the need to build the maximum

[1] Lindsay told me that he thought, if the Tories had been in, they would have
sent Sam Hoare or Eustace Percy to Washington. One reason why some in the
Foreign Service preferred a Labour to a Tory Government was because we put
fewer "outsiders" into high diplomatic posts. We were better trade unionists!

[2] I have kept a copy of this Minute which he circulated in the Office in June 1930.
"There was a recipe of 'public' writing, at its height under Lord Curzon, which
made two epithets—or substantives—to grow where one did before. I wish we
could make one grow where two have been growing—steadily. Our jargon is no
doubt a quality of the object and not of the subject; but our sentences often feel
like a fortnight without the option of a fine. The ear seems to be little used. A long
wind turns official production into a procession of whiches. The deadwood often
comes of dictation. That is an absolute necessity, but the results need pruning in
documents that go to the Cabinet or the Dominions.

"I feel it is an impertinence to offer any observations on other people's styles,
but I have to co-ordinate them—with some pride in the whole; witness a recent
Foreign Office Memorandum of 160 pages. Its manners were not as good as its
matter; and it is a minor ambition of mine that we should be as readable as possible."

strength of collective security against it. This thought ran through all his advice to Ministers. He was inflexibly opposed to attempts to "appease" the Germans by surrendering other people's rights and liberties. For this reason he was put aside, when Mr. Chamberlain took charge of foreign policy, and never once consulted by him, though he then bore the title, having been replaced as Permanent Under-Secretary by Sir Alexander Cadogan, of Chief Diplomatic Adviser to the Foreign Secretary.

Van and I became firm friends and, after I left the Foreign Office, we kept in touch, and in pretty close agreement on foreign affairs, until the war. Then he acted as one of my advisers, when I was Minister of Economic Warfare. He became a Peer in 1941.

"On November 19th, 1929, J. R. M. invites me to go to the House of Lords while retaining my present office! He has inadvertently broken the law by having seven Parliamentary Under-Secretaries of State in the Commons, whereas he is only allowed to have six. A Bill of Indemnity will be required in any case. We are all seven liable—or, alternatively, one of us is liable, but *which* one?—to a fine of £500 for each day we have sat and voted in this Parliament. This will tot up to about £19,000 each, or for the indeterminate seventh."

My initial reply is emphatically No, but, at his request, I agree to think it over and to give him a final answer tomorrow, speaking about it only to Uncle and Ruth.

Uncle doesn't press me to accept. His only point in favour is that, without a constituency and the need for constant attendance in the House, I should have more time for the Foreign Office. But I tell him that I find the whole idea repulsive, and that I should lose all touch, and influence, with the Party. Also that I should lose my Parliamentary salary when we go out of office. He advises me to base my refusal to J. R. M. on this last point.

Ruth, as I expected, is just as much against it as I am. She says, "I couldn't bear to hear Woods say 'Good morning, my lady'." Woods was the porter in our block of flats, and a good friend of ours. So I see J. R. M. next day and refuse, with thanks, on financial grounds alone. He accepts this without further argument.

Arthur Ponsonby accepted a Peerage, and moved from being Dominions Under-Secretary to be Parliamentary Under-Secretary at the Ministry of Transport, under Herbert Morrison, who, Ponsonby told me, first knew of the change when he read it in *The Times*. Russell—Bertie Russell's brother—already a Peer, became Under-Secretary for India, and two other Parliamentary Under-Secretaries were switched. And we were all legally advised to keep out of the House until the Indemnity Act was passed.

We had a second innings with the Egyptians in the spring of 1930. This time they sent a large delegation, headed by Nahas Pasha, their Prime Minister, and Makram Ebeid. It was a Wafd Government and I believed, and had often said openly, that, in carrying out an Anglo-Egyptian Treaty, if we could get one, only a Wafd Government could deliver the goods. Any other Egyptian Government, even if it signed a Treaty, would be outbid and upset by the Wafd.

The negotiations began in a big circus at the Foreign Office, Uncle in the chair, four other Cabinet Ministers, myself, Van and Loraine, six Egyptian Ministers, observers from Australia and New Zealand, and a swarm of lesser figures. The first day "Uncle was in fine form and we agreed on the first seven articles of the Treaty, subject to drafting. He frightened all our officials by going so fast, and refusing to worry about small points or all the little notes they passed up to him." He knew the big points on which the fight would come were the Suez Canal and the Sudan, and he wanted to get there quickly and settle quickly, if he could. Other Conferences have been spoilt through dragging on too long, while the Press and Parliament grew restive. He tried to get a Sudan formula in a small meeting, with only himself, Nahas, Makram and me present. A great deal of the negotiating in this Conference was done this way. Jebb had reported to me that he had heard every detail of what was said and done in the big circus from a member of the French Embassy and that it was leaking all over Mayfair. He also told me who was responsible for these leaks. When I reported to Uncle this admirable piece of intelligence work by my private secretary, he decided to close down the big circus as far as he could and to work in smaller groups.

We had several late sittings.

"April 14th. We begin at 4 p.m. today. The Egyptians come in at 5 p.m. and then, with an interval for dinner from 7 to 9 p.m. (in which Uncle and I go to the Strand Corner House), we go on till 4.30 a.m. on the 15th. Uncle was grand. The Egyptians were in the Ambassadors' waiting-room most of the night; he in the Secretary of State's room with a horde of observers, officials, etc. But some of these left early. Uncle went out by himself and talked to Nahas and Makram in a room at the back of the private secretaries' room. He came back and reported from time to time, and then went out again. He was out more than half the sitting. Meanwhile, there were biscuits and whiskies in the p.s. room. Through the door one could hear him shouting at the two Egyptians. Gradually they gave way on one point after another. We are gaining ground at the end through Uncle's sheer physical staying power.

"He and I walk home together in the small hours and are pursued by two journalists, who ask if he has any statement to make. Finding that one is from the *Daily Mail* which is attacking us furiously on Egypt, he says: 'No. I shall make my statement to Parliament.' " Before Easter he had settled everything except the Article on the Sudan.[1]

After Easter we were still stuck on the Sudan. And in spite of prolonged discussion of innumerable formulae, nothing could shift them. We had more late sittings, in one of which Uncle put his feet up on a couch and asked me to wake him when the Egyptians came back with their answer to his last proposal. I kept myself awake by alternating tea and sandwiches with Uncle and champagne with Van—and there was an amusing scene when in another room I found two Egyptians and two British Generals all on their hands and knees on the floor, over a large-scale map of the Suez Canal Zone, arguing about where the sand was hard, and therefore suitable for

---

[1] After a dinner at the Egyptian Legation, Jimmy Thomas tried to help. He harangued Makram in praise of 'Enderson and explained how he himself had often had to abate his demands in the light of necessity. He was once leading a strike and had to settle. He went down to address a mass meeting of his men. Police were guarding his car. They were afraid he would be thrown into the dock. . . . Makram, not quite understanding, but catching the word "dock", "Yes, yes, Mr. Thomas, I too have been to prison for my principles." Late that night we thought we'd got a settlement, but next morning the Egyptians said they must consult their Cabinet in Cairo.

"training and manoeuvres", and where it was too soft. But all such details were secondary to the Sudan. And on this, in spite of all our efforts, the final break came.

In 1930 we took the same delegation to the League Assembly as in 1929, except that Susan Lawrence replaced Mrs. Swanwick—an improvement—and C. R. Buxton replaced Sir Cecil Hurst, now elected to be a judge of the P.C.I.J. Malkin, who succeeded Hurst, was to be an adviser to, and not a member of, the delegation. This election of judges went partly by nationality and partly by legal merit. Thus it was generally agreed that there should be one judge, but not more, from the Little Entente—Czechoslovakia, Jugoslavia and Rumania. There was a Jugoslav and a Rumanian candidate. Uncle asked our legal advisers which was the better jurist. They said the Jugoslav. So we gave him our vote. Titulescu, Rumanian Foreign Minister, had canvassed me ardently for his candidate. I had said that we hadn't yet decided. In the result the Rumanian, and not the Jugoslav, was elected. That night, after the result was known, I went to a party at Titulescu's. I congratulated him on his candidate's success, even though I could now tell him that we had voted for the Jugoslav. "Hush!" he said, "I knew that. But I got a lot of votes for my man by telling people that you were voting for him."

In this Assembly we took few new initiatives. We were following through what had been begun the year before. But we completed the reform of the Secretariat, providing pensions, reasonable permanence of tenure, and a declaration, on appointment, of loyalty to the League. The increase in the number of Under-Secretaries was postponed, largely through German opposition because they thought any new post would be filled by the promotion of Rajchman, secretary to the Health organisation, who was a Pole. We finished off and signed, with twenty-four other States, the Treaty of Financial Assistance to the Victims of Aggression, its entry into force being made dependent on that of a General Disarmament Treaty.

The proposed amendment of the Covenant got bogged, and we postponed regretfully our accession to the General Act, since our Imperial Conference was due to meet in a few weeks' time and further consultation with the Dominions was required. Briand's proposal for European Union, very vague but supported by much rich oratory, was referred for further study.

Uncle made a strong speech on Disarmament. He heard very loud the ticking of the clock. Now that the London Naval Conference had, in large measure, succeeded, he urged that the Preparatory Commission for the Disarmament Conference should complete its work without delay and the Conference itself should shortly follow. The obligation, contained in the League Covenant, to disarm by agreement "has not yet been honoured," he said, "though it was incurred eleven years ago. The years are slipping by. And yet that obligation forms part of the Treaties of Peace, and is not less sacred than any other obligation which those Treaties contain. By that obligation every Government of the League is bound . . . The pace is slow, and the peoples of the world are growing impatient and doubtful of our good faith." This speech made a marked impression. It was in the old Protocol pattern—Security, Arbitration and Disarmament indissolubly linked. And there was still fair hope that this association of ideas would succeed. But the German elections, with big Nazi and Communist successes, came just afterwards and upset the French; while the Franco-Italian naval discussions were still sticking badly. So the atmosphere was not good, even for the Preparatory Commission.

None the less, this Commission met in November 1930, and at long last completed the framework of a Disarmament Treaty. Next year, in 1931, the date of the Disarmament Conference was fixed for February, 1932. How and why that Conference failed is not for discussion in this book. Here I claim only that, for the twenty-six months we were in office, we did our best to use the League as the most hopeful instrument at hand for peace and international co-operation.

But already, as 1930 wore on, disappointments grew and shadows deepened over Europe. The Naval Conference, though it had succeeded in April in reaching agreement, as between ourselves, the United States and Japan, on a limitation of naval building and an agreed ratio of 5 : 5 : 3 in capital ships, had not brought France and Italy into agreement on

their relative naval strengths. The Germans were responding
ill to the evacuation of the Rhineland, and the Nazis were
beginning to be noticed abroad. The strong impetus we had
given, in our first year, to the League of Nations seemed to be
weakening. And the economic depression, with its mounting
figures of unemployment, seemed to be beyond the control
either of governments, industrialists or financiers. On December
29th I wrote in my diary: "The economists can't yet make a
prophecy as to when the world forces will reverse. And, even
in the international field, there is fear in Europe and Old Adam
stalketh in the noonday. We go on signing new bits of paper,
but who believes in the undertakings they enshrine?"

And on November 11th, I had written: "Armistice Day.
It is growing terribly traditional. And Europe smells of a
smoulder, even though it may still be far from a flaming
explosion."

In 1931 both politics and economics got worse. At the
Foreign Office we politicians pressed on with our plans for
acceding to the General Act for the Pacific Settlement of
International Disputes. This would complete the work begun
when we signed the Optional Clause, and lay down predetermined peaceful procedures for settling so-called "non-
justiciable disputes". We were keen on signing this new bit of
paper and on getting others to do the same. In February some
of our officials suggested, in minutes, that we should delay
accession until talks, which were to be arranged with the leaders
of the other two parties on preparatory work for the Disarmament Conference, had taken place. So I too wrote a
minute.

"Another little halt wouldn't do us any harm! I have heard
this siren's song before. Sir R. Lindsay and others sang it to
us in 1929 over the Optional Clause. But we stopped our ears,
and sailed on to signature in a United Empire ship.... Twenty-
one months have drifted by since the Labour Party fought
and won a General Election on a policy, one of the *immediate*
objectives of which was accession to the General Act. . . .
Recently" (in October) "an Imperial Conference has met,
which agreed on this, if on little else . . ."I added in my diary.
"Damn these slow coaches and obstructionists!"

Uncle saw no reason for delay, and we went ahead and on

March 9th got a motion in favour of accession through the House against Tory opposition. The Liberals warmly supported us.

"A historic event!" I wrote. "Now we have done everything in *Labour and the Nation* (international policy), except General Disarmament."

On March 21st the Germans exploded the *Anschlüss* bomb. They just announced that there was to be a Customs Union with Austria. This clumsy, stupid provocation made sure that, when they needed help from France and others a few months later, they would not get it.

In May Uncle accepted a unanimous invitation from the League Council to be President of the World Disarmament Conference next year. In the same month the Credit Anstalt, the largest bank in Austria, closed its doors. This sent a new thrill of financial fear through Europe. Montagu Norman, without consulting the Foreign Secretary, had made large advances to this bank. This had been a move in the "independent foreign policy", anti-French and pro-German, of the Bank of England.

The flight from the mark gathered force. "July 1st. We are trying to fish Germany out of deep water. And we are trying, in support of the French, to make the Germans cut out their pocket-battleships and abandon the *Anschlüss*. The Americans are acting similarly in Berlin. But the Germans are intolerable. Bülow (sinister name) says that the abandonment of the *Anschlüss* is 'undiscussable'. And Curtius (small-minded and crafty) tells the Americans that to slow up the battleship programme is impossible because 'the aged Reichspresident Hindenburg has set his heart upon these new battleships'. Poor sobstuff this! When the Americans angrily return to the charge, they and we are told that slowing down would also 'undermine the loyalty of the Reichswehr!' "

"July 6th. Hoover plan" (for one year's moratorium on all payments, both of interest and principal, on inter-Governmental debts, designed to be a "psychological tonic" for Europe) "at last more or less accepted by the French." They had hesitated for a fortnight.

"July 11th. All-Party Disarmament Demonstration at the Albert Hall. Field-Marshal Sir W. Robertson in the chair,

J. R. M., Baldwin and L. G. Impressive, up to a point, as full Albert Halls always are, and yet something lacking. 'Rather pathetic, isn't it?' Baldwin said to me, when the cheering reached its height. L. G. mentioned with satisfaction the fact that A. H. is to preside at the Conference next year. How odd that J. R. M. should never make public reference to this!

"July 13th. Uncle leaves for Paris, en route for Berlin, where he is to be joined by the P.M. flying with two escorting planes." Another attempt to give the Germans a tonic; after this we wanted an international meeting of Ministers in London.

"But the financial news from Germany and Central Europe has been very bad. The Bank for International Settlements meeting at Basle yesterday heard Luther's" President of the Reichsbank's "account—he had flown from Germany to tell them—but ended by deciding that the bankers had done all they could and it was now up to the Governments to act. A story on the tape last night that B.I.S. had decided 'to take all necessary steps to maintain the mark'. No such luck!

"At Victoria to see Uncle off were Neurath and Cambon, German and French Ambassadors. The former stood afar off at the end of the platform and had to be fetched up by Van! How *clumsy* they are, these Germans! I had a very uncomfortable walk down the platform with N. on one side and C. on the other. Small talk wavered.

"July 15th. Dine with Royal Institute for International Affairs. I have a word with" Sir Charles "Addis going into dinner. He has been at the B.I.S. meeting at Basle and is gloomy. If Germany declares a moratorium on private payments abroad, we shall have to do the same, for our bills will be frozen. I hear later tonight that Norman is in a panic and has demanded an immediate public announcement of a meeting of Ministers in London on Monday, failing which he will demand legislation to be passed on Friday, the day after tomorrow, declaring a moratorium.

"July 16th and 17th. These are troubled days. Uncle in a very difficult position in Paris, between half a dozen devils and deep seas—including his colleagues at home!

"The visit to Berlin is cancelled—and this is announced by Uncle in a telegram, without consultation with J. R. M., whose vanity is terribly wounded. No flight in formation! Tyrrell should have prevented this slip. The French are putting out ideas for a Government-guaranteed loan to the Germans on stiff conditions—to be secured on German customs, with renewal of Dawes controls, political moratorium, etc. Germans must come to Paris on the way to London and accept in principle, or French won't come here. They are offended at our public proposal of London meeting without first obtaining their assent.

"Snowden, as usual, on his crippled hind legs, virulently anti-French. He and J. R. M. want to send Uncle instructions to prevent talks at Paris developing into a Conference, to reject without discussion any idea of British Government guarantee of any loan to Germany, etc. Van plays a good part in toning down, with Leith Ross, the form of these communications. P. S., I fear, may re-establish himself now, *à la* Hague, on a popular wave of anti-French feeling, already very strong in the City, in the Press and in some parts of all political parties. The Treasury are conducting sharp arguments with the French over the distribution of German reparations during the next twelve years. But this is not exactly the present point.

"I hear that on Friday (17th) a Tory M.P. asked one of our officials at lunch whether it was true that Uncle was being recalled from Paris. So the heats of No. 10 and No. 11 are becoming known to the enemy. I lunch with one of J. R. M.'s Private Secretaries and exercise great caution. *He* asks, 'How could we guarantee a loan to Germany, when we have refused to do the same for the Dominions?' So I infer that J. H. T." (now back at the Dominions Office, as a rest cure after Unemployment) "has been active at No. 10, as usual.

"July 19th. Meet Uncle at Victoria at 11 p.m. Stimson and Mellon also on the train. The French, Germans, Italians and Belgians come on tomorrow. Uncle, looking very tired, goes straight with P.M. to No. 10, where Snowden joins them. I hear afterwards that the conversation was a bit spiky!

"July 20. Uncle is very conscious of the jealousies of his colleagues, but comparatively quiet. He had undertaken, he says, to bring the Germans to Paris and the French to London. He had succeeded, and had committed our Government to nothing. But it had not been easy. Did we want French assistance or not? If not, he need not have gone to Paris at all.

The P.M. had had a mad idea of flying to Berlin and bringing the Germans back with him to London, thus 'keeping them out of the hands of the French'! He *had* told the P.M. of the impossibility of the visit to Berlin, before it had been finally cancelled. He had had to get the P.M. out of bed to tell him this; perhaps this was why the P.M. seemed to have forgotten it, he had seemed half-asleep at the telephone.

"If a Conference without the French had been desired, it could easily have been got. He would only have had to read them some of the telegrams he received from the Treasury. But he had used his discretion and brought these back, unused, in his pocket. Whenever he went abroad he had the same experience, lack of confidence, suspicion and jealousy on the part of his leading colleagues. He, at any rate, was pro-Peace and pro-Party, not pro-Self.

"July 21st. At 1.45 a.m. after finishing diary I hear the steady whirring of aircraft overhead. It is the R.A.F. doing their annual exercises over London. There is no defence against air attack on a large city. What shadows we are and what shadows we pursue!

"And a great financial crash is still possible. 'The Comet is upon us', as Brailsford headed his article in last week's *New Leader*.

"July 22nd. X of the *Daily Herald* to dine. Had absorbed all the Snowden stuff. Hundred per cent. anti-French. Why were they withdrawing gold from London? They had brains like razor blades. A. H., people said, was no match for them at Paris or Geneva. It was dangerous when he went abroad alone. X told a story, supposed to illustrate the present situation, of a German saved by a British Trade Union leader from drowning at Marseilles, and of a Frenchman on the shore who said, 'Why did you trouble to save him? He's only a German.' X also said that J. R. M. has told the Cabinet that, if a moratorium became necessary, there would have to be a National Government.

"The Seven-Power Conference in the end got nowhere, and passed the ball back to the bankers. But it was, perhaps, something that it met at all."

On July 27th, J. R. M. and Uncle paid their postponed visit to Berlin. It led to nothing beyond vague talk. On July 31st

Parliament adjourned. What happened in August belongs to my next chapter.

The period 1929–31 was, in international affairs, a very unusual one. Neither the United States nor the Soviet Union made any heavy political impact upon Europe. On the Continent France was the strongest power, in political influence, in armed strength, in finance. Stronger still, if all her Allies could be counted on to stand with her. This was no real threat to Britain, or to British interests. But it was an unanswerable argument for close Anglo-French co-operation. And it was not likely to last indefinitely. Germany, for the moment, was too weak to be an actual threat to France or anyone else. But all the old potential evil and harsh danger to her neighbours was still there. The League of Nations, on the other hand, was a new potential good. Henderson's aim was to make it actual and to use it, on the principles first laid down in the Geneva Protocol of 1924, to give to all, including France and ourselves and all the extra-European members of the League as well, the joint blessings of Security, Arbitration and Disarmament, and no more war. He pursued this aim with great determination and devotion. And he scored notable successes. In Parliament, in Cabinet, in the Foreign Office and in international conferences, he fought the good fight and he kept the faith. He did all that we had promised the electors in the field of Foreign Policy, except for that General Disarmament Treaty on which he was focusing all his efforts at the end of his term. Least of all men was it *his* fault that that Treaty was never signed. The promises he kept brought much less good than we had hoped. Our troubles washed away the basis of our hopes.

And in the end, in 1931 and the immediately succeeding years, our economic and political troubles, our domestic and international troubles, all flowed together into one great world-wide swamp—the Great Depression of trade and employment, the Great Betrayal of Democracy (in Germany), of Collective Security (first in China and then in Abyssinia) and of Disarmament by Agreement (at Geneva).

But I was very proud to stand at Arthur Henderson's side, both at the Foreign Office and elsewhere and afterwards, and do my best to help him in his fight for Peace.

CHAPTER XII

END OF THE SECOND LABOUR GOVERNMENT

As I have described in the last chapter, I was very much absorbed in 1929–31 by Foreign Affairs. The troubles on the Home Front were not my immediate concern. A Cabinet Minister cannot escape his share of collective ministerial responsibility, and is steadily fed—often overfed—with information, oral and written, of the joys and sorrows of his colleagues. But Junior Ministers, as a rule, do well to stick to their Departments. I had, indeed, an additional responsibility as a member of the National Executive of the Party. Therefore I tried, particularly as things got worse, to influence events on the Home Front.

The Second Labour Government's record abroad is a moderate success story, not lacking courage and skill. Its record at home is a hard-luck story, with failure almost unredeemed either by courage or skill.

On October 30th, 1929, I wrote: "Uncle is taken up with fights in the Cabinet to get the damned fellows to *move* in home affairs, industrial transfer, etc. It takes him much away from the Foreign Office. He has also Transport House on his hands. 'The only damned man of them who's any good,' says Tom Johnston." But there were a number of other good Ministers on the Home Front, if only some of their principal colleagues would let them start moving. My diary for October 30th goes on: "Spoke at Hackney for Herbert Morrison—a damned able chap this. I think he may be a future P.M." He was Minister of Transport throughout the life of this Government, and became a member of the Cabinet in 1931. And others, in whom I had great confidence at this time, were Arthur Greenwood at Health, my old friend Charles Trevelyan at Education, though he got into a terrible tangle over his Bill to raise the school-leaving age, and Christopher Addison and Tom Johnston, who got their chances later, on promotion to the Cabinet as Minister of Agriculture and Lord Privy Seal.

It was announced, when the Government was formed, that the Lord Privy Seal (Jimmy Thomas), would be "responsible for dealing with unemployment", and would be assisted in this task by the First Commissioner of Works (George Lansbury), the Chancellor of the Duchy of Lancaster (Sir Oswald Mosley) and the Under-Secretary of State for Scotland (Tom Johnston). This was a queer set-up. Of Thomas's three assistants, only Lansbury was in the Cabinet. The four, as anyone who knew them must have known, were most unlikely to work well together as a team. And none of the four had in his office Civil Servants of sufficient knowledge of the unemployment problem to be of any use to the Ministers, or of sufficient standing in Whitehall to deal on equal terms with the leading Civil Servants at the Treasury, Board of Trade, Ministry of Labour and other "departments concerned". This set-up, therefore, was doomed to work badly both on the ministerial and on the official plane. Just how these Ministers were serviced, I do not know, though I think I remember hearing that Sir Horace Wilson, then of the Ministry of Labour, was attached, for unemployment problems, to the Lord Privy Seal. And I recall, and have already quoted elsewhere, George Lansbury's account of meetings, with Thomas in the chair, "in a sort of semi-dungeon high up in the Treasury offices. We were surrounded by the reputed élite of the Civil Service. . . . There was always present one faithful watchdog of the Treasury, who . . . could always be counted on to find good and excellent reasons why nothing should be done."[1]

Thomas was soon persuaded, though the other three were not, that our election promises to keep young people longer at school and to take old people out of the labour market should not be honoured, and he quickly saw the point of every objection which any official raised to every scheme of new development.

The Treasury even resisted the revival of the Trade Facilities Act, under which new loans for development might be guaranteed by the Government, on the ground that this would "damage the national credit and hinder their conversion operations".[2]

[1] *My England*, pp. 142–3, quoted in my *Practical Socialism for Britain*, p. 12.

[2] *Practical Socialism for Britain*, p. 21, where I add: "Under the Second Labour Government the Treasury were always on top. 'How do you like your new Chief?' a Treasury official is reported to have been asked, soon after Mr. Snowden had succeeded Mr. Churchill. 'We are delighted at the change,' is the reported reply. 'We feel that we have moved up from the pantry into the drawing-room.' "

In 1930 the Prime Minister set up an "Economic Advisory Council", a mixed bag of Ministers, industrialists, financiers, Trade Union leaders and economists. He enjoyed presiding over the diffuse discussions of this body, which also spawned, as was to be expected, a number of sub-committees. Hubert Henderson was his favourite economist. He much preferred him to either Keynes or Cole—all three were on the E.A.C.—partly because he spoke with an attractive Scots accent, but still more because he explained, so clearly and with such insinuating charm, that nothing any member of the Labour Party ever proposed would do any good.

I heard that Snowden did not like the Council, which he thought would usurp his powers and those of the Treasury, and that he had objected to the Council enquiring into Free Trade as an immediate policy in Great Britain—on this his mind was tight shut—or into monetary policy, since the Macmillan Committee was still sitting on this, or into the functions of the State in relation to unemployment policy. Keynes had wanted this last enquiry, but the business men on the Council had backed up Snowden in resisting it, and Keynes had then hurt the Prime Minister's feelings by describing himself as "the only Socialist present". And Hubert Henderson had solemnly warned Ministers against the idea that unemployment could be cured by public expenditure, but had suggested a 10 per cent. import duty on all manufactured goods, half the yield of which should go to national development and the other half to the Unemployment Insurance Fund. And Colin Clark, then a junior member of the secretariat, had proposed a heavy export duty on gold.

Meanwhile, unemployment rose from 1,630,000 in June 1929, to 1,912,000 in June 1930, to 2,700,000 in July 1931, and to over 3,000,000 in September 1931.

There was an increasing obsession, among Ministers and politicians generally, with the question of the payments to be made to the unemployed; some wishing to increase and others to reduce them. But there was a terrible and growing defeatism, almost everywhere, about the possibility of reducing the *number* of the unemployed. That any schemes for new work could really make much difference seemed to more and more people less and less likely. In niggling discussions about "abuses" and "anomalies" in the payment, in a small minority of cases, of unemployment benefit, most Ministers and their officials quite lost sight of the major "abuse" and "anomaly" of mass unemployment itself. British unemployment, we were told, quite truly, was mostly due to world causes. There was a world-wide slump. So what could we do? None of the experts had foretold this slump, nor, as it grew worse, could any expert tell us when it would begin to mend. In fact, particularly towards the end of our term, we did much more than many realised, though much less than we should have done, in creating employment through schemes of new development. But for this, our unemployment figures would have been even higher than they were.

I recorded, on May 13th, 1930, a talk with Tom Johnston on the personal difficulties, and on the confused pattern of Committees—some not meeting for months at a time—which were supposed to be studying, or preparing to reach decisions on, unemployment and connected problems. There was no central directing hand or brain.

"'If the Party meeting only got to know of a few things like this, they'd all be climbing up the walls, not just the I.L.P. but the soberest Trade Unionists in the Party.' Meanwhile J. H. T. says that we can do nothing; we are in the hands of Providence; in America they have five millions unemployed, while we have only one and three-quarter millions."

Later that month Mosley resigned from the Government and ten months later, on March 10th, 1931, was expelled from the Labour Party, by a unanimous decision of the National Executive, for an "act of gross disloyalty in seeking to create a new party... with Parliamentary candidates in opposition to Labour members and Labour candidates in the constituencies".

In the summer of 1930 Jimmy Thomas retired hurt from the office of Lord Privy Seal and limped back to the Dominions office—a very quiet department at that time. He was succeeded, as Lord Privy Seal in charge of unemployment, by Vernon Hartshorn, who, when asked in November to tell the Consultative Committee of the Parliamentary Party what he had been doing about unemployment, replied: "How can I tell them anything? All my proposals were put in last August, and no decision has been taken on them yet." Hartshorn died in March 1931, and was succeeded by Tom Johnston.

"April 14th, 1931. House reassembles after Easter Recess. On Thursday, the day after tomorrow, there is a Tory vote of censure on unemployment. We are in very grave danger of defeat. We can't trust L. G., we have four Labour seats vacant through death and a long list of sick, and the Mosleyites and even the I.L.P. are uncertain. I put off papers in the office into a post-Thursday pile.

"April 15th. The prospects for tomorrow's vote seem a little better. I tell Gladwyn I think that statesmanlike odds are about three to one on the Government. He offers to take these in pounds.

"April 16th. T. J. following Baldwin makes a good speech, well arranged and containing new stuff—oil from coal, new plans for rural housing, electrification of railways, sitka spruce on Snowdon, etc. I congratulate him very warmly, and he and I and Adam McKinlay, his P.P.S., go out and eat welsh rarebits at a Lyons. He says he has had an amazing first fortnight in office. What a trail of strange characters, from L. G. to Saul Bron, coming to his room!

"Today L. G. promises support to the Government, praises T. J. and attacks the Tories and Simon. So the steam is out of the debate. We had a majority of 54!"

How easily we were cheered, for the moment, with quite small things, and by a Minister who had his heart in his job, and courage and energy, and hope that he could find men work!

Then: "April 27th. Snowden's Third Budget. A clever get-out. It will carry us on and rally the Liberals. L. G. as pleased as a child over the Land Tax. Frank Owen told me a few days ago that L. G. had told him that he would like 'one more big fight before I die', and the Land and the Lords look likely to furnish it. There was the same thrill in his voice, and the same phrase, tonight over the Land Tax, as over Addison's Land Utilisation Bill, 'it is a measure after my own heart'."

But it was a sick man's Budget, and strangely irresponsible. Just before Easter Snowden had had an operation, and had been lying ill in bed for weeks, practically cut off from all his colleagues. In February he had given solemn warning about the state of the national finances and of the heavy burden of unemployment benefit. And he had consented to, and indeed himself had half-suggested, the appointment of an "Economy Committee" of outsiders, with Sir George May of the Prudential in the chair. This Committee had been appointed on March 17th and reported on July 31st. They reported, first and foremost, a large prospective Budget deficit. Meanwhile, at the end of April, Snowden produced a Budget which purported to show a small prospective surplus, and contained no important immediate changes in taxation, nor reductions of expenditure. The chief difference between his estimates and Sir George May's three months later was in what items it was proper to charge to capital account. But what authority had the May Committee to settle this?

The Land Tax would bring in no revenue for two years. Though at first blush it greatly pleased the Liberals, it nearly led in June to the defeat of the Government. The Liberals put down an amendment, whereby payments under Income Tax Schedule A would be allowed against liability to Land Tax. Snowden fiercely resisted this. Most members of the Government and most Labour M.P.s thought the point was quite unimportant. I wrote: "June 12th. There is talk of a General Election next week. J. H. T. has been running about telling everyone that P. S. is a bloody fool and that he (J. H. T.) is to be the next Chancellor of the Exchequer. P. S. has heard of this, and is more mulish than ever.

"June 15th. The 'crisis' is not yet over. P. S. is very stubborn. Later tonight Uncle says it is decided that either P. S. will give in tomorrow, or his resignation will be accepted.

"June 16th. Snowden gives in. This is duly announced at a Party meeting amid congratulations. But this afternoon Dunnico ends the crisis by ruling the Liberal amendment out of order! So it can't come on now till new clauses are reached. The Tories very disappointed at the success of this 'intrigue', as they call it."

Snowden himself had for some time been eager to reduce unemployment benefit. He had hinted in his speech in the House in February that this might be necessary. This had caused a great row in the Party and at a special Party meeting he had beaten a retreat. I recorded: "Feb. 5th. Snowden tried to persuade the Cabinet to agree to reduce the rate of unemployment benefit! They declined, though some were much inclined thereto! So I needn't resign yet." And four months later: "June 11th. Party meeting on unemployment insurance. Cabinet policy announced by J. R. M. and Uncle. No cuts in benefit, nor increase in contribution, nor change in conditions of transitional benefit. But a Bill to deal with *some* 'abuses'. Politically unprofitable piffle! But the Cabinet has avoided, for the moment, the more obvious blunders."

As Molly Hamilton well writes: "There was no single issue on which feeling" in the Parliamentary Labour Party "was so decisive and so unanimous . . . while the rank and file would tolerate other sacrifices, if they were assured that they were necessary, sacrifices at the expense of the unemployed they would not stand."[1] This was a reef of granite. Snowden, and his associates in this proposed economy, had been warned.

So we swirled on into the much greater financial crisis, which started in Germany and Central Europe, but was soon transmitted with full force, through financiers' folly, to Britain too.

On July 28th, very early in the morning, they telephoned to me from Windsor that my father was dead. I went down with my sister. My mother was surprisingly calm. His end had been merciful and swift. He had read the lessons at Evening Service yesterday, then in the night he had begun to bleed from a haemorrhage in the stomach, and in a few hours he was dead. He had very little pain. The doctor, who came just before midnight, said he couldn't live through the night; gave him a drug to quieten him, and sent for a nurse. But the old man wouldn't have her in the room. "What do you want, young woman?" he said. "I shall be all right again soon." These, I think, were his last words.

He was ninety-one years and ten months old. For his own sake, it was well that he lived no longer. His sight and hearing were failing and his nerves were getting out of control. His disabilities were fast closing in upon him. For me his affection continued till the end quite unabated.

On July 30th, according to his wish, he was cremated. I went alone, in a car behind the coffin to Woking, and brought back his ashes in a casket.

[1] *Arthur Henderson*, p. 362.

On July 31st he was buried in St. George's Chapel, in the
South Aisle, where thirteen years later my mother's ashes were
laid beside his.

At the funeral in St. George's that day the King and Queen
were represented. My mother, Ruth and I, my sister and
brother-in-law, and three of my Evan-Thomas uncles and
an aunt were there. At the end Walford Davies, at my wish,
played on the organ part of Dvořák's *New World Symphony*,
including the Largo. This had been one of my father's favourites, and mine. We had often heard it together, sitting side by
side in the Nave in the dark, at evening organ recitals by
Walter Parratt. Then my mother went away for a fortnight
to stay with old friends.

"August 1st. The House is up, and Ruth and I go to West
Leaze,[1] where we find an infinite and pervading peace. Here
there still ring in my head the words we sang yesterday in
St. George's, very beautifully, 'This shall be my rest for ever.
Here will I dwell, for I have a delight herein.' "

But it was only to be a short peace before battle and storm.

Apart from three days with Ruth at Windsor, going through
my father's papers and looking after my mother's future arrangements, I was at West Leaze till August 20th—sleeping,
digging, sun-bathing, reviving.

But I knew that, following the publication, on the day that
Parliament rose, of the May Report, a Cabinet Committee of
Five had been appointed—J. R. M., Snowden, Uncle, Thomas
and Willy Graham—to consider what action should be taken
on it. And the Press were working up a crisis atmosphere. I was
inclined to be lazy and to contract out of all this. After all, I
wasn't in the Cabinet! And I had seen none of the official
papers. But Ruth prodded me to try to help Uncle, who, she
truly said, wasn't much at home in this field. So, about half-way
through the month, I sent him a short memorandum. I advised
that, if it was a question of balancing the budget, the Sinking
Fund should be suspended, and taxation increased—higher
income tax, surtax, death duties, perhaps an additional tax
on income from fixed-interest-bearing securities, since the
rentiers had been doing very well as a result of falling prices.

---

[1] Our small, modern house on the Wiltshire Downs, near Aldbourne. It had
been built in 1930 and we had entered into possession in January 1931.

But no revenue tariff—I had seen this suggested in the Press —and no serious cuts in the social services and, above all, no cut in unemployment benefit.

On August 20th, a few days after I had sent this document to Uncle, a special meeting of the National Executive was summoned in London. We met at 2 p.m. "I have a few words with Uncle just before the meeting. He says he has never gone through such a trying time as the last five days. The position is extremely grave. There has been a serious flight from the pound, which isn't over yet. The recent credits arranged by the Bank of England—£25 millions from New York and £25 millions from Paris—weren't intended to be touched. They were only secured, and announced, in order to restore confidence. But they *have* been touched already. The flight is not only by foreigners, but by some of our own nationals as well. The May Report figure for next year's deficit is too low, not too high, by more than £50 millions.

"He thinks I will appreciate how serious the position is, when he tells me that he has agreed to a cut of £1,000 a year in his own salary. They have been considering in the Cabinet Committee, and in the Cabinet, some drastic reductions in expenditure, including the pay of the police and the teachers. But they won't reduce unemployment benefit except, perhaps, by requiring a man drawing benefit to go on paying his contribution into an auxiliary fund for those on transitional benefit. There is a large majority in the Cabinet in favour of a revenue tariff of 10 per cent., as a preferable alternative to a cut in unemployment benefit. He and Willy Graham are both converted to this, in view of all the circumstances.[1] But,

[1] Harold Nicolson, deriving his information from some other members of the Cabinet, states that "a minority insisted that there must be no reduction whatsoever in the doles being paid to the unemployed and that additional revenue must be created by imposing a general revenue tariff of 10 per cent. . . . The Prime Minister made it clear that . . . all idea of a revenue tariff must be abandoned, since it would be obnoxious to the Liberal Party." (*King George V*, p. 457)

I am in no doubt, having been informed by three or four members of the Cabinet independently, including Arthur Henderson, that a majority of fifteen to six favoured a 10 per cent. tariff. But some of this majority were not prepared to resign rather than agree to a cut in unemployment benefit, though at least one of the minority against the tariff was. As regards the Prime Minister and the tariff, my information is that he was one of the majority in favour.

Nor were the approximate figures on the tariff kept secret. Mr. Churchill in the Parliamentary debates next month on September 8th (*Hansard*, col. 47) stated that "three-quarters of the late Labour Cabinet, lifelong free traders, were prepared to support a revenue tariff".

if the majority press too hard, there may be a batch of resignations. There can be no more borrowing for the Unemployment Insurance Fund. The source which previously lent the
money can and will lend no more." This, I suppose, is a reference to the Post Office Savings Bank—much exploited by
our opponents a little later. But the argument was nonsense.
It would, of course, have been perfectly possible to go on
borrowing for the Fund by way of the Floating Debt—
Treasury Bills or Ways and Means Advances. Here some of
our advisers had put a fast one over the non-experts.

"I say that I had been strongly opposed to a revenue tariff,
but, if it is really a choice between this and heavier cuts in
social services, I should perhaps change my mind. But *is* this
the choice? He says that everyone has been asking this question
about every proposal. He is convinced that it is. Both the Tory
and Liberal leaders want to cut unemployment benefit."

After an hour's meeting in the National Executive, trans-
acting routine business, we have a joint meeting at 3 p.m. with
the General Council of the T.U.C. Snowden, who is not a
member of either body, is also present.

"J. R. M. talks characteristically and says nothing, no figures,
nothing concrete. He blames the Press, including the *Daily
Herald*, for sensational and inaccurate reports. In the present
crisis first principles are of no use at all. But there is no change
in our policy or in our ideals. Let them remember that every
member of the Cabinet is a Socialist or a Trade Unionist, or
both. Faced with this lack of confidence in sterling, due to
mischievous propaganda at home and abroad, it is essential
to balance the Budget. There are three ways in which this can
be done: by economies, by fresh taxation, or by a combination
of the two. The Government have decided on the third method.
Perhaps someone would like to ask some questions.

"Snowden, invited to speak, says he has nothing to add.
Some members of the G.C. are now in a very angry mood.
Why have they been brought here, if they are to be told no
more than this? There is a succession of protests.

"Then Snowden, very unwillingly, rises and says a little more.
He can't disclose anything about new taxation. He thinks everyone will appreciate this. As to economies, Cabinet Ministers and
others with £5,000 a year or more will give up 20 per cent.

Other Ministers a smaller proportion. Teachers 20 per cent. Police some reduction. Civil Servants another bonus cut under the existing cost-of-living agreement. Personnel of the Fighting Services a reduction. They are looking for other possible reductions in the Fighting Services. Unemployment benefit is not to be reduced, but only to be paid for 26 weeks a year (sensation). £8 millions less on roads. Funds of Unemployment Grants Committee to be reduced. No reduction on Health Services. Increase in Unemployment Insurance Contributions.

"Then follow a few questions amid increasing clamour and confusion. Arthur Cook shouts above the din that we are being stampeded. Susan Lawrence asks whether, after 26 weeks, the unemployed are to go on to the Poor Law. There is no answer."

The joint meeting then breaks up, and the National Executive and the General Council meet separately. "As I go out, several of the G.C. say that this sort of thing is quite impossible. Bevin says he is for a revenue tariff in preference to cuts in the social services. The G.C. sit late, and then send a deputation, in highly critical mood, to the Prime Minister. The N.E., on the other hand, get through the rest of our business quickly, after deciding to leave the main question, for the moment, in the hands of those of our members who are in the Cabinet, i.e. Uncle and Clynes. This decision is reached as the result of a quite moving statement by Uncle, and a shorter statement by Clynes. Clynes assures us that heavier taxation of the rich is an essential part of the Government's plan. Uncle speaks much on the lines of what he said to me earlier today. And then he adds: 'You know who my colleagues are. You can imagine that I have had a tremendously hard fight. Mr. Asquith once said of me that I was always getting into situations in which I felt a double loyalty. I have been experiencing that again this week, loyalty to my Cabinet colleagues and loyalty to the Movement outside.' He adds that he is definitely for a revenue tariff in preference to a cut in unemployment benefit. A number of members of the N.E. stress their opposition to such a cut.

"And so away . . .

"I feel that it is impossible for this Government to live much longer. This is not the kind of thing that *we* can do. Better keep the Party together in opposition than break it up in office, and disappoint all the deep, simple hopes of our supporters. Let us put up a bold programme, let Tories and Liberals unite to defeat it, and then let us go out.

"And I ask myself, as to the background of it all, two questions. First, as to the flight from the pound, what persons, and what impersonal factors, are responsible? Second, as to the Budget deficit, when was this first discovered? Why Snowden's almost complacent Budget Speech only four months ago, with its little Churchillian devices, and its only extra tax an extra twopence on petrol? Who was deceived, and who deceived the public? Snowden, or the Treasury officials, or who?

"Back to W.L., thinking that very soon I may cease to be a Minister, and be able once more to speak my mind, and to pull my weight in the Party."

"August 23rd (Sunday). I am digging a hole in the chalk for a beech near my western hedge"—it's a fine tree now, more than thirty feet high, in 1952—when "in the dusk the village policeman appears, salutes and announces 'a message from the Prime Minister, sir'." We were not yet on the telephone. "I am requested to be at No. 10 Downing Street at 2.30 p.m. tomorrow. I ask the policeman to reply that I'll be there. Then Ruth and I classify the alternatives. A collective or an individual summons? A resignation of the whole Cabinet, or a partial resignation, either from the Right or from the Left, or an explanation of a policy now agreed upon without any resignations? A summons to me as a Minister, or, though this seems less likely, as a member of the National Executive to be further consulted?

"I may have to take a difficult decision at short notice, whether or not to resign; or whether or not to accept some other job. Ruth will come with me, to advise me on what may be one of the most critical choices in my public life. The heartbreak would come if Uncle stayed in, while I felt that I must come out. But I don't think this is likely.

"Whom in the Cabinet can I trust? Not many, wholeheartedly, on this sort of issue. Certainly Tom Johnston and George Lansbury in addition to Uncle. Probably Addison and Greenwood. That's only five. None of the others are better than possibles." Charles Trevelyan had resigned in January. I would certainly have trusted him.

"August 24th. By car to Hungerford, where we buy papers. The *Herald* gives eight names of those who will resign rather than agree to cuts in unemployment benefit—Adamson, Addison, Alexander, Graham, Greenwood, Henderson, Johnston, Lansbury. All my five are in that eight, and three more besides! All doubts vanish. 'That's my team,' I said to Ruth, 'I'll play with them against the rest.' There'll be no difficult decisions now. So Ruth goes back in the car to W.L. and the sunshine on the Downs.[1]

"Arrived at the F.O., I go to Uncle's room and congratulate him very warmly on standing firm. He is walking up and down in considerable agitation. He and those who have acted with him, he says, have taken their political lives in their hands. It's very uncertain how the thing will develop. They are to have their last Cabinet at noon. J. R. M. is determined on the formation of a 'National' Government, containing Tories and Liberals, with himself as Prime Minister. Uncle doesn't know how many of the present Cabinet will join. I tell him that I have come up in response to J. R. M.'s summons. He fears this may be an attempt to get hold of some of the Junior Ministers.

"The noon Cabinet is soon over. They are all to resign now, but J. R. M., Snowden, Thomas and Sankey will go with the

[1] Harold Nicolson (*King George V*, p. 464) quotes a letter from Sir Clive Wigram, from the Royal Archives, stating that on the Sunday evening "the Prime Minister" arrived at the Palace "looking scared and unbalanced. He told the King that all was up and that at the Cabinet eleven had voted for accepting the terms of the bankers and eight against. The opposition included Henderson, Graham, Adamson, Greenwood, Clynes, Alexander, Addison and Lansbury. In these circumstances the Prime Minister had no alternative than to tender the resignation of the Cabinet." The minority of eight named here differ from the eight named by the *Daily Herald*, by including Clynes and excluding Johnston. But the latter, as I know well, was most firmly with the minority. And I heard later that Clynes was too. Thus the minority was nine, not eight. There were twenty-one members of the Cabinet at this time. The others eleven were MacDonald, Snowden, Thomas, Sankey, Webb (Passfield), Parmoor, Wedgwood Benn (Stansgate), Tom Shaw, Amulree, Margaret Bondfield, Herbert Morrison and Lees-Smith. Probably, therefore, the voting was eleven (not including the Prime Minister) to nine.

The King may well have assumed that this ratio would roughly represent the voting within the Parliamentary Labour Party, or, at the least, that the Prime Minister would carry a substantial minority of his party with him in support of a 'National Government'. Had the King foreseen how few Labour M.P.s would follow their leader on this uncovenanted journey, he might have thought it more appropriate that Mr. Baldwin should become Prime Minister.

new Cabinet. 'And now,' he says, 'you'd better move about a
bit before this afternoon's meeting.' The Original Resigners
are lunching together in G. L.'s room. They stand a little apart,
at this stage, from the rest, morally a little above them.

"I lunch with Clem Attlee at Odone's. We prepare ourselves for the 2.30 meeting, to which he also has been summoned, by drinking a bottle of sparkling red Burgundy. He
is hot against J. R. M., for his indecision and his inferiority
complex, especially in all economic questions, and hotter still
against Snowden who, he says, has blocked every positive proposal for the past two years.

"At 2.30 the Cabinet Room is crowded. All Ministers not
in the Cabinet, and all Whips, are invited. J. R. M. sits alone on
the other side of the long table." It is as though a martyr was
speaking, just before a cruel death. "He had originally summoned us, he says, to tell us that our salaries were to be cut.
(This is not true, for the summonses went out only yesterday
evening, when the 'National' Government was already decided on.) But now he has to tell us that the Government is at
an end. He is very sorry. We shall curse him, and he is afraid
that he has caused us great embarrassment. But the gravity of
the crisis is not yet widely understood. We shall be told that it
is a bankers' ramp. But that is quite untrue. He has received
most valuable help from the bankers. No one, for instance,
could have been more helpful than the two representatives of
the Bank of England. 'Poor Norman has broken down under
the strain.' It was quite essential to get a loan quickly. Otherwise sterling would have collapsed. There would have been a
run on the banks, and then a run on the Post Office, and then
an attempt to cash thousands of Savings Certificates, against
which there is not a silver sixpence in the Treasury. He could
not bear to think of school children, who have put their savings
into these certificates, being unable to get them out. It is in the
light of facts like these that we must consider such a proposal
as a 10 per cent. cut in unemployment benefit. This would
leave the unemployed 1½ per cent. better off than two years
ago, for the cost of living has fallen by 11½ per cent. The
alternative would be equivalent to a cut of 50 per cent., or
even more.

"He thinks the crisis could have been avoided if the Cabinet hadn't changed its mind at a critical point. A plan had been drawn up and agreed, which would have sufficed to secure the loan required. But then the Cabinet went back on it. (This also is untrue and is much resented by Uncle and others, when it is reported to them.) This made necessary a Government of Persons, not of Parties. He is going through with this. He has not called us here in order to try to form any cave, or to ask us to join him. Most of us are young men, with our political careers before us. He realises that he is committing political suicide. He is not going to ask any of us to do the same, or to put our heads into the noose into which he will put his. But . . . perhaps some of us *would* be willing to travel the same road with him. The best plan will be for him to write to us individually and enquire. He would have liked to stay longer with us, but he must now go to the Palace.

"'But I have done one thing for you' (at this stage I almost anticipate a distribution of Savings Certificates) 'I have made it a condition that there shall be no reprisals against those who oppose us. There will be no coupon election when this is all over.'

"Then a question or two. Attlee asks what would be done to the rentiers. He can't answer that. It is impossible to anticipate a Budget statement. Shinwell asks whether the alternative was considered of the Cabinet resigning and leaving to the Tories and Liberals the responsibility of carrying through an economy policy. Oh, yes. Every possible alternative has been considered. Susan Lawrence asks whether formal resignations by Junior Ministers are necessary. Oh, no. All members of the Government will resign together, and then the new administration will be formed.

"And then we disperse. Going out, Willy Lunn and I speak vigorously against J. R. M. And I apparently am clearly audible, for a colleague claws my sleeve nervously and says: 'Don't speak so loud. There are a lot of Pressmen outside. They will hear you.' And I reply: 'I don't give a damn if they do!' To one Pressman I say: 'Just for a handful of panic he left us!' and to another: 'I am going into opposition now.' And so, by all the signs, are the great majority of us.

"Straight round to Transport House, where in Uncle's room is a council of war. With him are G. L., Bevin, Citrine, Stanley

Hirst, Middleton. The Trade Union leaders are full of fight. They speak of financial assistance. 'This is like the General Strike,' says Bevin; 'I'm prepared to put everything in.' They send for X of the *Herald*, to settle the line of tomorrow's leader. X —still under the influence of J. R. M. and P. S., who had been working on him very hard—had proposed to begin by paying a tribute to the courage of those who are staying in. 'And what about the courage of those who are coming out?' asks Uncle. So the whole emphasis is changed.

"The *Herald* in the days that followed, under Bevin's influence, gave a fine lead. Thomas threatened that, unless it changed its tune, there would be an advertisement boycott. This threat was ignored.

"There is a feeling in all our minds that Uncle is now the only possible leader. But he is very unwilling. He says that he is now 68; that they wouldn't have him fifteen years ago; that he must look after the party organisation, in view of an early election; that we mustn't drive J. R. M. and the others out; that this is only an interlude in the life of the Party, like the war; that Clynes is Deputy Leader and must not be pushed aside; and much more. But in the next few days he gradually yields to pressure from all sides.

"I speak to Gladwyn Jebb on the 'phone. He is in the country, getting a bit of leave before Geneva. I announce mock-pompously that a new Administration is being formed, to which neither the Secretary of State nor I shall be adhering. And so our Geneva trip together is off too. I tell him that he ought to take a turn of duty abroad now for a change. Which capital would he prefer? Berlin or Rome, he says. So I arrange, as almost my last official act, that he shall be posted to Rome.

"I go back tonight to W.L., breathing clearer air, happier than for many months.

"August 25th. To the F.O. to clear up. In the evening to Arthur Greenwood's flat. Evidence of practical unanimity in the Party is growing. Press estimates of J. R. M.'s Parliamentary following rapidly falling. How ignorant of our Movement the enemy Press is! They began by giving him 180 Labour M.P.s out of 280. Then this fell to 50. Now to 20 or 30. In fact, the figure will be less than a dozen. Jack Hayes, when taking leave at the Palace, had mentioned some such figure as this, and an officer of the Household had exclaimed, with disappointed surprise, 'Then it won't be a National Government at all!' And an officer of the Prince of Wales's Household had written to Jack Hayes some days before saying that he had been 'working for two years to bring about a National Government'. Not good form!

"August 26th. My birthday. I am forty-four; happy though weary. Finish at the F.O. Pay a round of visits with Gladwyn to the departments to say good-bye to the officials. A very nice lot, on the whole. For me Gladwyn and Van are in a class apart and I shall miss my daily contacts with them both. We have had great fun together. My last Minute, which I initial today, is on a letter, sent to all Ministers at this time of the year, according to an ancient custom, offering for a token payment a quarter of a buck from the Royal Parks. I minute: 'I pass this buck to my successor. H. D.' So, no doubt, Anthony Eden had it!

"August 27th. One of my friends in the late Cabinet to lunch. Awfully tired, but gives a very interesting account of some recent history. Greenwood, Johnston and Lansbury were against any dole cut throughout. Others only joined up later. Uncle deliberately held back, while others did the fighting. But he never finally assented to anything. He always said that he must first see the complete picture. Then at the end he dug his feet in against the dole cut, and then J. R. M. saw the game was up. The resignations would be too important and too many for replacement to be possible from the ranks of the Party.

"It was on the Sunday night that they heard from New York on the telephone that a loan would be forthcoming for a 10 per cent. dole cut, but not without it.[1] Seven of them had voted

[1] It was denied at the time by many speakers and newspapers that this particular economy, a cut of 10 per cent. in unemployment benefit, was made a condition of the loan from New York. But the evidence is overwhelming. Mr. MacDonald, asked in Parliament whether he would restore this cut, replied: "No. That was a condition of the borrowing." And now Mr. Nicolson, in his careful narrative in *King George V*, is quite definite on this point. (See pp. 450, 456, 457, 460, 462 and 463.) Indeed he goes further. On the Saturday, he says, "Messrs. J. P. Morgan had already hinted that" there might be reluctance to find the money "in view of the lack of confidence felt" in the United States "in Europe in general, as well as in the willingness of a Socialist Government to balance budgets or adopt 'sound' fiscal policies." And now on Sunday night, "in the concluding paragraph" of their telegram which Mr. MacDonald read aloud to the Cabinet, "Messrs. J. P. Morgan enquired whether they were correct in assuming that the economy proposals now tentatively put forward by the Cabinet had the sincere approval

against putting this humiliating question to New York at all, and no agreement had ever been reached that, even if a loan were the price, a 10 per cent. cut should be accepted.

"At an early stage Snowden had wanted to shove all the unemployed on to the Poor Law after 26 weeks. But this proposal had been dropped. The Tory and Liberal leaders had never agreed to a 10 per cent. cut as sufficient. They had reserved the right to move an amendment in Committee increasing the percentage.

"At a meeting of ex-Cabinet Ministers this morning, Uncle apparently agreed to accept the leadership, and Clynes, magnanimous as usual, will propose this himself tomorrow at the Party Meeting.

"Some of those who voted for the dole cut in the Cabinet are very angry with the *Herald* for spilling the beans and showing them up.

"But what a change it is to have good, or even passable, relations with all the leaders of the Party. These I now feel I have. With J. R. M., P. S. and J. H. T. I never had any relations at all, and was always conscious of suspicion and dislike, which I heartily reciprocated. It is a cleaner air I breathe today, and the prospects of a real Labour Government, full of youngish men, under Uncle's Premiership are bright, though still speculative, within one or two years. And I can hardly fail to be in the *next* Cabinet.

and support of the Bank of England and the City generally, and whether the latter regarded them as sufficient to re-establish confidence." "It was, it seems," adds Mr. Nicolson, "this last sentence that caused Ministers to cry aloud in pain," so that "to Sir Ernest Harvey," the Deputy Governor of the Bank of England, "waiting in the adjoining room, it seemed that 'pandemonium had broken loose' " (p. 463). To many of us it was, indeed, intolerably painful that our domestic policy should be dictated by a combination of American bankers and "the Bank of England and the City generally". In such conditions, we should have done without the loan and gone off gold instead—as the National Government, in fact, did three weeks later. Mr. Nicolson has taken great trouble to make his story of this political and financial crisis accurate. He states that he "has been much assisted by verbal discussions with Lord Wigram, Lord Hardinge of Penshurst, Lord Samuel, Sir Ernest Harvey, Sir Edward Peacock and Mr. Herbert Morrison". Also, no doubt, with Mr. Ramsay MacDonald, who, after the break, became his political leader. (Mr. Nicolson stood unsuccessfully for Parliament as a Mosley "New Party" candidate in 1931, and was elected as a National Labour candidate for Leicester in 1935.) But I regret that he seems to have had no "verbal discussions" with any of those Cabinet Ministers who stood with Mr. Henderson in resisting the cut in unemployment benefit. Four of these were still alive when he was writing this book, Lord Addison, Mr. Alexander, Mr. Greenwood and Mr. Johnston. At several points in his story it might have helped him to hear the other side.

"Meanwhile I must come back on to the economic front, while keeping one hand and one eye on foreign affairs, and write a best-seller on Finance and Financiers! But I am still very tired.

"August 28th. Historic meeting of the Parliamentary Labour Party at Transport House. Most arrivals seem very cheerful, though a few look apprehensively serious. Members of the General Council are invited to be present. This is an innovation, suggested by Uncle, to mark unity.

"James Barr from the chair gave an account of the joint meetings of the Consultative Committee earlier in the week with the National Executive and the General Council (there had been two of these which I had attended), of the resolution passed and of the manifesto agreed to.[1] A resolution was moved, on behalf of the Consultative Committee, approving their action and asking that we go into official opposition. On this, by request, Uncle makes a long statement, narrating events. He is followed by Sankey, the only one of the four remaining in the Cabinet who has the courage to attend the meeting. (J. R. M. had sent a querulous letter saying that he had had no notice of the meeting, but had read of it only in the Press, that he had already arranged to go to Lossiemouth, and that, if he *had* attended the meeting, he could not have told them anything, as confidences were always betrayed 'by one or two', and then

---

[1] The manifesto declared, in part,

"A new Coalition Government, for which the Labour Movement repudiates all responsibility, has been formed. It is a government of persons acting without authority from the people.

"It is determined to attack the standard of living of the workers in order to meet a situation caused by a policy pursued by private banking interests in the control of which the public has no part.

"Unemployment benefit is attacked because it strengthens resistance to wage reductions.

"A protracted Press campaign has created the impression abroad that Great Britain is on the verge of bankruptcy. Nothing could be further from the truth.

"Four thousand millions of British capital are invested abroad. Great Britain is still one of the greatest creditor countries. We are still adding to our capital assets. The taxable capacity of the country has not been exhausted.

"The immediate situation can be met without further depleting the slender means of the poor and without restricting national and local expenditure directed to development.

"If the will were present, we could overcome the immediate difficulty by mobilising the country's foreign investments, by a temporary suspension of the Sinking Fund, by taxing fixed-interest-bearing securities and by measures to reduce the burden of war debts.

"The proposals to economise at the expense of the poor are not only unjust but economically unsound. They will increase unemployment by reducing the consuming power of the masses."

a postscript saying that he had just received an invitation, dated August 25th, which must have been delayed in the post. P. S. sent a shorter and much more dignified letter, saying that he did not think it would serve any good purpose for him to attend, as he saw from the Press that a financial policy had already been decided on.[1] J. H. T. sent no letter.)

"Sankey began by saying that he believed J. R. M. had saved the country, but, here putting his hand on Uncle's shoulder, that Henderson had saved the soul of the Labour Party. He went on to justify his own action; partly on the importance and imminence of the Second India Round Table Conference, where he was again to be Chairman of the Structure Committee, and partly on financial policy. If you were in financial difficulties, you were wise to go to the best financial adviser. They had done that. He believed that the unemployed were willing to make a sacrifice, if everyone else did the same. They were only proposing a reduction in respect of the adult unemployed (a bad point this, which caused loud murmurs). They were none of them leaving the Labour Party. Nothing would ever drive *him* out. A brave speech, but remote from the Party's general mind.

"Then a few excited words from Sydney Arnold. Then I spoke. I said I did not often address the Party meeting. For more than two years my mouth had been closed, except on foreign affairs. I had been very happy in the F.O., but very unhappy outside it. The First Labour Government had been destroyed by a Red Letter, and the Second by a Banker's Order. (Loud approval from G. L.) We had had two magnificent speeches, one, Uncle's, magnificent for its content, the other, Sankey's, magnificent for its courage. We admired Sankey's courage, as he stood alone today, as we had admired it when he had come out in 1919 for the nationalisation of the mines. We thought he was right then, but wrong now. But let us not recriminate against those who had joined the 'National' Government. Let us not throw the first stone. But, if we were attacked, we would defend ourselves. Let us rise to the height of our opportunity, and re-unite our own ranks. I appealed, in

[1] These two letters were both read aloud, and I made these notes in my diary at that time. Snowden in his *Autobiography*, p. 953, states that J. R. M. sent no message to this meeting and that he himself was not aware of it till after it had been held. His memory was clearly at fault.

particular, to the I.L.P. to forget their bygone quarrels and merge their little group in the larger unity. Let us work now for a real Labour Government—not the sham thing we had known for the past two years—with an independent Parliamentary majority. But, for the future, slogans were not enough. We must hammer out a firm detailed policy of Socialist reconstruction in industry and in finance.

"There is a very good reception for this speech. Of those who follow" two—still alive in 1952—"make incoherent complaint and are ill received. Then Ben Tillett declares that 'the class war is here', and Jimmy Sexton regrets our departure from the ideals of Keir Hardie. Malcolm MacDonald announces that he will go with his father, and attacks Uncle for going back on understandings and on 'the report of the Committee of Five'. This brings Uncle to his feet to deny the accusation and, in particular, to repeat that the Committee of Five made no report. Finally the resolution is accepted and we are officially in opposition.

"Then Clynes moves that Uncle be the Leader. A beautiful speech, and a beautiful action, recalling his loyal acceptance of defeat by J. R. M. for the leadership in 1922. He says that Uncle has strongly urged *him* to be the leader, but he realises, in view of all that has happened, that Uncle is the only possible choice. For himself, he has been so long in the Movement that he has no longer any undue personal ambition. But he has not lost the love of service. He will serve willingly as No. 2, No. 3, No. 4 or in any other position which his colleagues may decide. Ben Turner seconds. No other nomination. Carried with five dissentients—Maxton, Beckett, Buchanan, Campbell Stephen and Jenny Lee.

"Uncle takes the chair. Regrets lack of unanimity. Since it is generally felt that there is a call to him to accept, he will give it a trial, in spite of his other work as Secretary and Treasurer of the Party.

"He moves that Clynes and Graham should be Deputy Chairmen. Agreed. Agreed also that an Executive should be elected. Meeting ends.

"Phil and I walk back with Uncle and offer our services, if desired, as at the F.O. He seems pleased and asks Phil to go on as P.P.S.

"We speak of the attack on him in the *Morning Post*, alleging that he had told Laval in Paris that there would have to be a moratorium in London, if there was one in Berlin. He says this is quite untrue. What he told Laval was that the situation in London was so serious that J. R. M. couldn't come to Paris, and that therefore the Five Power Conference must be in London. But J. R. M. had told him the same morning, on the telephone from London to Paris (which was probably tapped), that there was grave danger of a moratorium and that, in that event, there would have to be a National Government.

"I also recalled Addis' unguarded statement to me, within earshot of a whole crowd of people, going in to dinner at the Royal Institute of International Affairs, that there might have to be a moratorium." No wonder the rumour had got round!

"September 1st. To Bishop Auckland. First meet Executive and give them the inner story day by day. Unanimous and enthusiastic support. Then to public meeting in Town Hall. Crowded, and many can't get in. Expectant, deeply interested, responsive. But not electric.

"I speak for just over an hour, and end with an analysis of the effects of the falling price level. Bankers and financiers live in a gilt-edged world, divorced alike from the needs of industry and the realities of working-class life. We have been landed in a bog of national humiliation. The leaders who have left us have been gradually losing sense of direction, keeping strange company, listening to strange counsellors. I became a Socialist 25 years ago, because I hated social inequality and was disgusted by the spectacle of the rich riding insolently on the backs of the poor. Because I have not changed my views, I stand, unrepentant and unhesitating, behind Arthur Henderson, whose record entitles him to the country's full support. I would sooner go to Hell with the Durham miners and their heroic wives than share an Earthly Paradise with our three Lost Leaders. Vote of confidence carried with two dissentients.

"September 2nd. Back to London. Lionel Robbins comes in and talks after supper. Provisionally agreed that I go back to the School in the New Year. On the financial and economic situation, he is curiously unhelpful, though he would like, I think, to be otherwise. Sceptical about the possibility of raising the price level, or of mobilising our foreign securities, or of development schemes, electrification, etc. A prisoner, I feel, of his own subtle, but still incomplete, economic analysis. The only ray of hope he can shed is that there may be an American revival in the spring, with good repercussions here.

"September 5th. With Ruth to visit Cripps at his country house. He has been ill, and H. Morrison too, who has been staying with him.

"More light on the crisis. Cripps is the only lawyer in the House who has stuck to the Party, though he reports that Pritt is sound too. He shows me letters from his father (Parmoor) and from Beatrice Webb, his aunt, approving his attitude. Parmoor—I tell his son how grateful I was to him for his stand for the Optional Clause against J. R. M. and others, while Uncle was away at the First Hague Conference—thought on Friday, August 21st, that everything was settled, and a plan agreed without any cut in unemployment benefit. He went away, exhausted but content. Then, within half an hour, an attempt was made unsuccessfully to collect the Cabinet again. What had happened? Next day the Cabinet *was* collected again, and told there *must* be a cut in unemployment benefit. They wrangled all day, and it was finally decided—accounts differ as to whether unanimously or not—to sound the American bankers on a plan containing a 10 per cent. cut.

"Next day, Sunday, August 23rd, the Cabinet met at 6 p.m. to hear the American answer. The telephone message was delayed. J. R. M. asked whether they should disperse, or wait and talk. Agreed to wait and talk. Then Uncle said he would resign rather than agree to any cut. This was clearly the end. It was the first time resignation had been mentioned. Hitherto it had been thought that a minority would give way to the majority.

"Then at 6.30 J. R. M. reported that the Americans had agreed to a loan conditional on the plan put up, including the 10 per cent. cut. Cripps understands that, when J. R. M. offered his resignation on the Sunday night, Baldwin flatly refused to form a Government. But Cripps says also that J. H. T. had told Jowitt early in July that 'if there is a moratorium, our plans for a National Government are all ready'. So the idea was not new to J. R. M. when the King proposed it to him.

"Cripps says that, listening first to P. S., and then to Uncle, he could hardly believe that they were giving accounts of the same crisis. Sankey, he says, took his stand with J. R. M., partly because he felt that they ought to show that the Labour Party was not subject to dictation by the T.U.C. (What a silly attitude! The T.U.C. were only reasserting the principles of the Party, except as regards the revenue tariff, on which they were not united, and on which a majority of the Cabinet agreed with a majority of the G.C. in preferring this to a cut in unemployment benefit.)

"September 7th. New Parliamentary Executive meets at Transport House. I have been elected with an astonishingly high vote, which is really rather a moving tribute to the general belief in me. It is this sort of thing which sometimes frightens one, and recalls that Labour leader's prayer: 'God make me worthy of the men I lead.' Figures: Johnston 151, Lansbury 140, Dalton 137, Greenwood 131, Barr 125, Addison 109, Alexander 108, Ebby Edwards 95, Pethick Lawrence 87, Shinwell 81, Lees-Smith 79, Grenfell and Molly Hamilton each 68.

"These last two, having tied, were both put on. Uncle, Clynes and Graham *ex-officio*." These choices and these votes were a rough measure of our relative standing in the esteem of the Parliamentary Party at that time.

"In the next days we have heated and bitter Parliamentary debates. There is much assertion and counter-assertion by members of the late Cabinet." Never, certainly in recent times, has so much been said in public about proceedings and personal attitudes in Cabinet! "Our back-benchers are half rattled, half bored by all this. I make one speech—on September 15th, winding up from our side on Budget resolutions— which gives some comfort to our people. But I hate speaking in the House and am never at my best there."

Snowden's emergency Budget showed no flicker of ingenuity. He raised the standard rate of income tax from 4*s*. 6*d*. to 5*s*.; reduced all the personal allowances, except earned income relief which he slightly raised; added 10 per cent. to all surtax payments; and further increased the taxes on beer, tobacco, petrol and entertainments.

The new Government's policy—this Budget, taken together

with the economies on unemployment benefit, on the pay of the men in the armed forces, the police, the teachers and the civil servants, and on development schemes—was certainly unjust. It increased inequality.[1] It took power by law to break contracts with those who worked for the State, but not with those who received interest from the State, nor with those who worked for private employers. And its whole tendency, as Keynes, in particular, so cogently argued, was, by destroying purchasing power, still further to increase unemployment and to reduce future revenue.

In my speech I pointed out, as did other speakers from our side, that our crisis did not spring from an unbalanced Budget, for both the United States and France, our creditors in crisis, had unbalanced Budgets. It sprang from reckless over-lending, principally to Germany, by a number of finance houses in the City of London. These had borrowed short from the Americans and the French and lent, as they thought, short to the Germans. But they soon found they had lent long. When the German crisis broke, we couldn't get our money out of Germany. And so our foreign creditors hurried to get theirs out of London. They demanded to be repaid in gold, and some of our own nationals joined in the run on the Bank of England.

Lord Beaverbrook, among others, stated that many of our financiers had borrowed at 2 per cent. from the French and Americans and lent at 8 per cent. to the Germans. But, whatever the rates of interest, the thing was indefensible. None of our lenders knew how much the others were lending. They consulted neither one another, nor the Bank of England. A year later Mr. Montagu Norman at a bankers' dinner said that foreign concerns "have been able to borrow on short credit sums which, had the various lenders been aware of it, would have been quite out of the question and which have come as a surprise to all of us". He appealed for closer co-operation among finance houses, but added: "These are matters which

---

[1] "Take the cases", I said, "of three unemployed men, one with £5,000 a year, one with £500 a year and one with rather less than £50 a year—that is to say a man receiving unemployment benefit." The first was going to pay, in increased income tax and surtax, an additional £170 a year, or 3½ per cent. of his income; the second an additional £27 a year, or 5 per cent. of his income; the third, who was now to get 15/3 instead of 17/- a week, would have a 10·3 per cent. cut in his income. And this took no account of increased indirect taxes. "Equality of sacrifice?"

do not concern me very directly." Our crisis of 1931 was caused by grave faults of British private finance.

"September 11th. Davenport, 'Toreador' of the *New Statesman*, to lunch with me and Cripps. Intelligent and helpful. We of the Policy Committee are trying to meet as many City blokes as possible these days." This was my first meeting with Nicholas Davenport, with whom, and with his charming wife Olga, Ruth and I later became great friends. And so too a number of other friends of ours, who met them through us. We have spent many happy days, and also many useful hours, with them in London, at their house in Berkshire and at West Leaze. They will recur later in my story."

Our Policy Committee was meeting a great deal at this time, both as a full Committee and in sub-Committees. Graham was chairman. I took an active part, and so did Addison, Alexander, Attlee, Cripps, Pethick and Frank Wise.

"My first feeling of sheer joy, when the Lost Leaders decamped, and my belief that we shall have a majority at the next election, has subsided a little. I think we shall do well to hold our present strength—and may very nearly do this. Then after, say, two years of increasingly unpopular Tory government, a clear Labour majority at last?" I was slowly moving towards the cruel truth!

"September 17th. Beveridge to dine with me. He presses that the Labour Party shall say, at the forthcoming election, that, if we win, we shall not abandon the gold standard. It will give foreigners confidence in us, he thinks, if all parties united in saying that we should stick to gold. I said that we could give no such undertaking. It is held by many that we shall soon be forced off the gold standard anyhow. We, as a Party, shall no doubt demand the summoning of an international conference. But, if we are still on gold and the Conference fails to give us satisfaction, then I think we shall go off gold deliberately. He finds this answer very disappointing." As Director of the London School of Economics, he had at this time a very legitimate interest, since the School had just received a large instalment of dollars from the Rockefeller Foundation, and he was hesitating about investing it in sterling securities. Then, four days later,

"September 21st. We go off the gold standard this morning! The National Government has failed in its primary object. Everyone seems bewildered. Some think this will put off the General Election for some time. Later in the day this view weakens.

"September 28th. Meetings all day on Policy Resolutions for Scarborough (Labour Party Annual Conference). Parliamentary E.C. in the morning, National E.C. in the afternoon, with an interlude of negotiation by Graham and myself with Bevin and Citrine, who would like large alterations in our draft." We meet them on some points and stand out on others. "Graham and I do a redraft later this evening. The feeling earlier in the day is that the election is on. This weakens in the evening on reports of Liberal resistance.

"September 29th. Policy Resolutions reported to Party Meeting and accepted, on the whole, very well. One or two useful amendments suggested. Graham and I do a final redraft in the early afternoon. The feeling that the election is on strengthens as the day advances. The Tories all wear grinning faces. The Liberals are said to be 'finding a formula' and the promise of coupons. But Cabinet meetings are long, and apparently troubled. Herbert Samuel told Joseph Hunter that 'no decision has yet been taken'. J. R. M. said to be very angry, and more inclined than before to an election, because he has heard (quite correctly) that our N.E. yesterday decided, without waiting for Scarborough, that those Ministers, M.P.s and candidates who had associated themselves with the National Government could no longer be regarded as members of the Labour Party.

"Graham tells me that Snowden would never tell the late Cabinet anything about his financial plans, because he distrusted J. H. T. Also that J. H. T. not only wanted to succeed P. S. as Chancellor, but also wanted a knighthood for his stockbroker. J. R. M. was said to be sympathetic to both these aspirations."

I have already quoted a conversation, in February 1924, which shows that J. R. M., even at that time, was thinking, without distaste, about a "National" Government, with himself at its head. He may, of course, have entertained this idea even earlier.

I have no doubt that, as time passed, this tolerated thought grew into a strong desire. If I have correctly read the mind and the emotions of this strange man, he found most of his "followers" in the Labour Party less and less attractive, and many of his political "opponents" much more pleasing. He loved being flattered, made a fuss of, run after, by the polite and considerate rich. "Ah, Mr. MacDonald, if they were all like *you*!" he liked to hear them say.

And so gradually, and as these social circles widened—as they always will for rising politicians who desire to enter them—he contrasted to himself more and more sharply the drab, rude, coarse-grained, cocksure, uninstructed members of the Labour Party with those brighter spirits, the more elegant, refined, wealthy, thoughtful members of the aristocracy, with their wider interests and their more comfortable and hospitable homes. So he went to "the aristocratic embrace", as Webb, I think, first called it. And after that embrace, once or twice repeated, to the new political liaison, the "National" Government.

But though he wanted this badly, he wished to seem to have it forced upon him, by forces stronger than himself, outside himself, even against some faint gestures of resistance. Yet— and here, perhaps, is his greatest tragedy—when at last he got what he wanted, the first satisfaction soon passed, and he resumed his old unhappiness, his martyr's crown, his grievances against most of the world at home and abroad—including, of course, his old "followers" in the Labour Party. He never wanted to revive *that* dead relationship. But he had had his great new political love affair too late in life. When it came, at last, he was long past his best.

Of his desire for such a Government, and of his intention to form it, there is a great cloud of witnesses. I call only those who themselves gave evidence to me.

Webb[1] had been trying for months to resign on grounds of age, and in June, 1931, wrote to J. R. M. insisting that he must be free by the autumn. And J. R. M. replied, in June, begging him to stay on a little longer, "The truth is that we have not got the men, and I may soon take a decision that will surprise you."

This was an old song of J. R. M.'s, for Mrs. Webb told me in 1924 that he had said then that his difficulty was that so few of his followers were capable of taking charge of departments.

Molly Hamilton dined with us on November 5th. My diary

[1] See also his pamphlet *What Happened in 1931; a Record* (Fabian Society).

records that: "One night last March she went into J. R. M.'s room at the House, and he said, 'Baldwin was sitting in that chair an hour ago. He came to ask me whether I wouldn't form a National Government.' This was obviously a fly, but she only laughed and said, 'What a ridiculous idea!' and he dropped the subject."

On August 25th, Joe Compton, then M.P. for Gorton, Arthur Greenwood's P.P.S. and Chairman of the House of Commons Kitchen Committee, one of my closest comrades in the Trade Union Section of the National Executive, told me this story at Greenwood's flat. His official Chairman's room, on the Terrace Floor at the House of Commons, he seldom uses for private meals. But it is always the custom, as a matter of courtesy, to ask his permission before letting the room to anyone else. He now hears that his room has been taken for several nights a week by J. R. M. for small private dinners with Tory and Liberal leaders, and that one of J. R. M.'s staff gave special instructions that Compton was not to be informed of this, and that a trustworthy man was to be posted in the passage outside the door, to make sure that it was closed whenever any member of the Government went by. These small dinners had been going on for some time.

Who else attended them is not clear. Thomas, no doubt, and Baldwin, some other Tories and a Liberal or two. Snowden improbably. Henderson never. Lloyd George attended one and, observing that Henderson wasn't there, said it was no use discussing National Government and suchlike subjects without him. Whereat J. R. M. shut up like an oyster and L. G. wasn't asked again. L. G. told this to Uncle after the election.

Thomas, in the small hours of July 16th—during an all-night sitting caused by I.L.P. opposition to Unemployment Insurance Anomalies Bill—said in the Bar to Ernie Hunter of the *Daily Herald*: "What bloody folly it is to waste time like this, when within a few hours we may have to declare a moratorium and make big changes in the Government!"

And finally Snowden, who relates that "Mr. MacDonald at the Palace Meeting on the Monday morning agreed to the formation of a National Government, with himself as Prime Minister, without a word of consultation with any of his Labour colleagues" (I wonder about Thomas) . . . "When the Labour

Cabinet as a whole declined to agree to a reduction of un-employment pay, Mr. MacDonald assumed too hurriedly that this involved the resignation of his Government. He neither showed nor expressed any grief at this regrettable development. On the contrary he set about the formation of the National Government with an enthusiasm which showed that the adventure was highly agreeable to him."

His conduct at this time gives "ground for the suspicion expressed by Mr. Henderson and other Labour Ministers that Mr. MacDonald had deliberately planned the scheme of a National Government, which would at the same time enable him to retain the position of Prime Minister and to associate with political colleagues with whom he was more in sympathy than he had ever been with his Labour colleagues. He had always entertained a feeling of something like contempt for the Trade Union leaders. His mind for a long time before this crisis arose had been turning to the idea of a new party orientation and government by what he called a Council of State. Something of this sort had not altogether been absent from the mind of Mr. Baldwin, for I remember a statement he made two or three years before, that probably the time was not far distant when he and Mr. MacDonald would be sitting in the same Cabinet. This observation was probably due to Mr. Baldwin's shrewd appreciation of Mr. MacDonald's politi-cal temperament." . . . "The day after the National Govern-ment was formed Mr. MacDonald came into my room at Downing Street in very high spirits. I remarked that he would now find himself very popular in strange quarters. He replied, gleefully rubbing his hands, 'Yes, tomorrow every Duchess in London will be wanting to kiss me!' "[1]

And this may help to complete more than one picture. In January, 1930, Uncle and I stayed at our Embassy in Paris, on our way to Geneva. We had, I recorded, "a jaw, *à trois*, with

[1] *Autobiography*, vol. ii, pp. 952-7.

It is also interesting to read that in October 1930, Sir Arthur Balfour, a member of the Economic Advisory Council, wrote to the Prime Minister, forecasting . . . that grave measures, including some reduction in the unemployment benefit, as well as a 10 to 20 per cent. tariff on manufactured goods, would be essential if national bankruptcy were to be averted. He doubted whether any but a Coalition Government would be powerful enough to impose on the country the sacrifices that would be required, " and that the P.M. circulated this letter to the King and Cabinet". (Nicolson, *King George V*, p. 448.)

Tyrrell between tea and dinner. T. says that Morley always longed for the F.O., and when occasionally he sat in Grey's chair, when during the latter's absences he was acting Foreign Secretary, he was always very visibly happy." [Tyrrell at this time was one of the private secretaries.] "It was a lie that he didn't know about the war commitments before 1914. He was at the Committee of Imperial Defence when some of the most critical discussions took place. When Gladstone retired, Morley supported Rosebery against Harcourt for the succession to the leadership; not only because he hated Harcourt, but because Rosebery promised him the F.O.

"T. said that Morley was always pressing Asquith in later years to give J. R. M. a post in the Government. He said to Asquith once, shaking his finger as his habit was, 'You make a great mistake not to include MacDonald. He has the Front Bench mind.' (Terribly true! One supposes that J. R. M. would have taken it. I remember Ben Keeling saying to me about 1911, after he had some rather disillusioning talks with J. R. M., that the latter 'would bolt for the Treasury Bench like a rabbit for its hole, if he got the chance.')

"T. said that J. R. M. was also popular in those days with the Salisburys, and was a frequent visitor at their house in Arlington Street.

"Uncle then related how in 1910 there was much talk behind the scenes of a new Government, which should be created to settle the Irish Question. It would include, besides Liberals, Balfour and some of the younger Tories, and J. R. M. would be Chief Secretary for Ireland. Right in the centre of the picture, chief hero or chief scapegoat. J. R. M. was very anxious to go in. He asked Uncle to come and have a talk about it. He said that he, J. R. M., would be in the Cabinet. No other member of the Labour Party would, but Uncle could have any job he liked outside the Cabinet, if he would put the party machine at the disposal of the new Government. Uncle refused, and strongly advised J. R. M. to drop the whole idea. Anyhow, the idea dropped him!"[1]

[1] The author of this project of a National Government was Lloyd George. He wanted the leaders in such a government "freed from dependence on their party extremists" to settle not only the Irish question, but the constitutional question, and the social question, and to introduce compulsory military training. (Nicolson, *King George V*, p. 131.)

Of all the academic economists, only Maynard Keynes can claim any intellectual or political credit in the Crisis of 1931. But he came right out, in an admirable effort, both critical and constructive.[1]

He not only wrote, but spoke at a meeting in the House of Commons on September 16th, and attacked the Economy Bill and the Budget in great style.

With Norman Angell in the Chair, and flanked by Winston Churchill and Eleanor Rathbone, he described the May Report as "the most foolish document I have ever had the misfortune to read". Asked what he would do, if he were Prime Minister, in this crisis, he replied:

"Scrap the Economy Bill;

"Abolish the Sinking Fund;

"Summon an International Conference to promote the re-distribution of gold;

"Return to the Civil Servants and other people the salaries which have been unjustly taken from them.

"And I think that's enough for one night."

Sir John Simon said afterwards that it was tragic to see how Keynes had completely taken leave of his wits.

"On October 1st, Phil arranged a lunch—Uncle, Willy Graham, me, Keynes, Arthur Salter, Kingsley Martin and himself. Keynes had expressed a wish to meet Uncle. It went rather well, given some incompatibility of personalities.

"Keynes said that our export position, with the pound now at 16s., was tremendously strong. We should try for an International Conference that means business—finally settle War Debts and Reparations; a group of nations, including first and foremost a United British Empire, should stabilise a common currency among themselves; then bluff France and the United States in; work out a scheme for a co-operative pool of credits, guaranteed by all the Governments jointly, to do new work, not to pay old bondholders' debts. And so on, convincingly.

"J. R. M., he says, will soon be going 'to the place my wife calls Lousymouth'. And then he turns to Uncle and says, 'Here's a good ending for your next speech! "A week ago the pound looked the dollar in the face. Today it is kicking it in the

[1] Parts II and III of his *Essays in Persuasion*, published at the end of 1931, still shine brilliantly across the years.

arse." ' Uncle, obviously pleased after this lunch, said 'And when I quoted that chap in the Cabinet, Snowden said he was a fool!'

"'Conference'", says Salter, "has now become an indecent word at Geneva. One can't pronounce it in polite society." I cast Salter at this time for a high, if not the highest, post in the Treasury next time we come in. Uncle had tried to get him as head of a new Economics Section, which he and I were trying to form at the F.O. But J. R. M. and others had been jealous and objected. "You have the Department of Overseas Trade," J. R. M. had said. I then tried to get Austin Robinson, who I thought would fit very well in the F.O., both with Labour Ministers and with officials, to come and teach economics to the new entrants (and, if possible, to the Old Boys as well), but this too was bogged.

Uncle and Willy Graham were both very much against the Treasury officials at this time. Some had become very bitter partisans and showed it. Cripps told me later that he had had to say to two of them, who were abusing Uncle and Graham in front of him. "Remember, my dear fellows, you are Civil Servants. These people may be Ministers again some day."

Of Salter, who had been first class at Geneva, and not too bad after that as a Professor at Oxford, Uncle had once said: "A good Civil Servant, under proper political direction." But, when he heard that Salter wanted to be a politician, he was very sceptical. And, indeed, having come to Parliament as a University member and an Independent, he was rash enough, like all the other eminent "Independents" of the Coalition, to join Churchill's Tory Caretaker Government of 1945, and so scrubbed himself off our slate of possibles when we came in. Now, at the age of 70, he is Minister of Economic Affairs, not in the Cabinet, in the Tory Government of 1951.

From October 2nd to 8th I was at Scarborough for the Annual Conference of the Labour Party. The dissolution was hanging over us. It was being delayed, we thought, partly to cause us the maximum of inconvenience in our election preparations, partly because of the difficulty of "finding a formula" inside the Cabinet. There was a crack going round last week, "The Cabinet have been trying for a week to find a

formula which Sir Herbert Samuel will not accept. So far
they have not succeeded." There had been much running up
and down between Churt (Lloyd George's house) and Westminster. Lloyd George had remained inflexibly against an
election. But the absent sick soon lose influence. He was now
deserted, isolated and impotent. The rest of the Liberals were
capitulating to the Tories. In the constituencies anti-Labour
Pacts were being arranged everywhere. J. R. M. had arranged
for all his own little band of deserters to stand their ground and
fight their present constituencies with the aid of the Tory
machine and a private fund supplied by "certain friends".
Most of the National Executive travelled to Scarborough by
the same train as J. R. M., who was going to Seaham. At King's
Cross there was a carriage reserved for our party at the rear
of the train. I was wrongly directed to the front and coming
back became entangled in a crowd waiting for J. R. M. Trying to get through, and lugging a large suitcase, I asked:
"Where is the loyal section of the Labour Party travelling?"
This found its way into the *Evening Standard*.

The Scarborough Conference was an affair of quasi-
unanimities. (So it always is when the Labour Party is facing
an immediate election. So it was twenty years later, again at
Scarborough, in 1951. And I was still taking a leading part in
drafting manifestos and resolutions. But 1951, though a defeat,
was a most hard-fought, close thing and, on the whole, a
fortunate result, as against 1931, which was sheer rout and
ruin for the Party.) Our Policy resolutions were all carried
practically as they stood.[1] The I.L.P. were steam-rollered on

---

[1] We resolved, among other things, that "the banking and credit system of the
country shall be brought under public ownership and control", that we should
seek "an International Conference with the object of arriving at a concerted
monetary policy . . . to stabilise wholesale prices at a reasonable level", that there
should be "a vigorous policy" for "the deliberate organisation and development"
of the economic life of the country, that "as a first step the most important basic
industries, such as Power, Transport and Iron and Steel should be reorganised
as public utilities on the basis of national ownership and the participation of the
workers in the responsibilities of management and control", that there should be
"complete unification of the mining industry under public ownership and control
and a minimum living wage", that the cuts in unemployment benefit should be
immediately restored, and the other cuts in pay and social services as soon as
possible, that Britain should put forward at the Disarmament Conference due to
meet next February "proposals for drastic reductions, by international agreement,
in the numbers and equipment of all armed forces, and in military, naval and air
expenditure", and that India should have "full self-government and self-determination".

the issue of the acceptance by M.P.s of the Standing Orders of the Parliamentary Party. This was a rebuke to Parliamentary indiscipline, which had been giving the Government a lot of trouble, by no means undeserved, on the Home Front.

The National Executive elections resulted in few changes. But old Fred Jowett was defeated by T. E. Williams of the Royal Arsenal Co-operative Society in the Co-operative-and-Socialist-Societies Section. Harold Laski was a bad third. He got the Miners' vote (500,000), but little else. In the Constituency Parties' Section the voting was

LANSBURY	2,139,000
H. MORRISON	1,725,000
DALTON	1,573,000
DALLAS	1,524,000
ARTHUR JENKINS	716,000

Then followed, highest among unsuccessful candidates, Joe Toole 674,000 and Morgan Jones 592,000.

The new National Executive met on October 7th and approved an Election Manifesto drafted by Laski, good of its kind, but a bit too literary for some tastes. "Plan or perish" was a leading slogan.

"Citrine told me at Scarborough that early in the life of the Labour Government he went in one day to see J. R. M., who said he was very tired and couldn't go on leading the Party much longer. He had been thinking who might succeed him. He had thought of Mosley. How did Citrine think the Movement would feel about this selection? Citrine said it would receive practically no support, and would indeed be quite out of the question. 'Whom do you think the Movement would prefer, then, as my successor?' asked J. R. M. 'Probably Henderson,' said Citrine, 'we all feel he is doing very well as Foreign Secretary.' 'Doing very well!' said J. R. M. angrily. 'Look at this!' and he fished out a private cabinet paper, 'and you will see what a mess he is making over Egypt.' "

I leave London for the North on October 10th. Ruth is making the arrangements for my mother to move into her new house at Datchet and finishing the clearing up of my father's old house at Windsor, which must be vacated by the end of this month. This clashes very awkwardly with the election campaign and will keep Ruth away from Bishop Auckland until the last week.

On the way north I spoke, as at previous elections, for George Dallas at Wellingborough, and in two Yorkshire constituencies.

On October 12th I travelled from Leeds as far as York with Ernest Bevin, on his way to Gateshead, where a fortnight later he was defeated by a very large majority. "He tells me that J. R. M. said to him, going into No. 10 one day during the London Naval Conference, when the French were being very sticky, 'I never felt more like declaring war than I do today.' And Bevin replied: 'I shouldn't talk like that, if I were you. You might be overheard and misunderstood.' " Also that J. R. M. had said one day, at a small meeting of some of the non-Ministerial members of the Economic Advisory Council, 'You must remember the low mental calibre of those I have to work with,' and Bevin had said, 'Mr. Prime Minister, you shouldn't say that sort of thing in front of *me*.' "

I arrived that afternoon at Bishop Auckland and started my campaign with three meetings. Our organisation had been much neglected since 1929. My diary records that "from the very beginning I am unhappy and uncomfortable in this campaign, and I miss Ruth very much. Here, as practically everywhere, it is a straight fight. Curry (the Liberal) is running with Tory support. But, though unhappy and uncomfortable, I never contemplate the possibility of defeat, counting both on the solid tradition of this division and on the strength of the case against the dole cuts, to see me through. But many of the meetings lack enthusiasm, and I am conscious of a certain difficulty in getting the case over. Curry is late in starting and seems to be only fighting half-heartedly and spending very little. I speak outside the Division a good deal, at Darlington, Stockton, Billingham, South Shields, Sunderland and in the Barnard Castle Division. Also in Seaham against J. R. M. It seems impossible that *he* can win. Some of these are very fine meetings."

There had been trouble in the Atlantic Fleet at Invergordon —and a refusal to put to sea—owing to the pay cuts and the clumsiness of their announcement. Will Lawther in the Barnard

Castle Division issued a picture of warships looming up out of the murk, headed "Three cheers for the British Navy! They beat the Kaiser at Jutland and Montagu Norman at Invergordon".

"As the campaign proceeds, J. R. M., Snowden and others—particularly Snowden on the wireless and in an article in the *Daily Mail*—play ever more wildly on stunts. The German mark stunt is a special favourite with J. R. M., who displays a million mark note at his meetings and speaks of the horrors of inflation. Curry copies this, and tears up million mark notes and throws them in the fire in village schoolrooms. In the last days the Savings Bank stunt comes along, started by Runciman, backed up by Snowden and Thomas. The savings in the Post Office Savings Bank had been lent to the Unemployment Insurance Fund, which was now bankrupt. Therefore all these savings were in danger!

"There is no doubt that all this, especially the wireless talks, reaching voters who never come to meetings and seldom vote, contributed very powerfully to the results.

"October 26th. Eve of poll. I address more than twenty meetings, starting at Copley at 2.45 p.m.

"October 27th. Polling day. Go the rounds with Brian Bell (our agent). Curry has a lot of cars. We have only two, a third which was promised having broken down. Considering our complete lack of any proper organisation, we seem to be doing all right.

"That night Ruth and I go round to the Davis's to hear results on the wireless. I have a feeling that there will be many losses and am not inclined, as in 1929, to go and hear the results in public at a picture house. But the news, as it comes through, is overwhelmingly worse than I had ever anticipated. The towering 'National' majorities are the worst general feature. The defeat of Uncle at Burnley is the hardest blow of all, though not unexpected. But, when we leave in the small hours, I say to Will Davis: 'I'm not at all sure that I want to be a member of this House of Commons.' And this is quite sincere. But I still thought I was in, though I had marked down my majority to something just under 1,000.

"October 28th. At the count it was soon clear that it was pretty close, and fairly early I formed the opinion that I was just out. And so it was.

CURRY	17,551
DALTON	16,796

Liberal-National majority 755

(I had dropped 1,042 votes as compared with 1929, and Curry had added 3,407 to the combined Liberal and Tory votes.)

"After meeting our leading workers, some of whom were in tears, and thanking Brian Bell and others very warmly for all they had done, we caught the afternoon train from Darlington. There was no crowd on the platform today as there was in 1929, when J. R. M. and the rest of us travelled back in triumph, buying evening papers all the way. But, as in 1929, Harold Macmillan was on the platform, defeated then at Stockton, a lonely Tory in a Labour mob; now a victor once again. We had spoken then of ebbs and flows, and I reminded him of this today. He said, with some truth, that the tendency was for the electors to vote Left in days of prosperity and Right in days of depression. And I recalled Keynes' words that 'it is prosperity not adversity that makes the slave shake his chains'."

But through Durham and Tyneside, through the mining and shipbuilding areas, there was still mass misery, unemployment and hunger after two years of Labour Government.

My election expenses were £353 0s. 6d., a very moderate figure. But Curry's were only £199 19s. 4d. Clear evidence that, when he started, he didn't expect to win!

Another bit of non-revolutionary testimony. Molly Hamilton, who lost her seat at Blackburn, told me that when the dole cut came into force, in the middle of the election, the Employment Exchange manager expected a row, and asked for extra police, but not one murmur of complaint was heard, not even from those who were told to go away and come back next day, because the Exchange had run out of coppers. Such meekness is a mouldy miracle!

My blow was softened a little by the other results in County Durham. The loss of Blaydon, Durham, Houghton-le-Spring and Consett, all "safer" seats even than Bishop Auckland, showed the force of the tide. And J. R. M. held Seaham! In County Durham we held only two seats—Chester-le-Street and

Spennymoor—out of nineteen. The contagion of Seaham spread like a plague through Durham and Northumberland. South Wales, Yorkshire and some of the Midlands stood much firmer. But our numbers in the House were down to forty-six. George Lansbury was the only ex-Cabinet Minister to survive, and Attlee and Cripps the only other two ex-Ministers, in addition to five ex-Under-Secretaries, George Hall, Morgan Jones, Jack Lawson, Willy Lunn and Allen Parkinson.

Our casualties included, of ex-Ministers just elected to the Parliamentary Executive, Henderson, Clynes, Graham, Johnston, myself, Greenwood, Addison, Alexander, Pethick Lawrence, Shinwell and Lees-Smith; and of ex-Ministers not on this Executive, Herbert Morrison.

It is safe to say that almost any one of this list, had he been re-elected, would either have been chosen leader in the next Parliament in preference to Lansbury, or deputy leader in preference to Attlee—particularly as both of these were London M.P.s and the latter not a member of either the National or the late Parliamentary Executive. "Political success", as Tom Jones, I think, sententiously observes, "consists in the conjunction of personal qualities with fortunate events."

At the time I noted that "the factors which caused our defeat were:

(1) Disappointment (largely justified) at the general failure of the Labour Government on the Home Front;

(2) The story that our (loyal) leaders 'ran away' and went back on their undertakings to their colleagues;

(3) The inflation and 'fall in the value of the pound' stunt;

(4) The Savings Bank stunt;

(5) The stunt of the 'National' Government that was 'above Party';

(6) The confusion caused by the going over of J. R. M. and Snowden, whom we had boosted so long, and who had a great personal following;

(7) The staging of straight fights almost everywhere.

"This last point was very important in reducing our numbers so very low. We polled seven million votes to our opponents' fourteen million. Under P.R. we should have had two hundred members instead of forty-six, but we have always resisted that temptation.

"Underground fears sapped our foundations in the last few days. On the surface little of this was visible."

That summary, I think, was pretty accurate.

On November 3rd Uncle gave a lunch at St. Ermin's to the defeated Ministers. He said that, if he had to go through it again, he would take just the same line, but he would take it much sooner. And this is right enough. It was dallying with this proposal and that, and sometimes seeming half to agree, that undermined his position and that of others. And they had few firm alternative proposals. And they let J. R. M. and Snowden get away with it much too easily.

Addison, for instance, told me that once, when foreign loans to save the gold standard were being discussed, he asked whether it wouldn't be better and cheaper, and wouldn't get them out of many of their difficulties, to go off gold *then*. He said that at this point Snowden was more insulting to him than anyone had ever been in his life before, but, none of his colleagues backing him up, the Cabinet passed on. And Webb, when the "National" Government went off gold only three weeks after it was formed, said sadly: "No one ever told *us* we could do that!"

On November 9th, on the eve of the first session of the new Parliament, there was a Labour Party squash in the Suffolk Galleries. "Hosts of the fallen! Most of them absurdly cheerful. Tonight Ruth and I prefer the glum ones, such as poor little Willy Graham, who seems quite dazed and distressed. Poor old G. L., who is to lead the remains of the Parliamentary Party, sat most of the evening with his head in his hands."

Willy Graham had told me at the end of September that, when he took office in 1929, he resigned a Building Society Directorship, not indeed on a binding contract, but on a written understanding that he should come back when he left office. But now he learned that he would not be reinstated. This meant a loss of between £800 and £1,000 a year. He found also that a number of papers for which he used to write economic and financial articles will take nothing from him now. Such is the bitterness! He was obviously very hard up. In December I heard with pleasure that he had joined a firm of stockbrokers, one of whom was a friend of Cripps, as economic and statistical adviser. This, I thought, would give him not only some income now, but a practical contact with the City which might be valuable to him later.

But not so. In my diary of January 9th, 1932, I wrote: "Willy Graham died last night of double pneumonia. This is a very great political loss. On personal grounds I regret, not so much the ending of an intimate friendship—for it was hardly that, though we had been coming closer and closer together—as the ending of a relationship which I am sure *would have* ripened into a happy and co-operative intimacy. But on public grounds his loss is ruinous. He was only 44, just my own age. He seemed to have the sure prospect of high office and great usefulness when next we came in. He had a combination of gifts very rare in politics—an immense power of mastery of detail; a clear grasp of Socialist principles; a tremendous—perhaps too great —capacity for work; courage, which had grown visibly in recent years and months; great patience, gentleness and courtesy. He always commanded confidence in his presentation of a case. He was a first-class colleague, perfect to work with. He never lost his temper. He erred, if at all, by excess of modesty. 'Can you think of him living above his permanent officials?' Uncle once asked me.

"He had a heavy blow in his defeat at Central Edinburgh, where Snowden sent a special message of good wishes to his opponent. But, as his friends said, no bitterness; rather bewilderment. '1918–1931 has been a wonderful apprenticeship; we look beyond the ruins to the rising sun.' So he wrote, just after the crash.

"It is a stupefying irony that he should be taken, while Snowden is left, whom in the natural course of things he would have succeeded. He is gone before any of our Old Men, be they wicked or virtuous. And he is gone just when our Movement most had need of him."

I was told that, in his last delirium, he kept on repeating: "I can't think why Philip did it!"

First elected in 1918, and making his mark from the start, he had served Snowden like a faithful slave as Financial Secretary to the Treasury in 1923–4 and, as President of the Board of Trade in 1929–31, he had broken with his old chief only at the very end.

Snowden, I heard, had been very bitter at the majority of

fifteen to six in the Cabinet in favour of a revenue tariff, and particularly bitter against Graham. He had said: "William, there shall be a Free Trade candidate next time in Central Edinburgh." He had refused to accept the majority decision, and even demanded that the vote should be rescinded. "I can't stay in a Cabinet", he said, "where fifteen members are in favour of a revenue tariff."

Had Willy Graham lived, it is unlikely that I should have become Chancellor of the Exchequer fourteen years later.

I conclude with some afterthoughts on the financial crisis of 1931. We have had many financial crises since 1931, and the Tory Chancellor of the Exchequer in 1952 has told us that our overseas position has been deteriorating for fifty years. And we have learned much more about the causes and the cures of crises in the last twenty years.

Looking back to 1931, all we politicians on both sides seem very amateurish, and nearly all the experts—Keynes conspicuously excepted—very muddle-headed.

Since the Great Slump started in 1929 there had been no effective international action, either by Governments meeting *ad hoc*, or by Central Banks, or through the League of Nations. The essential action needed to stop the slump was to raise prices and so increase money incomes and purchasing power, and to increase investment. And this, of course, would have increased employment.[1]

If widespread international action on these lines was not to be had, national action, or action by a group of nations acting together, might be, for those so acting, a worthwhile second best. Certainly worthwhile for Britain and those who could be counted on to act with her, the Sterling Group of those days. But separate action of this kind would mean going off gold.

We should certainly have faced this possibility much sooner and not let ourselves be dragged so far down the deflationary slope.[2]

[1] Albert Thomas, with his idea of international public works, for electrification, transport, etc., under the I.L.O., was on right lines, but got little encouragement and worked out little detail.

[2] Harold Nicolson (*King George V*, p. 459 n.) observes that: "Those who recall the fact that, when a few weeks later we were driven off the gold standard, nothing

Our adverse trade balance in 1931 was not serious. We have often had it much more adverse, both before and since. It could have been met, as often in this period, by a quite small degree of disinvestment of our overseas holdings. Or it could have been checked, while we were still on the gold standard, by a tariff, though many of us were still absurdly prejudiced against this policy, which we associated, from past experience, with half-wits and with selfish vested interests. Or by a quantitative limitation of imports, as in the nineteen-forties, but we had not developed that technique in 1931. Or most smoothly of all, simply by going off gold, which, in the conditions of 1931, gave the necessary spur to exports and check to imports.

On the unbalanced budget, all we politicians were too simple. We all declared it should be balanced, though we argued fiercely as to how. Even Keynes gave no strong lead here against the current fallacy. Deliberate "deficit financing" in trade depression was an idea that came later. Looking back now, it is clear that, in the conditions of 1930–1, it was right to have a deficit, and wrong to try to balance the budget. The Americans already were setting us, in this respect, a good example.

Still less was it sensible to try to balance the unemployment fund. Clearly this should show a deficit in years of heavy, and a surplus in years of light, unemployment. But Labour Ministers had been talking awful nonsense on this subject for some time. Miss Bondfield had frequently said that it was "dishonest" to borrow for the unemployment fund. The official who had taught her to use this epithet in this context should have been sent away on very long leave. And, as I have noted already, Ministers, including the Big Five, were all humbugged by their advisers into believing that this fund could only borrow from the Post Office Savings Bank. Its borrowings could, of course, be merged in those of the Treasury as a whole.

very dreadful resulted, may be inclined to believe that in arguing (that the pound might suddenly drop to half its value) Mr. Snowden was not being sincere." But, he says, "Mr. Snowden, the Treasury and the City of London were obsessed by the terrible consequences that had accompanied inflation in Germany, when the whole middle class had been ruined." These pundits should have known that this was panic-stricken nonsense. Britain's position in 1931 was wholly different from Germany's and immensely stronger. Going off gold raised prices *slightly*, but this was most desirable and, with the fall in the exchange, eased the pressure both of unemployment and of an adverse trade balance.

The May Committee should not have been appointed. Ministers should carry their own responsibilities, not shift them to outsiders. Its Majority Report was crude and reactionary in spirit, and chock-full of economic fallacies, as Keynes showed, though many other economists were taken in by them. Its Minority Report, by Arthur Pugh and Charles Latham, got, and deserved, little publicity. It was hesitating and indecisive, not clearly seeing through the fallacies of the Majority, but not willing to follow them to their crude conclusions and with some sense, at least, of the gross injustices which the Majority proposed.

Snowden's conduct, on two points in particular, is quite amazing. First, he allowed Treasury officials to give evidence, in sensational language, which was later published, before the May Committee, to the effect that continued borrowing for the unemployment fund was undermining the stability of British finance. But this borrowing had been a feature of all his own Budgets, including that of April 1931. Second, when the Report was issued—the day Parliament rose for the summer recess, so that no debate could then take place upon it— he made no statement or comment of any kind.[1] The headlines and the leading articles, both in this country and abroad, rioted in talk of new revelations of unbelievable extravagance, of impending financial collapse and of national bankruptcy. The kindest defence of Snowden's silence at this time is simply that the man was ill. It was, in any case, *his* administration of the Treasury for more than two years which had brought us to this pass. He should have resigned long before, if only a fraction of all this was true. And yet he succeeded in establishing, within a few weeks, a heroic and complete alibi!

There is no doubt that the May Report, and the manner of its presentation by the Press, encouraged the run on gold in London, both by foreigners and British nationals. But this alone, bad though it was, would not have forced us to seek loans in New York and Paris on the terms discussed above. That came, as I have said already, from the financial crisis in Germany, which became also a financial crisis in Britain,

---

[1] Not even a simple arithmetical correction, to explain that the alleged prospective deficit of £120 million included a sinking fund of £50 million, which should, of course, have been subtracted from it.

because of reckless lending to Germans by leading financiers in the City of London. Our malady was money-lenders' madness. This was what finally turned the scale against the gold standard here and, before the scale finally tipped, put Britain in an intolerable relationship with foreign financiers and split the British Labour Government.

Hindsight is generally keener than foresight. Some of the problems we faced in 1931 were new, and full of political and economic dynamite. Our own understanding of them was limited and largely wrong, and so was that of our advisers, and of most of the commentators.

I hope it may be useful, both for students of the past and of the future, that I have here set down what I myself saw, heard and thought of these dramatic events. Thus ends this first part of my account of my life's journey.[1]

[1] Arthur Henderson told me that, when he went to Buckingham Palace to hand back his seals, he expected a very cold farewell. But, instead, the King said: "Thank you for all you've done at the Foreign Office. Our relations with every country in the world, except Persia, are better now than when you took over. And you're not to blame for Persia." These words were very deeply appreciated.

MY UNCLE HUGH AT JUTLAND

THE naval war, waged in the British Admiralty, did not end with the defeat of Germany in 1918. Naval and civilian writers, and talkers, kept it going for years, with much vigour and enmity.

Here I am concerned only with one of the brushes in these post-war hostilities, the debate on my uncle's handling of the Fifth Battle Squadron at Jutland. These four great battleships of the *Queen Elizabeth* class were stationed by Beatty at a distance, which some have thought excessive, of five miles from his flagship, the *Lion*. Beatty's biographer, Admiral Chalmers, says that the reason for this was that "the Fifth Battle Squadron was a supporting force, and neither the Commander-in-Chief nor Beatty had ever intended it to be used as an integral part of the Battle Cruiser Fleet until battle was joined. In his despatch Beatty gives Evan-Thomas full credit for his 'brilliant and effective support'."[1]

But when in the early afternoon of May 31st, 1916, Beatty suddenly became aware that German warships were at sea, and turned in pursuit of them, the Fifth Battle Squadron did not turn for another eight minutes, so that the distance between the *Lion* and my uncle's flagship the *Barham* had widened to nearly ten miles. Whose fault was this? Mr. Churchill blames my uncle. "It is common ground", he writes, "between all parties that Rear-Admiral Evan-Thomas, once he realised the situation, did all in his power to recover the lost distance, and that . . . he, in fact, recovered upwards of four miles of it. The result, however, of his eight minutes' delay in turning was inexorably to keep him and his tremendous guns out of the action for the first most critical and most fatal half-hour, and even thereafter to keep him at extreme range."[2] Mr. Churchill is supported in this view by the so-called *Admiralty Narrative* of

[1] Chalmers: *Life and Letters of David Beatty*, p. 268.
[2] *The World Crisis*, p. 598.

Jutland published in 1924. On the other hand, Jellicoe insisted on adding an Appendix, containing his own views, to
this *Narrative*, expressly stating that no blame rested on my
uncle and, according to his biographer, "was greatly angered"
at the "unfair treatment and insinuations" to which my uncle
had been subjected.[1]

Jellicoe, and my uncle, are supported on this point by Sir
Julian Corbett, the official naval historian, by Admiral
Harper in his pungent book *The Truth about Jutland*, and by
Admiral Bacon in his even more outspoken *Jutland Scandal*,[2]
while Beatty's biographer is more concerned to defend Beatty
than to criticise my uncle.

Sir Julian Corbett writes that "Admiral Beatty had already
(at 2.32 p.m.) turned the Battle Cruisers to SSE. . . . but the
general signal for this movement, which he made at the moment
his helm was put over, was not passed on to Admiral Evan-
Thomas and, being made by flags, could not be seen distinctly from the *Barham*. (At 3.5 the *Tiger*," the second Battle
Cruiser in Beatty's squadron, "signalled to the *Lion* that the
2.32 signal and signals made since had not been passed to the
Barham.) It was thus not till a few minutes later that the Fifth
Battle Squadron began to follow his lead."[3]

Admiral Harper, who, having been ordered to prepare an
official record of the Battle—which was never published[4]—
is exceptionally familiar with the evidence, attributes the
blame to "the failure of the signalling staff of the *Lion* to

---

[1] *Life of Jellicoe*, by Admiral Bacon, p. 445.

[2] Both Admirals criticise the *Narrative* severely. Both make the point that it was,
apparently, not officially approved by the Board of Admiralty as a whole. Admiral
Harper (pp. 149–50) says that it "bears the imprint of many hands and much
'chopping and piecing' to produce a desired impression. As an authentic record
it can only be described as thoroughly unsatisfactory . . . while Lord Jellicoe's
dignified, and fully justified, criticisms of its errors and defects", in his Appendix,
"are answered by querulous interjections, quite out of keeping with an official
publication". Admiral Bacon (p. viii, pp. 103 and 107) describes it as "an
anaemic production . . . . To the technical reader, versed in operations and terms,
as well as in the sentiment of the Navy, a nasty flavour pervades the whole narrative. . . . If intended as a serious staff production, it brings discredit on the
Naval Staff at the Admiralty. If intended as a popular narrative it fails equally,
as it is quite unintelligible to the man-in-the-street."
Beatty was First Sea Lord when this *Narrative* was published.

[3] *History of the Great War, Naval Operations*, vol. iii, p. 331.

[4] Though three ex-First Sea Lords—Jellicoe, Wester Wemyss, who had ordered
Captain Harper, as he then was, to prepare it, and Bridgeman—all urged, in
letters to the Press, that it should be published, the first two having read it.
Beatty was First Sea Lord when publication was refused.

transmit, efficiently and without delay, the signal to the *Barham* to alter course. A signal was made by flags which was not clear to the *Barham*, owing to smoke interference and the distance between the ships, and Beatty's staff knew, or should have known, it was not clear because it was not at once 'answered'. Responsibility for the reception of the message rested with him and his staff and with nobody else."[1] He goes on to praise the gunnery of the Fifth Battle Squadron as far superior to that of Beatty's battle cruisers.

Admiral Bacon notes that "the signal for the alteration of course was not passed by searchlight to the *Barham* . . . nor was the flag signal repeated by the *Tiger*, although flag signals from the *Lion* were very difficult for distant ships to make out, or even to see at all."[2]

Beatty's biographer writes:

"Beatty . . . at 2.32 p.m. turned the Battle Cruiser Fleet to SSE. The turning signal, made by flags, was not seen by the *Barham* owing to the heavy smoke belched forth by the battle cruisers in pressing on steam. In any case, the *Tiger*, as repeating ship, should have passed it on by searchlight. . . . Some critics have said that the *Barham*, on seeing Beatty turn, should have followed suit. Unfortunately Evan-Thomas did not receive the *Galatea's* signal" signalling presence of enemy cruisers "until some five minutes later than Beatty, and since his last orders were to look out for the Grand Fleet, he might reasonably have assumed, at first, that Beatty was probably adjusting his position prior to meeting Jellicoe. At 2.38, Evan-Thomas, realising the true situation, also turned to SSE. This was six minutes after Beatty, but . . . for Beatty to have waited for the battleships would have been unthinkable. It was his first duty to locate the enemy at the earliest possible moment."[3]

It appears to me that my uncle comes well out of this.

Further criticism is levelled at him by Mr. Churchill at a later stage of the action. "From ten minutes past four, the Fifth Battle Squadron had begun to fire, at the long range of 17,000 yards,[4] upon Admiral von Hipper's last two ships. . . . The four mighty ships of Admiral Evan-Thomas threw their 15-inch shells with astonishing accuracy across the great

---

[1] *The Truth about Jutland*, p. 155.
[2] *Life of Jellicoe*, p. 260.
[3] Chalmers, p. 227.
[4] Actually 20,000.

distances which separated them from the German rear. . . .
That they were not 5,000 yards closer was entirely due to their
slowness in grasping the situation when the first contact was
made with the enemy. However, they now came thundering
into battle; and their arrival within effective range would,
in less than an hour, have been decisive—if no other German
forces had been at sea that day.''[1]

But the main German fleet was now approaching, and
Beatty tried to lead them up to Jellicoe. So, Mr. Churchill
continues, ''Beatty turned about so swiftly that his ships soon
passed the Fifth Battle Squadron, coming up at full speed, and
still on their southerly course. As the two squadrons ran past
each other on opposite courses, the *Lion* signalled to the
Barham to turn about in succession. The *Lion's* signal of recall
was flown at 4.48. She passed the *Barham* with this signal flying,
at 4.53, and Rear-Admiral Evan-Thomas responded to the
signal three or four minutes later. Perhaps the Rear-Admiral,
having been slow in coming into action, was inclined to be
slow in coming out.[2] Brief as was this interval, it was sufficient
at the speed at which all the ships were moving to expose the
Fifth Battle Squadron to action with the van of the German
Battle Fleet. . . . The four *Queen Elizabeths* were now subjected
to tremendous fire concentration, particularly upon the point
where each turned in succession. The two leading ships, the
Barham and the *Valiant*, were engaged with the enemy's battle
cruisers; the rear ships, the *Warspite* and the *Malaya*, fought the
whole of the finest squadron in the German Fleet. This apparently unequal conflict lasted for over half an hour. All the
ships, except the *Valiant*, were struck repeatedly with the
heaviest shells. . . . Such, however, was the strength of these
vessels that none of their turrets were put out of action and
their speed was wholly unaffected.''[3]

On this last phase Beatty's biographer comments: ''Beatty
warned Evan-Thomas by flags of the bearing of the enemy
battle fleet, and at 4.48, just before the two squadrons came
abreast of one another, he hoisted the signal ordering him to
turn 180°. Evan-Thomas did not turn till 4.57, and this delay

[1] *The World Crisis*, p. 603.
[2] This criticism also is expressly rebutted by Jellicoe in his Appendix to the
Narrative.
[3] *World Crisis*, pp. 605–6.

brought his squadron under the fire of the battleships in the van of the High Seas Fleet. On the other hand, he was able to give as good as he got,"[1] and later, from 5.12 p.m. "the Fifth Battle Squadron now bore the brunt of the action until 5.30 p.m., when it too drew out of range. Evan-Thomas had succeeded in the difficult task of keeping the German battle cruisers fully occupied, and also inflicting punishment on the van of their battle fleet."[2]

Sir Julian Corbett gives the following account. "At 4.40 Admiral Beatty swung back 16 points in succession . . . to join the C.-in-C. by the shortest possible course. The signal was 'general', but it was made by flags, and Admiral Evan-Thomas, who was eight miles astern, could not see it. He was busy at the time with the enemy, and was just making a signal to concentrate in pairs from the rear. He saw the turn, but, being in hot chase, he rightly judged it his duty to hold on as he was."[3] A little later "*Warspite*'s steering gear began to give way under the wounds she had received. . . . She stopped in a forest of water-spouts, doomed as it seemed to destruction, but replying to the enemy's fire with all her guns, an inspiring sight for the destroyers. With his other three ships Admiral Evan-Thomas led on, and dropping neatly into his station, reopened fire, the accuracy and the effect of which were the admiration of friend and foe."[4] Nor did *Warspite* perish, but was ordered, and made her way, back to harbour.

Finally, more than ten years after the battle, my uncle, now retired, himself went into action against Mr. Churchill. The latter was publishing in *The Times* a series of articles on the history of the war. On February 9th, 1927, he published an article on Jutland, containing the criticisms of my uncle already quoted. My uncle replied in a letter published on February 15th, as follows:

"This account is written by Mr. Winston Churchill, who holds one of the most important positions in the Government, and therefore his writings are read by a very large number of people, quite apart from the fact that he is such an able writer.

"As that first part of the Battle of Jutland concerns me, and as no remarks from me have ever been asked for, by either the

[1] Chalmers, p. 239. [3] Corbett, p. 340.
[2] *Ibid.*, p. 242. [4] *Ibid.*, p. 363.

Chief of the Naval Staff or those under him, who I presume have written the so-called official account, it appears necessary for another and more detailed account to be given of the time when German light craft had just been sighted by *Galatea*. The signal for 'Steam for full speed' had been made, and all the battle cruisers were drawing their coal fires forward and making a tremendous smoke, which made it impossible to distinguish flag signals from Fifth Battle Squadron stationed five miles off, except possibly on very rare occasions. Had signals been made by searchlight, as they had been on other occasions on the same day, they would have been seen immediately.

"So far as the Rear-Admiral Commanding Fifth Battle Squadron was concerned, he knew that two enemy light cruisers had been reported and that the battle cruisers were turning, but to what course it was impossible to see; and they rushed off into space without his having received any signal from the Vice-Admiral in command, neither searchlight nor wireless having been used by *Lion*.

"The only way I could account for no signal having been received by me was that the Vice-Admiral was going to signal another course to Fifth Battle Squadron—possibly to get the enemy light cruisers between us. Anyway, if he wished us to turn, the searchlight would have done it in a moment. It was not until *Tiger* asked *Lion* by wireless whether the signal to turn was to be made to *Barham* that the Vice-Admiral seemed to realise the situation. But those lost minutes turned out afterwards to be a most serious matter. After all, isn't it one of the fundamental principles of naval tactics that an admiral makes sure that his orders are understood by distant parts of his Fleet before rushing into space, covered by a smoke screen? Also, if, as I believe, he knew that German heavy ships were at sea, should he not have seen that his most important ships were close at hand?

"With regard to the remarks of Mr. Churchill about the later stages of the Battle of Jutland, I would submit, as one of the Flag Officers who were there, that they are a mixture of armchair criticism, want of vision from a sailor's point of view, an utter disregard of the effect of smoke, gunfire and fog, added to a terribly partisan account."

Mr. Churchill did not reply.

INDEX TO NAMES OF PERSONS

311

INDEX

Abbey Division of Westminster, candidature for (1919), 124–5; withdrawn, 125

Adamello, trenches in solid ice, 88

Admiralty, views on Princes' voyage, 13; uncle's service at, 19–20

Agnez, Town Major of, 87

Agnosticism at Cambridge, its fashion at King's and Oscar Browning's counterpoise, 56

Albert Bridge Road, second married home, 73

All-Party Disarmament Demonstration of 1931, 254

Anglo-American Naval Negotiations (1929), MacDonald's statement on, 225

Anglo-Iranian Oil Company, dispute with Persia (1952), 239

Anglo-Russian Parliamentary Committee, on Bilinski legend, 154

Anglo-Soviet Trade Agreement, signed April, 1930, 154

Anschlüss, 254

Arbitration, General Act of, passage through Cabinet, 224; at League Assembly and in F.O., 251–3

Armentières, 82

Army Council, Walsh's opening meeting of, 147

Army Service Corps, commission in, 80, 81

Arras, 84

Artists, Socialist policy for the encouragement of (paper by Rupert Brooke suggesting), 43

Asiago Plateau, actions on, 97

Asquith Coalition Cabinet (1915), Henderson's impression of being a Minister in, 147

Auckland Park Mine, visited (1910), 69

Australia, father in, 21

Australian Commonwealth, First Parliament of (1901), 21

Australian Expeditionary Force, in France (1916), 82; discipline, 87

Austria, visited (1927), 165; Customs Union with Germany, 254

Austria-Hungary, German responsibility for, in 1914, 80

Aycliffe, 109

Bacchante, H.M.S., the young Princes' ship, 13, 13 *n.*, 14, 21

Balmoral, father's annual visits to, 24

Bank for International Settlements, meeting at Basle, 255

Bank of England, investigation proposed by Labour Party, 179; pro-German and anti-French foreign policy of, 254; Norman's uncontrolled advances to Credit Anstalt, 254

Bantam Division (35th), service in, 81; discipline, 86

Battersea Polytechnic, tutorial work at, 112

Battle of Britain, Polish airmen's part in, 169

Beaumont and Fletcher's *Maid's Tragedy*, read at Fish and Chimney, 44

Belgium (1914), invasion of, 73, 80

Berlin, Brooke's letter from (1912), 77–8; MacDonald's mad idea of flying to, 257

Bimetallism, Shaw Lefevre's speech on, 23

Birmingham (1928), Annual Labour Party Conference, author's advocacy of Bank of England nationalisation, 181; re-elected to National Executive, 181

Bishop Auckland, first contacts (1910), 70; nominated for, 201; campaign and election for, 201–17

Blackpool, Annual Conference (1927), 171

Board of Education, Edward Wood